FORD

BOOTON HERNDON

DID YOU KNOW that the Ford Motor Company, one of the seven wonders of the modern industrial world, was losing money soon after World War II at the staggering rate of $10,000,000 a month?

Booton Herndon, in this new and utterly absorbing book, investigates the fortunes of the great automotive company from its founding, when the money rolled in, through its darkest postwar days to the present. In so doing, he portrays the two remarkable men named Henry Ford; the talented managerial people like Tex Thornton, Ernie Breech, Robert McNamara, Bunkie Knudsen, and others, brought in at high salaries and vast stock options to reorganize and redirect the postwar firm; and the colorful times and sometimes severe crises each of the two Fords struggled in turn to manage, lead, thwart, or overcome.

The major part of this uncompromising biography focuses on Henry II and the incredible corporate renaissance that he was able to direct after the company seemed destined for oblivion. It's an earthy tale, and not everything worked or came out right. But in terms of size—of the men, the company, the decisions, the ultimate success—it is a heroic tale. And it is also as close a look at a modern industrial entrepreneur in all of his moods as we are likely to get in our lifetime. Herndon's engrossing narrative is a major achievement in direct, empathetic, newstyle reportage.

is the author of some over a thousand ar- he was editorial con- or on *Rickenbacker:* . Born and raised in rginia, and educated Missouri, he began a which was interrupted fter having taken part vasion and the Battle Herndon returned to now lives with his n the *Charlottesville* their two children.

BOOTON HERNDON

FORD

An unconventional

biography of the men and

their times

WEYBRIGHT AND TALLEY
NEW YORK

Copyright © 1969 by BOOTON HERNDON
All rights reserved, including the right to reproduce this book or portions thereof in any form.

Published in the United States by
Weybright and Talley, Inc.
3 East 54th Street
New York, New York 10022

Published simultaneously in Canada by
Clarke, Irwin & Company Limited
Toronto and Vancouver

Library of Congress Catalog Card Number 72-87068

PRINTED IN THE UNITED STATES OF AMERICA

To Bonnie, who helped with the research, organization
and editing of this book, typed my notes and four
drafts of the manuscript, and provided encouragement,
understanding, inspiration and love while concurrently
cooking, keeping house and entertaining our many friends,
handling our involved finances and figuring our taxes,
putting up with my crazy whims, moods and activities,
being a complete mother to our two teen-aged children,
caring for our menagerie, writing her own column for
the local paper, helping her community through participation
and leadership in a dozen different organizations, some
of which she created, being deft at the net and steady
in the bow, and all the time a good-looking, well-groomed
and desirable woman—my thanks, wonder and love.

Contents

photographs appear after page 184

Men of paradox

1

ONE PLEASANT DAY in May, Henry Ford II and I sat down to luncheon in the small, private dining room on the 13th floor of the glass and aluminum building that is the heart of the Ford empire in Dearborn, Michigan. Beneath us an expanse of green, dotted with an occasional tree, extended hundreds of yards in every direction; even with the inflated value of real estate in greater Detroit, he can afford to work in an oasis. He can also afford the ultimate in esthetics. Where we sat a single steel column once stood for a brief time. Mister Ford had had it erected, and when it reached 207 feet, the proposed height of the building, he had driven over to his grandmother's house to determine whether one glimpse of the tower from any part of the estate would offend her eyes. Only after personal reconnaissance proved it to be totally concealed from her view did he authorize the ground to be broken for the building in which we were now ordering filet mignon and fresh strawberries.

As the waiter left with our order, Mister Ford looked at me with almost belligerent directness and said, abruptly, "I was thinking about this last night and I wrote a whatchamacallem, a preface, to this book you're writing. Here's the way it goes: *I'm not interested in this damn book. I'm only cooperating because I've been asked to. I don't care if anybody reads it or not. Signed Henry Ford II.*"

I sat there with my mouth hanging open for a moment, and then I thought, *Why the hell not?* I started writing it down in my notebook. "I'll go along with that," I said.

He hesitated. "Well, maybe you'd better not," he said. "It was just something I was thinking about last night."

"I'm going to put it in the book anyway," I said.

"I don't care what you do with it," he said. The waiter arrived with the first course and that was that.

Though Henry Ford II is clear and precise to his executives, to the writer trying to understand him as a complete personality, he is a paradox. Here I was, his guest, taking up his time. With us was his vice president for public relations, Theodore H. Mecke, Jr., a personable blend of sensitivity and efficiency, whose time was also valuable. On that day, as on many others, I had appointments set up with Ford's permission with executives whose salaries (salary-plus-bonus incomes) range up to more than $200 an hour. The appointments had been made through appropriate channels by my official shepherd, an ebullient Irish redhead named John E. Sattler, the staff director of a floor full of talent. Apparently no restrictions were put upon anyone who talked to me either about Henry Ford himself or the company and sometimes I was amazed at the candor I encountered. Mister Ford thus graciously and generously opened wide the doors to himself, his executives, his family, and his friends— and then said he didn't care whether I used the information or not.

Like his grandfather, Henry the One, Henry Senior or

Grandfather Ford, as he is usually referred to in the inner circles, Henry II is a farrago of contradictions. He, incidentally, is referred to only as HF II, The Chairman or Mister Ford, even by his top executives, and you can tell from the way they say it that they mean *Mister*. "I used to think that when a guy calls you by your first name you call him by his," a vice president told me, "but I got rid of that idea quick with Mister Ford."

My sources of information on this one man number several hundred—from gossip column tidbits to lengthy and intimate conversations. With the qualifications that much of my knowledge is vicarious, I guess I know Henry Ford II about as well as anybody does; most people's knowledge of him is restricted to their areas of mutual interest. His wife and daughters, for example, know next to nothing about his business; his executives, whom Mister Ford does not see socially, know little more about his personal life than what they and their wives read in the society columns and pass on in the executive dining room and at Bloomfield Hills cocktail parties. But with all the information I have gathered, I still find him paradoxical.

"I know how hard it is for you," his daughter Charlotte told me. We were sitting in a high-ceilinged, red-velvet-walled room in her Sutton Place duplex, overlooking the East River. There was a little sadness in her blue eyes and direct voice. "I don't understand Daddy either. I love him and I admire him, but I don't understand him."

Another day, after luncheon with the younger Ford daughter, Anne, in her McMillen-decorated Park Avenue apartment, I repeated Charlotte's remark. She gave a little squeal of surprise. "Charl said *that?*" she demanded. "How could she? Why Daddy's the easiest man to know in the world. I can see right through him."

John R. Davis, who worked closely with Henry Senior for a quarter of a century and was one of the most trusted of all Henry Ford II's associates for many years, spent several hours with me talking about both of them. Attempting to understand either one, he said, was preposterous. "The only thing to understand about Henry and the old man both is their utter inconsistency," he said. "Both of them could be charming, gracious, wonderful one minute, and totally inconsiderate the next. There's one difference—young Henry inherited a touch of sweetness from his mother and father that the old man never showed. Complete chameleons, both of them. But two more interesting people never lived."

Nor controversial. Surely no other industrialist has been the subject of so many printed words as the patriarch—and they range from sycophancy to venom. One reason, of course, is that like so many of the Great-Man genre Henry Ford made the mistake of living too long. Of his many contributions to mankind, two were of such magnitude as to immortalize him. One was the practical means of low-cost transportation exemplified by that marvelous piece of hardware, the Model T. The other was the concept, which formed the basis of twentieth-century mass production, that payment of high wages to industrial workers—even enough to enable them to buy the automobile they were making—would in the long run benefit both industry and the total economy. Both of these contributions, however, were made before his 51st birthday. In the activities and philosophies of his remaining third of a century on earth he did not maintain his batting average.

The fact remains that Henry the One is looked upon today with reverence by some, hatred by others. Both emotions pop up in the most unlikely characters. I expected a man like labor leader Walter Reuther, who was brutally beaten by Ford guards, to show some bitterness. But I wasn't prepared for the gentle little Detroit artist, who, though he would not harm a termite if it were eating his viola, ranted about Ford—who'd been dead for more than twenty years and whom he'd never seen—with such fury that spit flew all over my face.

Young Henry calls forth the same range of reaction. Shortly after *Fortune* magazine omitted his name from its list of 153 Americans worth at least $100 million, a retired top executive dismissed his personal wealth as meaningless. "So he's worth a hundred million, maybe a few hundred million. That's only a fraction of his *value,* what he contributes to the Ford Motor Company, its stockholders, and the economy of the United States and much of the world."

Max M. Fisher of Detroit, a personal friend of Ford, himself the head of a multimillion-dollar company, said, "Henry is the new breed of businessman. His interest in our domestic problems and his willingness to speak up and do things about them—stand up and be counted—have influenced the entire business community. We in America should thank God for his leadership, sensitivity, intelligence, and guts."

But an eminent figure in the New York publishing world said, "I don't know Henry Ford myself but I know *what* he is, a fat playboy who's got his mind on broads and booze. How can a slob like that run such a company?" And the chairman of the board of a major brokerage house told me bluntly that he discourages customers from buying stock in the Ford Motor Company. "Some of the things Henry Ford does through his company and his pinko foundation threaten the free enterprise system that this country and my business are built on," he said.

I'd like to try to tidy up the record on these two men who built the third largest industrial company in the world. The largest, of course, is General Motors, but GM is the product of many combines and many managers, most of whom have remained behind the scenes. Ford's, or the Factory, as many employees call it, has always been run—or mis-run—by someone named Henry Ford, with a charisma and flair that has grabbed the attention of the world. For many years every other car sold in the world was a Ford. In many countries today an automobile is still *El Ford,* even if the name on it is Volkswagen or Chevrolet. The increasing penetration into both the domestic and international market by General Motors and others was in itself due in part to the peculiar nature of Henry I, who permitted himself to be overtaken. A farm mechanic, unconsciously operating within the sociological system of his times, the Puritan Ethic, he remained static among the vast changes in the world he made.

His grandson, product of Yale and heavily influenced by its Department of Sociology, which stressed the continuing adjustment of mankind to environment, has rebuilt the company under the principles of his times, the Social Ethic.

The automotive industry supports one out of every six Americans. (On the other hand, more Americans have been killed in automobiles than in all our wars combined.) On a personal level, the automobile represents the single most important purchase after the home. Charles N. Barnard, who covered the automotive beat for 15 years before becoming editor of *True,* says it more strongly. "A car has a mystique. A house just sits there. A car is a wife, a mistress. You fall in love with it, dream exotic fantasies about it. If it fulfills your expectations you remain steadfastly faithful; if it doesn't, you're hurt and mad. Automobiles are more than a business. They're an emotion."

Despite their all-out role in the automobile industry, both Fords refused to stay within the confines of business, however huge. They became active in other areas of their community— which to them is the world. It took a Ford to hire an ocean liner, stock it with a hodgepodge of sincere pacifists and self-seeking odd balls, and take off for Europe in an effort to stop a whole damn war. His grandson never tried anything quite so spectacular, but he has become personally and outspokenly involved with the biggest issues of our day. Martin Hayden, editor of the *Detroit News* and a sensitive observer of his town's leading citizen, points out that Henry Ford II not only can say and do things other industrialists would not, but he can get away with it, too. "We're used to the Fords taking stands on issues around here," he said.

In their social lives there seems more variance in the two Henry Fords. The first courted his childhood sweetheart from the Michigan farm country at sleigh-riding parties; after their marriage, there was never a hint of scandal. The second met his bride-to-be on an ocean liner returning from Europe and courted her in the exclusive New York and North Shore Long Island society in which her family was prominent. After two decades of marriage rumors began popping up in the international jet set that there was another woman. The Fords were divorced and both remarried.

As for diversion, Henry I enjoyed bucolic pleasures; he liked camping trips and revived the almost-forgotten art of square dancing. His grandson has gone in for other social pastimes, like being the life of the party and leading the band. There's a big difference, but is it in the two Fords, or in the times?

Lee Hills, publisher of the *Detroit Free Press* and president of Knight Newspapers, Inc., said it well. He went to the trouble to write out his thoughts for me before I came in, then amplified them in discussion. His memorandum was most perceptive. "There's a touch of the old Populist in both of them!" it began, went on to spell out how each had contributed to the betterment of people, and summed it up: "Both were men for their times."

The first of these men for their times is now long dead, his memory spotted by the anti-Semitism and anti-labor actions of his later years. Those who knew him during his great period are long gone. Studies of him as a young man reveal the charm, magnetism, and enthusiasm that attracted to him all those who helped him. Friends and associates of his grandson see those same qualities in him.

Other similarities in the two Henry Fords make it possible to study each through the other, to see not two people, but one multisided man for his time. Enlarging on this, we can see the times themselves, and the industry which, more than any other, changed our times—an industry which would be important and exciting even if it had made only a fraction of its contribution to civilization.

No name in modern times has had such positive and exciting meaning to so many people over so long a time as Henry Ford. That statement is cheating a little, maybe, because it had two standard bearers, I and II, to carry it on into well over a century. Other super names during the period—Edison, Marx, Wilson, Roosevelt, Churchill, Hitler—had, effectively, only one. And what a hell of a century these two Henry Fords have had to work in. When Grandfather Ford was born, this country, the overall leader in the development of the twin bedrocks of transportation and communication, was connected only by thin lines of rivers, one-track railroads, and rutty wagon trails. Other automotive pioneers, most of them long since forgotten, made some contributions, but it was Henry Ford's Model T which, more than all the others combined, assembled the people of America and subsequently the people of every country and land mass of the world. The Ford empire grew commensurately: the English boast that the sun never sets on the British Empire; the present Henry Ford can say that he never sets on the world. Seventy-two years after his grandfather pushed his homemade motor buggy out into a rainy Detroit street at midnight for its first run, eight communications satellites bearing the name Ford were boosted into orbit in one shot to make a total of 26 silently swooshing around the globe. One of them may be over your head right now.

To anyone interested in finance, the name Henry Ford has continual fascination. He organized the Ford Motor Company in 1903 without putting up one cent of his own money. A quarter of a century later, it was worth one billion dollars and by that time Ford owned it completely. He was the first, and, what with income taxes, probably the last, self-made billionaire. (Not that he cared; he continued to wear the socks his wife darned.) Along the way, the eleven other stockholders—who put up a total of $28,500 in cash—collected many millions in dividends, and when Henry cagily maneuvered them into a position where they had to sell out, sixteen years after the formation of the company, they got even more. A lady who was coerced into putting up $100 collected $95,000 in dividends, mostly tax free, over the years and $260,000 for her stock.

Years later the second Henry Ford gave his own dazzling industrial performance. He set out to save a company that was losing $10 million a month. He was 28 at the time, about the same age his grandfather had started building an internal combustion engine before anybody had invented such conveniences as spark plugs. Young Henry II had no more knowledge of the modern tools of business—financial controls, personnel, organization—than young Henry I had of a 4-venturi carburetor, but he did have the same attributes: the proper background to assimilate the knowledge that was needed, the charm to attract talented people to help, the leadership to keep them and use them, and the physical and mental stamina to keep going.

In 1968 the Ford Motor Company, 415,000 people strong, $9 billion in assets, and Henry Ford II in firm command, produced a record year. Sales totaled more than $14 billion. That's more than most of the nations of the world take in, more than most of the states, and more than the United States itself in any year up to 1942. Henry Ford II made his share of millionaires, too. The most prominent of the many older men on whom he leaned, the managerial genius Ernest R. Breech, earned many millions of dollars through his association with Ford.

Henry Ford I created the company and made it big; Henry Ford II saved it and made it bigger and more extensive. Henry I began the River Rouge plant in Dearborn. Today this one compacted fraction of the company, covering twelve hundred acres, comprises the world's largest industrial complex. It has its own 85-mile railroad, with 19 locomotives, and a food service that serves 100,000 lunches a day. Yet only a comparatively small number of cars, all Mustangs and Cougars, are actually assembled there, in a building put up in 1918 to build boats.

Ford's glass plants comprise the country's third largest glass producer and the size of its steel operation usually ranks in the top dozen. If you look at the overall organization chart, you'll see, dangling like a participle over on the right hand side, two little squares representing the Ford insurance and credit companies; together they do business in the billions.

The computer center is the largest in industry, as is the Ford communications network. If a Ford manager in Copenhagen, say, wants to talk to the plant in Cologne his call is routed through London to Dearborn, then to Cologne. It's a lot simpler and easier than trying to go direct.

Even before the Model T, Ford became international, moving first into Canada, then England. Young Henry carried on the international expansion. As just one example of the size of Ford country, up until 1968 Ford of England brought more income into the British Isles than any other company, English included. The plant at Dagenham is half the size of the Rouge; the German complex, at Cologne, is a third as large.

The company is concerned with more than hardware. A small department containing over two hundred Ph.D.'s is doing basic research on anything that seems challenging to anybody at any time. One of them was telling me about some complicated discovery that may have some bearing on the metastasis of carcinoma throughout the human body. I asked him what that had to do with automobiles and he looked at me as though I had said something dirty. "We do more here than just bend metal," he said.

Maybe so, and Henry Ford II proudly proclaims his three P's—products, profits and people—but when I think of Ford I still think of an automobile, and I'll bet you do, too. The analogy may seem paradoxical at first, but even in the wildly dissimilar models of, say, 1910 and 1970, the theme of the two Fords is continued; both represent cars for their times, made by men for their times. Henry I and the group of crony-mechanics who alternated work and horseplay with him around the clock worked for twelve years, for a period of that time defying his directors and stockholders who wanted big, expensive cars, until in 1908 he brought out the Model T. It took that long to make something so simple. There was little that could go wrong and just about anybody could fix it if it did. This was the vehicle that connected people, made neighbors, brought the farmers to town, first on Saturday, then any old day. Three years after it came out oil companies began selling greater quantities of gasoline than kerosene. People began demanding roads, and got them, complete with filling stations, motels, and shopping centers.

Sixty years later the Ford line of cars was so complex, with so many different models of different colors with different options—*CJ 428 cu. in. 4V V-8 ($336.80) * (Available only with 4-speed Manual or Select-Shift Transmission) * Over price of Base V-8*—that the huge assembly plant at Mahwah, N.J., could run for a whole year without duplicating a model.

Both Fords liked speed and competition. Not many men are racing at forty today, but that's how old Henry Ford was in 1904 when he became the first man to go 90 miles an hour in an automobile. He didn't even have a steering wheel, but a kind of tiller. "When I can't see ahead," he explained, "I can tell if I'm going straight by looking down at the steering handle." Racing went into the doldrums after World War I. The 1932 flathead V-8 engine, the old man's last engineering marvel, was a major factor in making stock car racing what it is today, a large segment of what may be the country's most popular spectator sport. After the Automobile Manufacturers Association

13

put the brakes on high-performance cars in the late Fifties, Henry Ford II defied the ban and went back in, "with both feet," in 1961. Three years later Ford cars were in the forefront of racing over the world.

The assembly line is generally thought of as the creation of Henry Ford I. He actually inspired and directed its development from an existing idea. Henry II can hardly claim a similar individual influence in modern managerial techniques, but there is nevertheless a parallel of some degree. Building on the profit-centered, decentralized organization of General Motors, he inspired the development of the modern Ford organization. I can't testify to its superiority, but neither can anyone else outside the company. According to Edwin D. O'Leary, vice president in charge of personnel and organization, Ford is so far ahead of everybody else that it's going to stay that way. In other words, the system is not open to study.

By their contribution to transportation and by their enthusiastic reception of new ideas and their willingness to try them out no matter who thinks they're nuts, both Fords have made economic and sociological impacts on civilization. I'm not quoting the Ford PR department, but rather someone who has reason to bear animosity toward the elder Ford, having been beaten up and dragged down thirty-nine steel steps—"The end of my spine hit every one of 'em and I can still feel it"—while the old man then ostensibly ran the plant. I refer to Walter Reuther, former Ford employee, active organizer in the plant, and later president of the United Automobile Workers.

Reuther and I talked in his office in Solidarity House, UAW headquarters in Detroit. Compared to the meticulous spotlessness of Henry Ford II's offices over the world, the place was a shambles. Reuther was coatless. In his early sixties, he looked twenty years younger with hair still red, eyes sparkling, and bubbling exuberance. As he talked he'd jump up, stick out his

14

chest, strut back and forth, and orate—not with pomp, but with honest enthusiasm.

"Henry Ford," he said, referring to the founder, "was responsible for the great shift in production philosophy on the part of American industry. He was the first to realize the value of the mass market for his products—for everybody's products. I'm convinced that he was sincere in his motivation for the $5 day. It doesn't make any difference how many of the people who were with him then tried to take credit for the idea, the old man had to approve it and he knew what he was doing. It was his most fundamental contribution to our economy, even more valuable than the Model T. Only after Henry Ford showed the rest of them how, did industry begin to build for the large number of consumers. He structured the idea of the mass market which required mass production which made it possible to utilize the advanced technology that science was beginning to furnish at just that time. Some people say Henry Ford was only a good mechanic but he was much more. He combined his personal mechanical genius with a unique understanding of this basic fact—mass consumption makes mass production possible. He was sound mechanically and he was sound economically, and he brought the two together at just the time when scientific advances were becoming available to make the combination work. . . ."

Bringing the idea up to date, Reuther naturally gives the union credit for the current extension of Henry I's economic principles into today's economy, but he also concedes some measure of cooperation to Henry Ford II. "On some of the progressive features the company now brags about I sometimes say, 'If they're so good, why did you fight us when we first proposed them?' But it is to their eternal credit that when we kept pushing for these things the company became interested, hired their own experts, looked into the situation with an open mind, and came around to our way of thinking. Our union and the Ford Motor Company pioneered the guaranteed annual income for the automobile production worker. Even during the periods of cyclical layoffs he and his family can maintain their standard of living and pay their bills. Do you realize what that means to the American economy? It's carrying on the same idea that Henry Ford developed, the idea that makes this great flowering of production possible. You couldn't have the benefits of mass production and technological advances without purchasing power on the part of the consumer, and that consumer is nobody but the American worker. Working together across the bargaining table, Ford and the union have hammered out a most secure base for the American economy to continue to survive."

Henry Ford II has also received extravagant praise from more neutral observers. When he first took over the company, it had a well-deserved reputation for vicious anti-unionism; he made the proposal, a managerial blockbuster in the immediate postwar era when labor and management castigated each other on a round-the-year basis rather than just at bargaining time, that each accept the other, and the responsibility that went with acceptance. Not long after Edward Cushman, director of the Wayne University Institute of Labor Relations, went out on a limb with the statement that Henry Ford II was leading industry and the nation into democracy in the economic system.

The two Henry Fords have been up to their ears in their country's problems, almost across the board. In some cases it's hard to differentiate between activities in which their own self-interest was involved, and those which were purely altruistic. I've been told by tough-minded Ford executives that they are proud to be part of an operation with social consciousness whether it shows up on the ledger or not. I've also been told by do-good personnel recruiters assigned to ghetto areas that a better life for people of these areas means an increasing market for Ford cars. But both groups give full credit for the immense amount of time, money, and effort contributed to interracial problems to the man at the top.

Within their respective eras, both Henry Fords have shown a striking blindness to the color of a man's skin. When, in 1890, the first Henry was supporting himself and his bride by cutting and selling timber on his Michigan farm, he frequently was on one end of a cross-cut saw, a Negro helper on the other. He later brought this same co-worker into the Ford Motor Company and influenced the rest of the new industry into opening their doors. The old man, however, drew the line at social equality.

His grandson expanded the Ford influence in work opportunities into the entire American community, and draws no racial line. In June, 1968, he prevailed upon the prominent black leader Whitney M. Young, Jr., to speak to several hundred of Ford's Grosse Pointe neighbors on the need to expose the school children of today to all other children, regardless of ethnic or economic background, in order to prepare them for the world in which they will live. As a personal friend of the Youngs—the two couples are frequent dinner companions—Ford knew of an event taking place back home in Westchester County, New York: Whitney's 14-year-old daughter, Lauren, was graduating from junior high school that afternoon, as class president. After the speech, a Ford car rushed Young to the airport; a Ford plane took him to New York; another Ford car got him to the suburban school so that the proud father was there for his daughter's commencement address.

And thanks in large measure to Henry Ford II and his influence in big industry, opportunities for blacks have increased over the entire country, and Negro executives are In. "I worked on inner city problems in Cleveland in 1967 when I was president of the Euclid Division of General Motors," Robert E. Hunter, subsequently president of Philco-Ford, told me. "But I

17

didn't dare bring it to the attention of the company. After Mister Ford got interested GM poured Holy Water over it and now it's just another company program."

The original Henry Ford drew another firm and heavy line. Though he devoted much of his energy to making work for people of all races, and demonstrated an interest in their welfare which was paternalistic to the point of meddling, he proclaimed and maintained audibly a harsh aversion to charity. His refusal to contribute to the Detroit Community Chest, even during long layoff periods and the soup-kitchen days of the depression, is one of the strongest of the denigrating truths about him. At the same time he was criticizing and withholding his money from organized charity, however, this contradictory individual was spending tens of millions of dollars, far more than the tax-deductible limit, on his own personal do-good projects. He built an orphanage, the large, highly respectable Henry Ford Hospital, several schools, the Henry Ford Museum, and Greenfield Village, preserved landmarks and relics of bygone days, and saved and developed two deteriorated communities. Some of his activities reflected what seemed to be a pretty screwball approach at the time, like sifting Edison's personal trash heap, but almost everything worked out magnificently. The day after a young Detroit pseudointellectual told me scathingly that the Henry Ford Museum was a pantechnicon of junk and she wouldn't go near the place, I met Arthur Hailey, author of *Airport* and *Hotel,* and asked him how he was coming along with his research for his next book, on the automobile industry.

"Not so good," he said, "I went to the Henry Ford Museum and couldn't get out for three days. It's marvelous."

The Ford Foundation was set up primarily as a tax gimmick to keep ownership of the company in the family, and started out as a poor relation in the family of foundations. Though it grew to be larger than any other foundation and was placed under independent control, Henry Ford II, as a dynamic

18

member of the board of trustees, has had strong influence in the disposal of a sum approaching four billion dollars in both controversial and well-received projects, here and abroad. The thrust of the Foundation is to help people help themselves through constructive projects and grants to institutions of basic and higher learning. Ford has more than a touch of his grandfather's aversion to charity *vis à vis* creation of employment, but he has nevertheless personally given away millions.

Henry the One was born July 30, 1863. HF II was born September 4, 1917. In between the two, whether as a link or an expander, was Edsel, the only son of one, father of the other. Little has been written of Edsel Ford, or of his wife, the former Eleanor Lowthian Clay, cultured member of a prominent Detroit family. Edsel was overshadowed and overwhelmed by his father. Just as he was a good baby when he was loved by doting parents, so was he a dutiful son when he was demeaned by the tycoon tyrant his father became. I have never heard anyone say anything unkind about Edsel. Those who came to hate The Old Man but who admire his grandson (a combination of opinions surprisingly prevalent among Ford workers and union leaders) try to write off the hereditary influence of Henry I completely and give all the credit to Edsel and Eleanor Clay Ford; those who can look back across the years to the achievements of the patriarch do not minimize those of his characteristics that appear in his grandson, but see them sort of filtered through the forbearance and sweetness—a word often used—of Edsel and Eleanor to produce the perceptivity and understanding of the grandson—who deserves some special study on his own.

2

BEFORE LOOKING at both Fords and all their operations, industrial, public, and social, let's narrow the focus to the one that's available, Henry Ford II.

I've gone out and gotten information for about a thousand magazine articles and fifteen books, but never before have I worked on a story in which there was so much curiosity on the part of my friends and neighbors. I live in a pleasant community where everybody tries to keep up with everybody else's business, usually without malice. When I return home from a visit with Henry Ford II or someone connected with him, friends, acquaintances, and sometimes people I've never seen before come up to me at the supermarket, filling station, tennis court, or cocktail party and ask me what kind of a guy he is.

I hope these people don't get together and compare what I told them because they'd all think me the biggest liar in town.

21

There would be some major contradictions. This is because a writer is a reflector. He reflects the impression made upon him by his sources of information, he reflects his own emotions and judgments, and finally, he reflects on what he reflects. When people ask, what kind of guy is Henry Ford, I can't answer objectively; both directly and vicariously, he has had a tremendous effect on me. Nor can I answer with consistency; I have seen him through too many pairs of eyes.

For example, I can't say that I like Henry Ford, or that you would like Henry Ford; what I can say is that a lot of people whom I like very much, warm, lovable people, like Henry Ford very much. They've given me good reasons, from their hearts and their minds, for liking him. But before going into their combined eulogy, let me express my own dyslogy. He scares me. And well he should, for he is a man of enormous power.

For most people, the type of people industry wants, a career with Ford is challenging, exciting, and, if you make it, rewarding. But I remember one well-paid executive who suddenly started trembling when I asked him a question about Henry Ford which only he could answer—and Mister Ford would know it. For as a brilliant and articulate vice president and one of the unterrified observed with grisly humor, the sword that can bestow knighthood upon the vassal—he extended his arm and lowered it, palm down—can also, with just one quarter of a revolution—he turned his hand to resemble a karate chop—cleave the poor devil in two.

Another perceptive executive idly commented that he sometimes stands at his great expanse of glass in the Central Office Building (COB) at Dearborn at ten minutes to eight (they get to work early in the automobile industry) and watches the three thousand inhabitants scuttle toward the entrances. "It always reminds me of the Eloi in *The Time Machine,*" he said. "You remember—they are the people who live on the face of the earth and when the bell rings they happily flock to the temple to be eaten up by the Morlocks." He was bemused by his own picture of the human tidbits coming into the meat grinder.

Only a few minutes later, on simultaneous impulse, we visited the men's room. He was telling me a mild little anecdote as we entered. I noticed that his eyes flicked over the toilet stalls behind us to make sure that they were empty before he continued with the story. After that, I made a habit of observing other executives as they entered the blue-doored men's rooms in the COB. In an action so automatic that Pavlov would rub his hands in satisfaction, every eye always checked the doors of the stalls. I'm not trying to imply that the suspicion and tale bearing so common in the Factory just a generation ago still exist; they don't. But discretion does, for every employee on every level is subject to the periodic personnel review. "We can't have people just floppin' around here," Ford told me.

Ford's eyes are a bright blue, and when he looks directly at you they have a piercing quality that makes the color even more intense. Along with the swinging colors of the '70 Maverick —Thanks Vermillion, Freudian Gilt—they ought to have Ford's Eye Blue. Often I felt I was being unpeeled like an orange. He ducks his head forward, brow wrinkled, and sights over the rims of his Ben Franklin tortoiseshell glasses with a look that cuts right through all pretense. Several times I tried to stare back at him over my own half glasses, but I always felt, even though we are about the same size—six feet and overweight—that I was looking uphill. I know from what others have told me that there is a tremendous warmth behind those unflinching eyes, but I only rarely felt a great deal of it. This is not resentment; I have been exposed to people of great wealth before and I understand their problem. They can't let their guard down.

Ford relaxed with me as much as I could expect. In our sessions we frequently joked and laughed. He was courteous, and when he refused to answer or elaborate on a question, it was usually with a little embarrassed laugh or a halfway apologetic explanation. Yet at the end of an interview, I never felt as I have with hundreds of other people a warm eagerness to see him again.

Ford has a high-pitched voice which, under even mildly unpleasant circumstances, can rasp on the ears. While I was prowling through the Factory, I was told several times of an incident in which Mister Ford snapped at a minor executive in scatological language. I inferred from the amount of comment on this one nasty crack not that Ford snarls obscenities at underlings but that on the contrary, as people in Ford offices all over the world will testify, he customarily does not. The correctness with which Ford treats his employees almost without exception must require an inordinate amount of self-control from a man who has been described by so many people as impulsive and bluntly outspoken.

But for me, being in the presence of all that power and of those under that power, no matter how well controlled, has had a cumulative effect. On occasion, then, I would tell those friends curious as to what sort of guy Henry Ford is that he is an overwhelming sort of guy.

Yet I've seen all that power put to good use, and have again reacted to it subjectively and emotionally. I know that he spent several weekends in Washington, alone, helping set up the National Alliance of Businessmen, put his own high-powered executive in as its executive director, and cancelled a safari in Africa in order to stay with it. Through this organization, he believed, a positive blow could be struck at one of the most malignant causes of racial unrest in America, unemployment. He proposed to find jobs for 500,000 hard-core unemployed, mostly Negro, some proportion of whom just might get somewhere if they had an honest-to-God fighting chance. Ford led the way both in his own company and in the national organization.

Though I don't usually cover public meetings anymore—they're not only dull but predictable—when I learned that Ford

24

and the Ford staff were staging the kickoff of the NAB, I went to Washington to see the performance. Before it began, I could tell it was going to be worth it. Rudi Fischer, a Ford old-timer who'd come down to attend to the routine details, told me he'd gotten sick of the clock watchers assigned to the job and told them to go away. "They wanted to go home at five o'clock," he said. "I haven't gone home at five o'clock for forty years." The way things were going was smooth, smooth, smooth.

Several hundred people were in the ballroom of the Sheraton Park Hotel when the meeting began at ten o'clock Saturday morning. On the dais were cabinet members, public officials, and men prominent in the human relations area. One of them was Whitney Young, Jr., executive director of the National Urban League. I noted that as Young finished his brief talk, Ford gave him a warm little punch on the arm as he turned away to return to his seat.

During one of the speeches, Ford, in response to a signal, left the platform and proceeded to a side entrance. Shortly after, he started back, along the side wall. He was walking fast, purposefully, his stomach protruding a little. Behind him, more at ease, came President Lyndon B. Johnson. Ford mounted the platform, took the microphone, and, with the public address system magnifying the sharp quality of his voice, said, "Ladies and gentlemen, the President of the United States!"

We all stood and applauded the President. I looked around; the large room was almost completely filled. There were 750 selected men here, from all over the country, executives of the nation's largest corporations and trade associations, keeping the operators of the fifteen television cameras busy. This was a Saturday morning; most had flown in the night before. There would be no golf for them this weekend, no drinks at the club tonight (how many wives had called off how many dinner engagements?), but not one face showed any emotion other than enthusiasm and determination to do the job that Henry Ford was asking them to do. The President could have begged off; even as he was speaking, Senator Robert F. Kennedy was announcing to a nationwide television audience in a special press conference that he would be available for the Democratic nomination in opposition to the President. Yet Johnson was there; his friend Henry Ford had asked him to be there. As I looked around, I felt proud of my country and its leaders, proud of being a witness to the formation of something of such great potential, and proud of my association, however tenuous, with Henry Ford II. He had been given a job to do, and he was getting it done. (A year later, on the first anniversary meeting of the NAB with President Nixon and his cabinet in attendance, Ford was given a rare reward for his efforts: a silver platter with the engraved signatures of both Johnson and Nixon.)

These, then, are my own impressions, reflected from the personal encounters with Mister Ford himself and with many of his executives. No great warmth, even a touch of fear in the gut, but great admiration and appreciation for his ability, dedication, and accomplishment.

But when I'd visit with his friends and family, and sometimes with those of his most perceptive executives, I'd bring back a different reflection. Seeing the real Henry Ford through the eyes of those who know him personally and like him and love him, I feel a personal attachment to the man. He's as human as anybody else. The hard, tough image, the defensiveness, that he imparted to me softens in the light of what others say and feel about him. He told me, for example, that he never brought his worries home from the office, that on only one occasion, involving a protracted legal suit in the Fifties, had he lost one wink of sleep over the Ford Motor Company. When I quoted him to his wife, however, her eyes grew wide and she exclaimed, "Oh, but that ees not true!"

This was in 1968, just after Ford, in one of the great industrial dramas of the decade, had hired Semon E. ("Bunkie")

26

Knudsen away from General Motors and made him president of the Ford Motor Company, replacing Arjay Miller. Knudsen was placed in salary grade No. 28, the same classification as Henry Ford himself.

Miller was a grade below. (Actual 1968 compensation: Ford, $200,000 salary plus $400,000 bonus; Knudsen, $180,-952 (eleven months) plus $400,000; Miller, $175,000 plus $295,000.) A special title was created for him, vice chairman of the board, and he was given a particular and most important area of responsibility especially fitted to his high intellectual capabilities and his great concern for social progress. (A personnel executive told me that Arjay Miller could be the dean of any graduate business school in the country. When he left the company it was to take over that very position at Stanford University.)

Thanks to his salary, bonus, stock options, and other opportunities at Ford, Miller had become a multimillionaire. But Miller is a person of sensitivity—what about his pride? And so, Mrs. Ford told me, her husband, who would have me believe he has an elephant hide so far as business is concerned, turned and tossed, night after night, worrying about those involved in the change in command.

Mister Ford's daughter Anne told me a similar story about her father. One of the leading characters in the too-incredible-for-Hollywood events of Henry Ford II's battle to gain control of the company in 1945 was John Bugas, a brave and loyal comrade. At one time the situation was so dangerous that both Bugas and Ford carried guns. Bugas was rewarded with increasing responsibility, pay, and opportunity. He also, as is almost automatic in the case of anyone of such position, became worth several million dollars. However, he was not cut out for his penultimate job with the company, vice president in charge of international operations. He was relieved of that duty, given the specially constructed box on the organization chart entitled vice president and consultant, and continued on at a rate of pay which in 1966 amounted to $125,000 salary, $100,000 in bonus, with the usual fringe benefits. But here again, a good man's feelings were hurt.

On the night of February 18, 1965, Anne was in Detroit visiting a friend. Of the three Ford children, Charlotte, Anne and Edsel, Anne is the closest to her father. "They get together and talk until four in the morning," Charlotte once told me without envy, but a little wistful.

"Daddy and I are awfully close, just as Charlotte said," Anne said, "but I'm afraid it is pretty much a one-sided conversation. I do all the talking, he does all the listening. This is the only time that I ever recall Daddy talking about business. He didn't talk about what he and Mr. Bugas had been through together—none of us has ever heard that story first hand— but he did say how close they had been, what good friends they were. And now he had to reassign the duties of this good friend. He was really concerned about it."

At no point in this conversation, Anne recalls positively, did her father mention another, and certainly far more intoxicating event than the impending transfer of John Bugas. In less than 24 hours, her father married the woman he loved. Why didn't he tell Anne, of all people, about his impending happiness?

"I think he wanted to," Anne told me. "I think he started to a couple of times, but he just couldn't bring himself to go through with it. Daddy is terribly shy, even with me."

Henry Ford is singularly blessed with the love of four beautiful, charming, and intelligent women—his mother, his wife, and two daughters—and I have been fortunate in that three of them talked to me with surprising candor.

There has been severe criticism of Henry Ford for his divorce and remarriage, but from what his friends and daughters

28

say I think a case can be made that some of his actions are a credit to him.

The triangle began at a party given by his uncle, Ernest C. Kanzler, in Paris in March, 1960, where he met Maria Cristina Vettore Austin, a blonde Italian divorcée.

"We actually met the night before the party," Cristina told me, "but it was only how do you do. Then at the party, it was at Maxim's, he told me he wanted to sit by me. That was when the romance began. It just happened. I did not want to break up his marriage. Believe me, I did not break up his marriage. This marriage, it was already broke."

It is impossible to reproduce Cristina's accent phonetically; I will only say that it is a delight to listen to her. She's the only woman I ever met who kept me waiting forty minutes and made me forget it in forty seconds. She should really not be described in prose, either—a painting would be more appropriate—but I'll try. The night before I met her I had been reading up on the painters of the Impressionist school in order to impress her husband, a connoisseur, if I got the chance. Seurat could have done a beautiful job with Cristina's eyes: the amber flecked with blue and yellow with traces of green. She is blonde, with a small face and a wide, warm mouth.

She's something of a nut on diet and physical fitness: she likes to ride her bicycle around Grosse Pointe Farms, tinkling her bell as she glides to a stop at the homes of friends. The Fords were given a set of his-and-her bicycles, and she tried to get her husband to ride with her, but even Cristina couldn't swing that. Henry Ford's ideas of recreation do not include a great deal of exercise. But she continued to pester him about his health, and I think he loves it.

There was also a touch of pride in Cristina's voice as she told me of an episode concerning her husband's health. "He is supposed to see the doctor, you know, for a checkup, every six months," she said. "I beg him, but he will not go. So last Monday I make an appointment for him. Then I call him and tell him there is something wrong with me, that I must go to the hospital, he must go with me. He say that he have many appointments, that he cannot go, that he will send a driver and he will call the hospital and I will be all right. 'Oh, no,' I say, 'I have so much fear. I cannot go alone. You must go with me.' So he break all his appointments and meet me at the hospital and then I tell him, 'It is not me, it is you!' So he have the examination and he is perfectly okay."

She sat back and smiled triumphantly.

The Monday she was talking about was just three days before the 1968 stockholders' meeting. The chairman of the board had a few things to attend to that day, but Cristina got her husband to the doctor.

Cristina and Henry Ford had been seeing each other for about two years, Cristina said, when the newspaper people in Rome and Paris, a particularly nosy breed, began getting close to the situation. "He thought we had better not see each other again."

A close personal friend of his told me that this self-enforced deprivation continued for about a year, and that it was based on all the right and good things: the sanctity of marriage, the necessity to preserve it for the benefit of the children, and, very important to a man with hundreds of thousands of people dependent upon him and the whims of the car-buying public, the aversion to scandal. As one observant and articulate vice president commented, being Henry Ford is a difficult personal assignment; he can't do all the things you and I can do. It was not a happy time. "I'll call you a liar if you say I said it," one of Ford's older New York friends told me, "but though I didn't know about Cristina, I could tell something was eating on him. I figured his marriage was going to hell but I understood. I'm a two-time loser myself."

As for Cristina, she felt the separation was pretty silly. "It was his idea," she said. "I never ask him to marry me. All I want is to be happy. As for his marriage, pfft! It was dead. I don't think a woman should let her husband know she is suspicious. Then the other woman becomes forbidden fruit. You know what I mean?"

After not seeing Cristina for some time, Henry Ford could not stay away.

I got more of the personal picture of Henry Ford on another visit to his daughter Anne. Happily married to a Wall Streeter named Giancarlo Uzielli, and mother of an active little boy, Anne looks as though she'd have trouble ordering a drink in a cocktail lounge; in a gray miniskirt, white blouse, and with her long blond hair flowing, she'd be taken for a teen-ager. We had lunch together one day shortly after Jackie Kennedy married Aristotle Onassis. Everybody in New York was gossiping about the wedding, and the event had brought up the marriage, three years before, of Charlotte Ford to another Greek multimillionaire, Stavros Niarchos.

"Do you know what somebody said to me last night?" Anne said indignantly, and repeated an untrue rumor about Charlotte. "Can you imagine that?"

"I've heard that one and a couple of dozen more," I said. "All I know is what I read in the papers. I don't think I can stamp out all rumors, but if I knew the real story maybe I could help."

That's how Anne came to tell me of her father's role in the Niarchos marriage.

One thing is necessary to remember. Henry Ford II is a busy man. Charlotte often protested sadly that she rarely saw her father; he was always busy, a prisoner of the company. He travels constantly. As Cristina had told me, "The poor man, he never sleep three nights in the same bed."

This is the man who received Anne's call from New York.

31

She and Charlotte had discussed Charlotte's romance with Niarchos and the two girls decided that Anne should call their father.

"Can you come to New York tonight, Daddy?" Anne asked.

"Is it important?" he asked.

"Well, yes it is," Anne said. "Charlotte and I really would like to see you tonight."

Anne paused in telling me this story, looked at me for emphasis, and then said quietly, "Daddy was here with us *in two hours*. He listened to us, got the story straight, and then he said, 'Well, I guess we'd better go talk to Stavros.' Stavros was in London and we flew there the next morning. Mother just happened to be there, too, and so was Stavros' wife. Both of them were as understanding about it as they could be. Mrs. Niarchos agreed to get a divorce. But it was Daddy who handled everything. He was there when we needed him."

Calm, strong . . . here is another reflection of Henry Ford.

In most of Europe, Ford is left pretty much alone, and he is at home there. In the United States there are few places where he can be himself. One of them is P. J. Clarke's, a popular Irish pub on Third Avenue in New York.

I have never seen Henry Ford at P. J. Clarke's—indeed, I make a point of not going there; I have poked into his life enough without spying on him in saloons—but here again I am able to reflect him as seen by other eyes. Ford's pal at Clarke's is Patrick J. Doyle, a police reporter for the *Daily News* from 5:00 P.M. to 1:00 A.M., and after that a movable fixture among the horde of humanity that jams the place in the late hours. The small center room of the dimly lit cavern—somewhat reminiscent of a London bomb shelter in World War II—is officially known to the In group as the Pat Doyle room. It was Henry Ford himself who suggested that I talk to Pat Doyle, and it was a good thing, too, because if the word had not been sent along the pipe from Dearborn to New York, I don't believe Pat would have given me the time of day. As it was, after we shook hands for the first time at P. J. Clarke's, Pat started the conversation with, "Let's get one thing straight. I'm not going to say anything critical about Henry Ford!"

I had expected a large, jolly, red-faced, redheaded Irishman. Instead I found a slender, quiet, black-haired Irishman loyal to Henry Ford to the point of humorlessness. He had brought with him a three-page description of his friend which he had typed up for me on copy paper. One of the sentences that jumped out at me had to do with Ford's colorful language. After swearing me to secrecy, Pat mentioned a couple of Fordisms, and he was right: some of Ford's choice expressions wouldn't look good in print even today. When after a few drinks he gets involved in a furious argument over nothing with Pat, they shout at each other happily in bawdily masculine phraseology. Mister Ford loves it.

Each basks in the other's friendship, and contributes in his own way. Pat doesn't fight for the check—"Wouldn't that be kind of silly, especially since I don't drink?"—but other than that they might be financial equals. After all, neither one of them can fire the other.

Pat is convinced that Ford saved his life. Pat's ulcer perforated while he was driving to work, in his Volvo, and he was in bad shape when he finally arrived at the hospital. Ford went into P. J. Clarke's that night looking for him, was told what had happened, and immediately went to the hospital. Doyle was in a coma and Ford couldn't get to see him. He had to return to Detroit without visiting the patient.

In the meantime, Pat was bleeding to death. He refused to have the operation which the doctors assured him was his only hope. ("I thought I could cure it myself.") Finally his wife, Frances, thought of Henry Ford. It was at night and she could not get his home telephone number, so she called the FBI, which

33

could. Ford couldn't get away, but he immediately sent a long telegram beseeching Pat to have the operation. It was this telegram which influenced Pat to give the doctors permission to operate. They did, he recovered, and he gives credit for his life to Henry Ford. (Ford, when I asked him about this, waved his hand and growled, "Aw hell, one lousy telegram?")

One night Henry and Pat rambled over to the *News* and spent a couple of hours in the city room. Ford, warmly received by Pat's other friends, was fascinated.

Pat Doyle was obviously in a position, the times I talked to him, to show a picture of Henry Ford that few other people have seen. Pat has seen him nuzzling Cristina like a teen-ager in a parked car, kissing her neck and ear until she giggled and pushed him away. He has heard him roar with laughter and shout in colorful language and has seen him become irate and pound on the table over some nasty paragraph in a gossip column. But the most poignant picture of all was the one Pat painted of Henry Ford II, industrial tycoon, after reading an unpleasant gossip item about Charlotte. He threw his head forward, cupping his face in his hands, and cried out, "Oh, Charl, my Charl, what are they doing to you?"

A far different glimpse of Henry Ford comes from Whitney Young, Jr., a man who is equally at home with denizens of the black ghettos, presidents, and fellow Harvard-educated executives.

Young has always been favorably inclined toward both Henry Fords and the company. His father was an electrical engineer with Ford in 1919, making $300 a month; it would have been hard to find another Negro with a like position or salary at that time. The Ford Motor Company was the pioneer in equal opportunity in the automobile industry, if not all industry.

Henry Ford II and Young met in Paris on a tour of Eastern Europe sponsored by Time-Life Incorporated and composed of leading American industrialists. They had a few drinks in interesting places and started a friendship which deepened over the years. During the tour, their group arranged to cross the Iron Curtain the hard way, in a bus, instead of flying from capital to capital. At the check point at Nickelsdorf-Hegyeshalom in Hungary, a Communist guard, fully aware that the bus was filled with capitalists of the very worst kind, rich ones, swung on board scowling to inspect the passports.

"Henry and I were sitting together, in the back of the bus, of course," Whitney said, "and we watched the guard coming down the aisle. He'd hold out his hand for the passport, look at the picture, then compare it with the face of the bearer. He'd look mean, then come on to the next. You ought to have seen his face when he saw my picture. A black man! One of the oppressed! His face lit up. He gave me a great big smile. Then he came to Henry Ford. Everybody in the world knows that name. He looked at us sitting together and his face fell. He must have figured I was Henry's valet, and I'd probably get off the bus dragging my ball and chain.

"Well, he went on down the aisle and out the door, and stood there watching us get off. As I stood up I reached for my bag, but Henry was quicker. He grabbed it, and his too. So I got off the bus, and here comes Henry Ford right after me, carrying my bag. Man, you ought to have seen that fellow's face *then.*"

Frequently, in gathering information about a person or institution it's difficult to pin the really important people down to definite appointments, and when you do, they don't always keep them. But the eagerness on the part of almost everyone to talk about Henry Ford was in itself a reflection of their opinion of this man. Edgar Schmidt, a professional leader of the Detroit United Foundation, recounted with municipal pride the complete story of how Ford developed and put into effect Ford's own idea of the one-donation campaign on which every United

Fund in the country is based. When I thanked Schmidt for his time he was silent a moment. Then he said, "Anytime I can speak of a great man it is a privilege to me. Henry Ford is a great man."

Earl Newsom, now retired from the plush Madison Avenue public relations firm that bears his name, insisted upon making the three-hour drive from his home in Connecticut in order to see me. He received me in his duplex office with the circular staircase, and started to talk about Henry Ford. "I'm very fond of that young man," he explained in his gentle voice, and gave me the story behind the story of Ford's first enlightened dealing with labor.

William Randolph Hearst, Jr., had had two impacted wisdom teeth blasted out in the morning, but he kept his appointment in the afternoon. Hearst, a colorful character in his bright red suspenders, displayed a strangely proprietary interest in Henry Ford II. Hearst is the son of one dynamic tycoon, Ford the grandson of another. Long the custodian of some of the most revealing gossip columns in the world, Bill Hearst knows of many a rich man's heir who has gone sour. But he also knows the story of how young Henry Ford II moved in boldly and wrested the control of his own company away from the entrenched interests. "We were all so proud of him," he told me, "so proud." That was an interesting use of the word "we." One of our boys had made it.

Nathan Cummings, head of the industrial giant, Consolidated Foods, was in the midst of a complicated merger when I called him in New York. "I tell you what you do," he told me on the phone from his headquarters in the Waldorf-Astoria Towers. "You go on home to Virginia. Sunday morning you get up, have a nice breakfast, read the paper, and then call me here collect at eight o'clock and we'll have a nice long chat about Henry."

It was indeed a charming, unhurried conversation—although I managed to pay for the call. Cummings told me of a cruise that he, Max Fisher, and Ford and their wives had taken in the Aegean Sea the preceding summer.

"Everything about the cruise was idyllic," Cummings said, "but what I looked forward to most was breakfast in the morning. I'm an early riser, and I was always first in the dining salon. Then Henry would come in. Max had to be away a lot—that was the time of the Israeli-Arab war—and the girls wouldn't come in until much later, so Henry and I would sit there, drinking coffee, and talk for hours. We talked about painting"— Cummings is one of the world's foremost collectors of the Impressionist and post-Impressionist schools—"and I was constantly impressed by his appreciation and insight into art. It's hard to do justice to the charm of this guy. Here, let me tell you a story. We stopped in at some tiny little island, I don't even remember the name, and went ashore. Henry wanted to call his office on some important matter. The only phone in the village was in a little grocery store, and it was during siesta time. An old fellow and his wife ran the store, and didn't want to open up. They were pretty surly, as a matter of fact. They didn't speak much more English than Henry and I speak Greek, but somehow or another Henry charmed them into opening up the store and letting him place the call. And before we left they insisted on our sharing a glass of wine with them."

Sidney Weinberg, senior partner of Goldman, Sachs & Co., and one of the great names in finance, also graciously squeezed me in on a most difficult day. It wasn't until after I had spent over an hour with him that he asked to be excused. He had to meet the vice president of the United States, Hubert Humphrey, and escort him to a banquet. It was at this banquet, I read a couple of days later, that Weinberg secured pledges totaling millions of dollars for the impending Humphrey campaign. Henry

Ford was one of the donors; Sidney Weinberg, several people have told me, has had great influence on Ford's political thinking.

Weinberg said he was tremendously impressed with Ford as a board chairman. "I've sat on the boards of over twenty-five corporations," he said, "but this one is unique. Usually the chairman of the board just wants his directors to rubber stamp what he's already decided to do. But Henry Ford welcomes dissent. He encourages it, employs stratagems to make us speak up and give him our opinions. He's the most impressive board chairman I've known."

Weinberg added to his financial laurels when he became the architect of the plan under which Ford went public. The plan had to satisfy the Foundation, the Ford family, the Securities and Exchange Commission, and the Internal Revenue Service. Weinberg worked on it for two years and drew up over 50 versions before the final plan was approved. A marvel of simplification of complexity, the prospectus was issued in 1956. Weinberg's fee was estimated at a million dollars, which he turned over to his company. "What would I do with it?" he asked. But during my visit with him he got up from behind his desk and escorted me into a smaller private office. There he pointed to a small picture frame hanging on the wall. Behind the glass was a personal note of appreciation from Henry Ford II. The million dollars meant little; the personal note was the ultimate in reward.

Nobody closely associated with Henry Ford, particularly on so high a level, had any criticism whatever of his personal life. The criterion by which he was judged by his multimillionaire peers was whether he got the job done. The value of the Ford stock is an indication. According to Sidney Weinberg, when it was first placed on the market it was overpriced at $64.50, owing to the attendant furore and glamor. Since that time it split and then went up into the 60's, a value Weinberg now felt was underpriced.

J. Edward Lundy, member of the board of directors, executive vice president in charge of finance, and a man so dedicated to the job and esteemed by his subordinates that he can always be found at 7:45 A.M. having breakfast and holding court in the executive dining room, gave the pragmatic answer as to the effect of Ford's extracurricular activities. "People come out here from Wall Street," he said, "and ask me how Mister Ford gets his work done, with all the socializing they say he does. I tell them what I'm telling you right now. I can send a complex financial problem up to him in the afternoon and the answer is delivered to me early the next morning, in clear, positive language. As far as I'm concerned, he's always here, and he's pretty nearly always right."

When Levi Jackson, the Yale All American of the late Forties, was graduated, not one of all the corporate recruiters beating the New Haven bushes even said hello to the captain of the Yale team; Jackson is a Negro. Ford was the only company that offered him a job on the basis of his academic training, and he liked it so much that he chose it over professional football. He had become a Grade 11 personnel services manager in the $15,000–$20,000 range plus bonus, when he was asked to work with the New Detroit Committee formed after the 1967 riots to deal with interracial problems, and first met Henry Ford.

"He asked me who I worked for in the New Detroit Committee," Jackson told me. "I may have taken the question the wrong way, but anyway I got my back up a little bit and I told him that I didn't work for anybody on the New Detroit Committee. 'I draw my paycheck from the Ford Motor Company,' I said, 'but I reserve the individual freedom to express myself as I see fit.' He just gave me a little smile. You know, thinking about it since then, I think I told him what he wanted to hear. And I don't think his question was just making conversation, either."

"What do you think of Mister Ford?" I asked him. Then I stopped myself. "Forget it. I guess you could hardly tell me you thought he was a horse's ass, could you?"

Jackson glared at me as though I were a Harvard linebacker. "If I thought Henry Ford was a horse's ass I'd tell you he was a horse's ass," he said. "Furthermore, I don't think he'd care what I told you. So now that you've asked me I'll tell you. I think he's the most perceptive person I've ever met, considering the position he holds. We've got a lot of people, even professional social workers, who can't perceive the depth and measure of the problems which face us. He can. He's got decency and compassion, and he's smart."

In the industrial pyramid that is Ford, Jackson's relationship to the chairman is about like that of a major to the Secretary of Defense. Nevertheless, it was Jackson who made the initial presentation of one of the most far-reaching socioeconomic proposals in history, that the Ford Motor Company go into the ghettos and hire the people of that world. He managed to get close enough to Ford at a luncheon of the New Detroit Committee to hand him a typewritten copy of his proposal. Ford skimmed through it, and immediately suggested that Jackson come in and talk further after lunch. Jackson did, and his plan was accepted that afternoon.

Most people probably take it for granted that the members of Ford's corporate family are loyal to him, but one man's allegiance is so strong that it made an unusual impression. Leo C. Beebe, a man of such strength and intensity that Ford, man and company, has used him as a troubleshooter in several situations, saw me on the seventh floor of a federal office building in Washington, where Beebe's current assignment for Ford was running the National Alliance of Businessmen. Beebe gestured with his cigar to the window. "If he told me to jump out of that window, I'd do it, and think about it on the way down," he said. "I'm always having to remember the way I feel about him, so that I won't be blindly obedient to whatever he asks me to do. I've got to put more thought on the problems he hands me than that. He's completely idealistic, and sometimes I've got to be more practical. He's a strong leader, strong as a horse. I'm a worshipper."

I could hardly reflect the opinion of each of the hundreds of thousands of Ford people about the boss and his company but one reaction is worth passing on. "See that redheaded guy there?" Alfred Krause, general manager of the steel division, said to me one day in the Rouge. "He's one of our most militant shop stewards, always bellyaching about something. But he and everybody in his family drive a Ford and if you go up to him right now and make a derogatory remark about anything or anybody named Ford he'll knock you flat on your butt." I took one look at the scowling heavyweight and accepted Krause's word without personal verification.

When I get back home after conferences with eager Ford executives, I can't help but reflect to my friends their determination to turn out good products. Most of the women couldn't care less—they want to know what Cristina wore where. But somebody always wants to know whether I recommend that he buy a Ford car, and if so, which model. On the basis of technical automotive knowledge, I can't tell him very much. I'm not an automobile buff—and the cars my wife and I happen currently to be driving, a Plymouth and an MG purchased before I had my interest in Ford, will probably continue to satisfy our non-status-seeking transportation requirements for some time. Henry Ford II himself was no help in this regard, either. He personally likes to drive skillfully on European highways in cars with stick gear shift, manual steering and stiff suspension, cars in which he can get the feel of the road.

"Americans like to blast along over interstate highways at 80 miles an hour in big cars with every kind of power attachment, windows up, air conditioning on, radio going, one finger on the wheel," he said. "That's what they want and that's what they buy and that's what we manufacture. We build the best car we can to meet the taste of the American people."

He never even bothered to mention his own car, a four-on-the-floor Cougar, maroon with black leather upholstery. I just happened to hear about it from Anne.

Ford himself gives the impression that he just popped up one day and started running the Ford Motor Company, but other sources have been able to put together his personal history. A woman who used to clerk at Hudson's, the big Detroit store, for example, remembers him as a pudgy little rich boy in a camel's hair overcoat. His brother Benson, two years younger, said that even as a youth Henry was always a leader. In the teen-age crowd in Grosse Pointe he was called "The Chief." William Clay Ford, eight years younger than Henry, shares Benson's filial love for their big brother, but is a little less reverent. He remembers another nickname, "Lard-ass." George Van Santvoord, former headmaster at Hotchkiss School in Connecticut attended by all three Fords, spoke of Henry affectionately and with respect.

"He came in with the handicap of being Henry Ford," Van Santvoord said. "He had a remarkable father and his mother is a woman with a powerful personality, but he was branded with the name and fame of his grandfather, the billionaire automobile manufacturer. Henry was self-conscious about his background. He could have been self-indulgent and tried to throw his weight around, but instead he was modest, good natured, and showed regard and respect for his classmates and his teachers. This boy was not notable for his intellectual brilliance, and, as he was overweight, he wasn't a great athlete like Billy. But everybody liked him. When he graduated I recommended him to Yale University and I think he performed creditably there even though he didn't graduate."

One Ford anecdote is especially popular in academe. According to the story, when Henry's sociology professor at Yale picked up the surprisingly well-written term paper on which his student's graduation depended, a slip of paper dropped out. It was the bill submitted by the chap who wrote it. The professor blew the whistle and then the question came up as to whether Henry would be permitted to graduate. The administration, aware of the potential of having Henry Ford II as a graduate, placed tremendous pressure on the professor and the entire department, but both courageously resisted and academic integrity was preserved. Young Ford did not get his degree.

It's a wonderful story, but as in any anecdote involving either of the two men named Henry Ford there's a good chance it didn't happen. One way to check was to ask Henry Ford II. I was leading up to it when he suddenly interrupted.

"Well, I'll tell you one thing, there wasn't any bill that dropped out," he said. "I may be stupid, but I'm not *that* stupid."

"But did you get help with it?"

"Yeah."

"How'd they find out, then?"

"Well, they called me in and told me that the paper seemed to show a knowledge that I hadn't displayed in class and wanted to know if I'd gotten any help. I said I did so they didn't pass me. But that wasn't the only reason I didn't graduate. I busted another course, too."

When I asked the professor who taught the course about it, he didn't want to be involved and suggested that I simply accept Ford's version. Pressed a bit, he said, "It was not necessary for me to see a bill to know that the paper was not written by the student. It was on Folkways and Thomas Hardy and I had sense enough to know whether the paper represented the student's actual knowledge of the subject. It would have required reading all fourteen or fifteen of Hardy's novels, for example."

43

Was there a big flap between the administration and the sociology department? "If there was I never heard of it. All I did was report the matter to the dean and as far as I know that was the end of it."

As it was, Henry stayed on after the commencement exercises in which he could not participate. He was manager of the Yale crew and the big race came after the school year. The nongraduating manager stayed behind to fulfill his duties.

Just 29 years later, appearing before the Yale Political Union in the spring of 1969, Ford started to read his prepared speech, then grinned and interrupted himself. "I didn't write this speech, either," he said.

During the summers while at Yale he worked in the Ford plant. One year he and his brother Benson were assigned to the experimental engine department where they worked under a Negro foreman named Leonard Williams. It was rough, dirty work tearing down engines. There's a story, perhaps apocryphal, that a top executive with the company sought to curry favor with their father and grandfather by attempting to transfer the boys from this demeaning position. The two older Fords kept them there. Benson told me that though the work was hard and Williams was a taskmaster, they both benefited by the experience. "He was a wonderful man," Benson said.

In World War II, Henry was commissioned an ensign in the Navy and assigned to the Great Lakes Naval Training Station in Chicago. It was in the Navy, according to Leo Beebe, that he became a man.

"I'll never forget the first time I saw him," Beebe said. "I was a high school coach, signed on as a chief petty officer in the Navy physical fitness program. Then I was assigned to the training station, and told to report to B Barracks. When I walked in there was this pudgy ensign with a squeaky voice chewing the tail out of some sailor he had backed up against the wall. I knew then that I'd drawn a good officer. He was green, but he learned. We had some pretty tough guys in that barracks. I'd come up the hard way: I worked my way through Michigan washing dishes, was captain of the basketball team, and then went into coaching. I was used to tough guys. Ford wasn't, but he learned fast. Some of these guys would come in drunk on Saturday night, and would get pretty obstreperous. He handled them beautifully. A lot of officers would duck out and leave all the work to the chief petty officer, but he and I worked together, for hours every night, planning the program for the next day. I didn't realize it then, but now I know I was watching a miracle, a boy turn into a man. We had the best barracks in the whole damn station."

Ford left the Navy against his will—he had hoped for sea duty—when the federal government became concerned over the increasing inability of the company to deliver its wartime commitment of bombers to desired specifications. Young Henry was deactivated in a procedure that required cabinet action. He was placed in the plant in hopes that like a sealant in a tire he would slosh around and somehow settle in the leak.

As president at the age of 28, he realized that he needed more managerial expertise than he possessed. He persuaded Ernest R. Breech, the executive's executive from General Motors, to join him. Breech told me about it.

"He was smart enough to see that he had to put an organization together," Breech said, "and that's what we did. We made an excellent team. In 14½ years with the Ford Motor Company, I had nothing but complete support from Henry Ford. With his name and position he could have thrown his weight around, been much more difficult, but then, of course, if he had, he wouldn't have had Ernie Breech. Both our doors were open to each other, and to the other executives who were trying to put this company together. He listened, he took advice, and he learned. He may not have been a great student at Yale, but he certainly was a great student of how to become an executive and he became one."

All this required prodigious effort and long, hard days. Yet even when the company was in its worst shape, there was enough money in the Ford family for all of them to live like millionaires without turning a finger. Why did he let himself in for this titanic burden? One time I was talking with him about Gauguin's *The Brittany Coast,* which he owns. I asked him if he hadn't ever thought about going off to the South Seas like Gauguin to loll on a beach. "Oh, I guess so, at times," he said.

"Then why in the hell didn't you?" I asked.

He gave the little embarrassed laugh which I had come to learn meant that he wasn't going to answer the question. "Oh, I don't know," he said.

I guess if I weren't fascinated by people I wouldn't have chosen to spend my life digging into theirs. Even more interesting than what people do is how they came to do it. How did Henry Ford develop these characteristics of dedication, mental energy and bravery so superior to those of most of the rest of us? How did this scion of world-sprawling wealth develop sensitivity and compassion?

Before I ever saw Henry Ford II, I spent months reading about him and the dramatic events of his life. I made a list of characteristics in which he stood out from the crowd, and I naively thought that when I asked him about them he would think a bit and then muse about himself out loud. But trying to pry this type of information out of Henry Ford proved to be one of the most frustrating experiences of my professional career.

How, for example, could this man who never had to fight anybody or anything muster the great physical courage and determination it took to take the Ford Motor Company away from a tough guy in an entrenched position? How could a person who spent his boyhood in homes in Grosse Pointe, Maine, and Florida develop a compassionate understanding for those who grew up in the slums? How could someone exposed as a youth to the reactionary policy of the Ford Motor Company of the Thirties choose to combine with a labor union—which cost him billions in benefits and strikes—and provide pioneering and progressive steps toward financial security for his employees? How could a man who has never purchased an automobile make the hundred-million-dollar decisions not only to produce the Maverick and the Mark III, but to determine what they'll look like and who will buy them for how much? Why does he work so hard, so long on public as well as corporate projects?

I just didn't get any answers at all, least of all from Henry Ford II. "I'm not very introspective," he explained.

Asked some of these questions, his brothers Benson and Billy Clay said that they were all raised to work hard. Anne and Charlotte could not even surmise. Cristina said she had no idea how her husband got that way, but that's the way she wanted him. Leo Beebe, speaking particularly in reference to Ford's personal bravery, used a kind of you-climb-a-mountain-because-it's-there analogy. A malignancy existed in the Ford Motor Company; Henry Ford II was the only man who could cut it out; he did so.

And so there will be few further attempts at psychoanalysis of Henry Ford II in this book. A Ford is a Ford is a Ford. Before departing the subject for good, though, I can suggest one possibility, proposed with some hesitancy because of its simplicity: maybe a man does this because he has the self-confidence to think he can do the job and the pride to continue. This is security. I know that I wouldn't take the Ford Motor Company, with its awful attendant responsibility, if they gave it to me.

Through the lives and careers of both Henry Fords runs a kind of don't-give-a-damn characteristic. The original displayed it on numerous occasions. He bucked his own directors to bring out first the Model N and then the famous T, and the whole industrial world when he more than doubled wages in his plant. He barged into things with utter disregard for the possibility of ridicule—tried to stop a war, tried to establish a TVA-like operation years before the federal government did, proclaimed that "history is bunk," tried to change the thinking of the entire Jewish people, tried to make people quit smoking, proved that railroads could be run efficiently by buying one and doing it, set up educational systems without bothering to get a high school diploma himself, established one of the world's great museums without much caring that people were laughing at him for purchasing a bunch of spurious trash in the process, stated publicly his firm belief that the Du Ponts, Roosevelt, Wall Street, Communists, Jews, and unions were all in cahoots . . . and so on.

Nor does Henry Ford II get too upset about popular opinion. In one of my efforts to pump him, I used the argument that by telling me the real story he could dispel some of the canards about the company and his grandfather. "Oh, let the fairy tales continue," he said. "Who gives a damn?"

In the meantime, one of my own personal experiences with him might indicate the complete lack of insecurity in the Henry Ford personality.

It occurred during the spring of 1968 when he was setting up the operation to find JOBS (acronym for Job Opportunities in the Business Sector) for the hard-core unemployed. Thanks to a lot of hard work and the magic of the name, Ford prevailed upon a number of the top-flight business leaders of the nation to go along with him. The day before he was to address the Chicago group, dragging such notables as the mayor of Chicago and the president of the phone company out for an 8:00 A.M. breakfast, Ted Mecke called me to suggest I come to Chicago to see The Chairman in action. "From there he's flying to New York and you can ride with him," Ted said.

This was the way I usually saw Mister Ford, in bits and pieces of time grabbed here and there thanks to Mecke. I had convinced Mecke that I was going to write a book on Ford whether he cooperated or not, and Mecke had decided that the company would stand up under my scrutiny. After an hour's chat with me, in which he showed a genuine interest in how books get written, Mister Ford apparently agreed. From then on I had full cooperation with Mecke and his department— itself larger than many corporations—in seeing the people and places I wanted to. But as far as talking with Mister Ford for eight-hour days, five-day weeks, during the better part of a year, as I had done with Captain Eddie Rickenbacker in the book I'd just finished, that was out. I could see Mister Ford when Mister Ford didn't have anything more pressing to do, and Mister Ford had a lot of more pressing things to do.

So I jumped, or, rather, flew, to Chicago at the opportunity and attended the breakfast. Ford had made this speech to other groups and he delivered it in a perfunctory manner; he is too intelligent not to be bored by the repetition of even his own words. After the breakfast, which was successful, he was put through one general televised press conference and then five separate TV interviews. Hard-core politicians can remain charming and cheerful, colorful and cooperative, after the third or fourth interview by someone who hasn't done his homework, but Mister Ford is not a politician. "You asked me that before and I told you," he informed Interviewer No. Four, on the air. "Do you want me to tell you the same thing all over again?" The interviewer cowered and muttered he guessed so. "All right, I'll tell you what I told you before," Mister Ford said, and did so.

A company limousine—black Continental with less than

6000 miles on it; they replace chauffeur-driven limousines at approximately 6000 miles—was waiting and after the last interview we drove to the airport. On the way we talked. Although he had just finished repeating several times that the first year's goal was JOBS for 100,000 unemployed, he was more concerned with three men he saw lounging on a street corner. Three men standing there doing nothing. The abhorrence of idleness, combined with an obsessive determination to do something about it, is a characteristic shared by all the Fords I've talked with. I think it's one of the reasons he was letting me ride along with him at the time; he respected my desire to do a job. At the airport he remembered that the chauffeur was on the verge of retirement after many years of personal service and made a point of shaking hands with him and wishing him well. "I wonder what he's going to do with himself now," he mused to Mecke, with concern.

The company plane was waiting—Ford has ten US-based planes, including five jets, more than some airlines—and we flew to Detroit. All the time, of course, I was firing questions at my host. I had done my homework, several million words worth, and at least the questions weren't stupid. He was courteous, as he has always been with me, and either answered each question, said he didn't know (after all, I've read a lot more Ford history than he has), or fielded it gracefully. But Mister Ford keeps his guard up with nearly all people at nearly all times and I was not one of the exceptions.

"Man, you're a lousy interview," I've told him a couple of times, laughing but meaning it, and he laughed back, though clearly with no intention of being a less lousy interview. From the way his friends talk about him, he's got to be one hell of a likable guy when he is confident he can let his guard down. It's just that until he reaches that point, he keeps it up. His grandfather at one time was getting 10,000 letters a week, all attempting to put the bite on him. Today's model comes with a built-in degaussing apparatus.

At the Ford hangar—bigger than the terminal buildings at many airports—Mister Ford's factotum was waiting with some important papers for him to sign. Charlotte, vivacious and pretty, was waiting with some bargains she'd picked up shopping in Detroit to hop a ride back to New York. Finally we were aloft again, this time in a bigger jet.

During the course of the Detroit–New York hop, a young man appeared and set two tables with linen and silver. We had shrimp cocktails and filet mignons. Over luncheon Ford and Charlotte laughed over some of Cristina's difficulties with the telephone. Ford observed that Charlotte didn't really need a telephone, not with her voice. "Just open the window," he said. "I wonder where I got it from," she said. Charlotte, who is interested in business—"I should have been a boy," she told me. "I'd be next president of the company"—asked how the negotiations were going to get Jean-Claude Killy, the French Olympic skiing champion, to join Ford. Not so good, her father said; now an agent was involved. "But what does he want?" Charlotte asked. "Money," Ford said.

After dessert and coffee Mister Ford leaned over against the side of the plane, looking out the window, relaxing. That's when the incident occurred that convinced me that Henry Ford II is not insecure, and that he inherited at least some of that don't-give-a-damn characteristic of his grandfather. He reached into his left-hand coat pocket, pulled out an ordinary book of paper matches, and tore one out. Then, in front of God and his biographer, Henry Ford II proceeded to pick at his teeth. This is emotional security, in the fullest sense of the phrase.

But with all this, Mister Ford sometimes lets comparatively minor things irritate him. One newspaper profile made him furious. Published in *The New York Times,* it discussed the three

51

sides of Henry Ford II: Henry the swinger, drinking champagne in water glasses over ice; Henry the chairman of Ford Motor Company; and Henry the man aware of social problems. I thought it a perceptive piece but it burned Ford up to the point that he wrote a letter to the *Times* protesting it. The profile contained some frivolity which he did not consider to be in accordance with the dignity of the *Times,* and it called attention to his former continental coiffure, long in back with full sideburns. But what made him really mad was the insinuation that he had his hair cut to make a good impression at a stockholders' meeting. As I've said, this is an unpredictable man.

However angry the article made him, I like its framework and will use it for my own examination of both Henry Fords as industrialists, men of social conscience, and swingers in order to compare two charismatic individuals bearing one familiar name, two men who have both reflected and affected their world and times.

Men of industry

3

EVERY YEAR the big business magazines bring out special editions, loaded with full-color advertising, analyzing the performances of the major corporations during the previous year for the Monday morning quarterbacks of the greatest game of all, big business. Participants and spectators, chairmen of the board and wives of the aspirants, sagacious investors and nickel-stock speculators all join in the great American pastime of second-guessing. Why didn't I get in on Mohawk? How did I get stuck with Curtis?

From the early 1900's, no industry has provided the fiscal fascination of the yo-yo course of the Ford Motor Company. If you'd like to take a minute off to eat your heart out, think for a moment of an indolent, incompetent young lawyer named John W. Anderson. Although he'd already been burned a couple of times on improvident investments, he conned his father into lending him $5000 to back a two-time loser, Henry Ford. Over the next sixteen years this one investment brought Anderson $17,435,000, most of it tax free. Others who have watched the Fords go by over the years have seen the company overtaken by a one-time pipsqueak of a competitor, thanks to the stubborn refusal of Henry Ford to build a competitive car to replace the outdated Model T, and have seen blatant mismanagement and contempt for modern business methods, corruption, and viciousness, losses of $10,000,000 a month, and, even during a period of rebirth and magnificent accomplishment, a quarter-billion-dollar mistake immemorially called the Edsel. Just about anything that has happened in any business, good or bad, has happened at Ford, and in the extreme.

I don't know of any recognized business expert who doesn't place management at the top of the list of ingredients that make a successful enterprise. But in the case of Ford behind that corporate word, management, are some individual human quirks without which the big picture might have been totally different. If Billy Durant of General Motors had been able to take advantage of Henry Ford's upset stomach one morning in 1909, the Ford car would be just another GM product and practically nothing in this book would have ever happened. If a young captain in the Air Force named Arjay Miller hadn't read an article on Henry Ford II in *Life* one day in 1945, he and his fellow Whiz Kids might have gone to work for Allegheny Corporation instead of for the Ford Motor Company, and where would he and the others, including Tex Thornton and Robert McNamara, be now? If it hadn't been for the intense enthusiasm of a fellow named Jack Reith you probably would never have heard of the Edsel, either. And suppose Eugene Bordinat, the flamboyant vice president in charge of design, who wears cuff links the size of hub caps, hadn't cooked up an elaborate scheme to persuade Henry Ford II into reversing himself and approving the Mustang?

Give a man the spark of leadership and, whether he is Henry I who never finished grammar school or Henry II who never finished college, he can use those who did the way a mechanic uses a set of wrenches. Select the right one, do the job with it, and replace it when it shows signs of wear. Both Fords have had that spark, and have displayed it in ways that are both similar and diverse, according to their times. The real story of the Ford Motor Company is that of its people, their dreams, their work, their accomplishments, their bloopers. Not all those people are named Ford, but the relationship of those who aren't is symbiotic with those who are.

Studying the history of the dynasty is easy in one sense; it's all there, complete with the muddy footprints, filed away for public scrutiny in the Ford Archives. In actuality, however, it's impossible. There is so much material that no single pair of human eyes could ever read it all. The strange genius who founded the company must surely have been one of the most egocentric men of all time. He made and preserved notes on himself as a child: as a mature man of wealth and extreme curiosity he hired researchers to go back and check out his entire life, both personal and business. In addition to Ford on Ford, the archives contain stacks of reminiscences from hundreds of people associated with him, many of whom seemed inclined to augment their own roles or justify their own grievances. After becoming steeped in Fordology, however, I found that some of the most outrageous and self-serving exaggerations often contained a nugget of valuable truth.

Thanks to Henry Ford's intense interest in Henry Ford, we have a clear picture of a likable kid growing up in rural America just after the Civil War. He was born July 30, 1863, on a farm a few miles west of Detroit. At first glance he seems the epitome of the normal American boy in that he was mischievous, he liked to putter around with tools, and he hated his chores. But deeper excavation into his activities reveals an offbeat characteristic: he had to make a production of things. He couldn't just jab somebody with a pin; he drilled two tiny holes in the seat of a school desk, inserted a threaded needle in one, then ran the thread up that hole, down the other, and across to his own seat. One twitch and ouch.

Most kids take things apart and then can't put them back together. Henry could. He was 13 years old when he made a small screwdriver out of a nail and a pair of tweezers out of one of his mother's corset stays, and fixed his uncle's watch.

And while every red-blooded boy hates his chores, Henry's distaste was so intense that he began dreaming of machinery that would lighten the farm boy's load. He didn't care who knew how he felt, either. He bitched about his jobs bitterly and in writing. "Chicken is for hawks," he noted, "Milk is a mess."

His grandson, Henry II, was also outspoken as a boy, though in vastly different circumstances. When he was 7 years old he had to go through the rigmarole of getting ready for company. The company was Edward, Prince of Wales. The whole house was in a dither. His baby sister reflected the tension as infants often do, and his maternal grandmother, after hours of preparation, lost her normal composure at the last moment. His Royal Highness came into the nursery where Henry was waiting, all dressed up.

"How is everything?" asked the Prince.

"My sister just threw up and grandmother is hiding behind the screen," Henry answered.

As a farmer of moderate success, the father of Henry the One wanted him to follow in the furrow. Instead the boy, fascinated with machinery and steam engines, went off to Detroit as an apprentice. He learned his trade so well that he became an engine repairman, an excellent position in the Eighties for a young man, but his father lured him back to the land with the loan of a forty-acre tract to clear and farm. Henry took it, married his sweetheart, Clara Jane Bryant, cut the timber and built a house to his happy bride's specifications.

In Europe, engineers were beginning to develop the internal combustion engine. One of the best, invented and built by Nicolaus A. Otto, used illuminating gas and was called The Silent Otto. It was exhibited in the United States and people paid good money to watch it sit there and turn its flywheel. When it reached Detroit Henry Ford went into town and joined the crowd ogling the engine. The sight of it shook him up. We know from his later accomplishments that he had the rare capability of mentally syncretizing disparate objects. His imagination must have put the stationary Silent Otto on wheels. But he realized his limitations. It took an electric spark to ignite the gas, and he didn't know how to make one. He immediately got a job with the Edison Illuminating Company in order to learn how and then told Clara she was leaving her pleasant and sociable rural life and moving to Detroit. As for the farm, he left it there.

He was 27 when he had that experience that changed the course of his life. His grandson was 28 when his future opened up. He became head of Ford. From the accounts of the people who were with Henry II at the time, as well as his own, he accepted it calmly. But one man, of sensitive perception, felt the change like a pulsing electric current.

"Henry was the chairman of our major industry unit in 1945," Edgar Schmidt of the then Community Chest told me. "I called to remind him of a unit meeting. He said, 'Edgar, haven't you heard? I've taken over the company. Mother and I are sitting here now making plans for the future.' He went on to talk about the new era coming, but it wasn't what he said as much as the way he said it. I could feel it as well as hear it. There was a freshness, a buoyance, as well as determination. I was talking to a different man!"

It's one of the odd little ironies that keep popping up in Henry Fordiana, but at earlier ages under the same general set of circumstances the grandson fled from what his grandfather had fled to. His grandfather left the farm in his teens to learn rudimentary engineering. Henry left engineering to learn sociology. Why? All I got out of him was "Well, I was flunking engineering, and they said sociology was easy so I transferred, but I flunked that too."

It seems to me that the real answer is that Henry II needed technical information on engineering about as much as his grandfather needed a course in farriery. The Henry Ford of the late 1880's had to develop his potential as a mechanical genius; the Henry Ford of the late 1930's had to develop his aptitude for modern corporate leadership. He couldn't have chosen a better place to learn it than in the nation's first sociology department at Yale. Its philosophy was conservative, but the professors hammered away on man's need for constant adjustment to the changing times. "When men are content to do just as their grandfathers did," the Yale student read in his textbook, "they merely repeat the past, errors and all, because it is easier to imitate than to discriminate." He learned the importance of cooperation, of association, and above all, of adaptation to change, such as that made necessary when a fellow comes along and puts the world on wheels. In conversation with me years later he placed even more emphasis on his extracurricular activity as manager of the Yale crew, in which he experienced the practical application of helping people literally pull together.

Meanwhile, back in the nineteenth century, the built-in high-powered personality, standard equipment with both Henry Fords, ran wide open. Henry I was a gregarious fellow. Tough and wiry, he loved to wrestle and box and play elaborate practical jokes. One time he nailed a friend's shoes to the floor, another time he pumped sulfurous smoke into a basement where some of his cronies were working. He was rarely alone during the long hours he spent in his workshop. Friends dropped in, and not just to watch. Henry I could get more work out of one buddy for nothing than most men can get out of a paid staff. Often his friends would put in an entire night working in his workshop, only it wasn't work, it was fun.

But even the Ford magic wasn't enough to bring the boys in on Christmas Eve, 1893; he was alone when he finally had his first engine ready, he hoped, to run. It looked something like a toy cannon mounted on a board. The cylinder was a piece of gas pipe a repairman had left at the electric plant. Henry had made a plug for one end, drilled a hole, and squeezed in the butt end of a piece of wire. It would make and break contact with another butt end in the hand-fashioned piston, so that a spark would jump to ignite the mixture of air and gasoline.

The only way to get gasoline into the firing end of the cylinder was for someone else to dribble it in through a hole he'd drilled in the top. He took the crude little gadget into the house and put it on the kitchen sink. He attached the cylinder wire to the cord of the kitchen light, and grounded it to the water pipe. Clara was busy in the kitchen getting things ready for guests coming for Christmas dinner when he took over the sink, but she stopped and accepted the can of gasoline he handed her. She was used to him. Henry spun the flywheel, and she let a few drops of gasoline trickle in. Nothing happened, and they tried again. The engine started. Flames shot out of it and it made an awful racket, but it did run. Ford watched it for a minute or so, and then waved Clara and the gasoline away. It ran—why waste gas?

The next step was a bigger and better engine, and a vehicle in which to mount it. He worked on both for two and a half more years. Even in the 1890's a self-powered vehicle was, at least in comparison to bicycles and buggies, a sophisticated apparatus. He couldn't just take a buggy frame, mount it on bicycle wheels and have the chassis for a motor car. The mere

decision as to the number of wheels required heavy consideration; Henry put quite a bit of thought into the possibility of a
gas-powered bicycle before abandoning the idea.

Since there were a few horseless carriages already running
around the streets of Europe and the northeastern United States,
you might wonder why Henry started from scratch. One reason
was that most horseless carriages were powered either by steam
or electricity, and he had made up his mind to go with gasoline.
A few years later he met his idol, Thomas A. Edison, at an
electrical convention, and the great inventor encouraged him,
banging on the table for emphasis, to continue with the internal
combustion engine. The conversation fed his ego and reinforced
his decision, but he was already committed. Another reason was
that Ford was a perfectionist, and in the 1890's there were more
bugs than cars. Most of the automotive pioneers in America
were working out of tool sheds, just like Henry, and each sput-
tering result reflected its breeding place.

One night in the spring of 1896, he completed what he
called a quadricycle. It looked like a box on four oversized
bicycle wheels. It had a two-cylinder engine, two speeds forward, no reverse, and no brakes. Henry sat on a buggy seat
and steered by means of a tiller. Its major immediate defect was
that it was too big for the tool-shed door. He had to knock down
part of the wall to get it out. He started it by spinning the flywheel, got in, and drove off with more racket than speed
through the rainy deserted streets. Rude and crude as it was, he
later got $200 for it, and it ran for several years. In the mean-
time he was building another one.

By the time the second car was finished, sometime in 1898,
Henry Ford was pretty well known in Detroit and the automobile was beginning to attract attention in Europe and the east.
His patient perfectionism showed; his car was lighter and
stronger than most already in existence. To produce it a group
of local businessmen got together and organized the Detroit

Automobile Company on a total of $15,000 cash investment. At the same time, the Edison Illuminating Company was completing plans for a major expansion. Henry Ford could be a part of those plans; he was offered the position of general superintendent. He turned down a solid future with a major corporation for a job with a local group gambling on a horseless carriage. It turned out to be a lemon. The men with the money insisted on bringing the car out anyway, but the purchasing public had more sense and the company went out of business.

Henry Ford was now 38 years old, with a wife and child, and out of two jobs. He could have gone back into the electric business. And by this time, there were 50 or so automobile companies trying to get going and he could surely have latched on somewhere for a monthly paycheck. Instead he went into racing.

Automobile racing was just beginning to be glamorous. It had begun in France and was working its way west. There could be money in it—if you won. But I think that Ford's motivation was the improvement of the product—the chance to test a car under the strain of competition. In the body of both automobile and man, ordeal proves strength and reveals weakness. Even in 1900 a man of extraordinary foresight like Ford could perceive this. He had never really had an opportunity to test his handmade product. When he took his car out on the bumpy streets he was frequently preceded by an advance guard, a friend on a bicycle who warned people driving horses that a strange object making a big noise was coming.

The first test was of his own personal magnetism; he had to secure both financial backing and a team of expert assistants. Some of the men who worked with Henry Ford during those days later claimed that they had contributed more than he had. C. H. Wills received a percentage of all Ford's personal income for many years for his early contributions to both chassis and engine. Ed "Spider" Huff, who broke up with Ford regularly, took credit for much of the electrical work. But whatever the justification of their claims, it was Henry Ford who inspired them and made the final decision on their creations and modifications. Somebody had to add direction to the ingenuity demanded by the vacuum in existing knowledge. For example, an efficient method of igniting the gasoline in the cylinder had to be devised. Huff got the idea of a coil encased in porcelain. Who could mold and bake porcelain in Detroit in 1901? Easy: the first spark plug was cooked up, but literally, by a dentist. But it was done under Ford's direction and inspiration.

The engine had two cylinders, each 7 inches in diameter. It made so much noise that they had to hitch up a horse to tow it out of town to test it. As with most automobiles of the day, the engine was mounted under the driver. He perched up there like a farmer on a bale of hay.

The car was finished on October 10, 1901, which by coincidence happened to be the day of the first automobile race held in Detroit. This meant, of course, that Ford had no opportunity before then to drive on the dirt one-mile oval horse track with its flat curves. Several years later Eddie Rickenbacker came along to become the winningest racer in the great days of racing before World War I, with a reputation of driving like a fool. Rick kept his secret for fifty years before confiding to me that before every race he'd sneak out to the track and practice until he knew the exact speed at which he could take every curve— and even then it was a hazardous operation. Ford, by contrast, drove just two practice laps, slowly, with a bicycle racer hanging on the running board giving him pointers, before the race began. He sat high up with nothing but the wheel to hang on to. He had no brakes, no windshield, no goggles. As he was neither stupid nor ignorant about automobiles, he must have been brave.

His only competition was Alexander Winton, a pioneer automobile manufacturer from Cleveland who had driven his racer in France, all over the east, and in Chicago. The promoters of the Detroit race permitted his advance man to pick out first prize, an elaborate punch bowl, as a inducement to enter. Nobody expected much from the hometown entry of 1901.

Winton skidded around the first turn in a cloud of dust and pulled away. Ford's lighter car, however, surprised everybody on the straightaways; after three miles he was only a fifth of a lap behind. He went into the curves faster and faster, and gradually cut down the lead. Winton's engine began to smoke, and Ford closed the gap fast. The hometown folks began jumping up and down and screaming. Ford went out in front and stayed there. He passed the finish line, coasted to a stop, got out and leaned against the car. He'd averaged 44.8 mph. Before the crowd swarmed to congratulate him, two boys who got there first heard him mutter, "Boy, I'll never do that again. I was scared to death."

But winning is a pleasant sensation, and Ford built another car, this one designed strictly for racing. It had four cylinders as big as fireplace logs. The engine was so huge it wouldn't fit under the driver's seat, and he put it up in front. This lowered the driver so that the car no longer looked like a buggy, but like something new, an automobile. In motion it was a dragon, spitting fire and roaring. Ford called it 999, after a famous locomotive. Driving it, he said, was worse than going over Niagara Falls. There was no hood, no casing for the crankcase, no windshield, and hot oil splashed back against his face.

Ford had more sense than to try to race it himself, but in 1904 he took a crack at the world speed record, 77.13 miles per hour. The place he chose for the attempt was a frozen lake. Local farmers scraped the snow off the surface in a narrow track three miles long, and cinders were sprinkled over part of it for traction. The temperature was near zero, and Ford didn't even have goggles. He was 40 then, which was old enough to know better. As the car picked up speed, the fissures in the ice began to throw it around. It would come down with a thump, often sideways. He'd skid into the snow piled on the side of the track, bank off, straighten up, and keep going. At least the ride didn't last long. He was officially clocked at 91.37 miles per hour, the first man to hit 90. After the race he celebrated with a muskrat dinner. Ford was very fond of muskrat.

To drive the car in competition, Ford in 1902 had found a young bicycle rider, Berna Eli Oldfield. The combination of Oldfield's recklessness and the car's power caused Ford to have some softhearted second thoughts. He seriously suggested to Oldfield, just before the first race, that he get out of it. "This chariot may kill me," Oldfield said, "but they'll say afterwards that I was going like hell when she took me over the bank."

Oldfield won by a full lap. The crowd broke down the fence and carried him off the track on their shoulders. Years later, after the name Barney Oldfield had entered the English language as the epitome of the fast driver, Oldfield and Ford laughed about how each had made the other. "But I did a better job of it than you did," Oldfield said.

For Henry Ford II, the test of courage came not with a race but with a human confrontation. His grandfather had brought into the company a tough ex-sailor and pugilist named Harry Bennett and had come to lean upon him more and more during the years until, in his dotage, both he and the company were under Bennett's control. With spies, henchmen, and a small army of armed thugs, gangsters, ex-convicts, former policemen, and professional athletes, Bennett tyrannized the entire plant. Men were fired without reason, terrorized, and beaten, and there were stories of actual disappearances. Both Henry II and his friend John Bugas, the former FBI man, wore guns when they came to work.

When the showdown came, Bennett and Ford faced each other, alone. One was stocky, muscular, a veteran of violence and given to unpredictable rage. The other was a slightly pudgy young man of gentle upbringing. Bennett was working himself up into a wild fury.

"You're taking over a billion-dollar organization you haven't contributed a thing to," he shouted.

Henry had to be frightened but he didn't back up. He kept control. He told Bennett that Bugas was taking over his duties. But he was no fool and he told Bennett he could stay on the payroll.

"Frankly," he told me later, "I was afraid to fire him outright. I might not have been able to make it stick."

Bennett whirled, walked swiftly to the door, and almost ran down the hall toward his office. How close had Henry come to physical injury or even death? He will never know.

After the meeting, Ford drove out into the country with Allen W. Merrell, a friend since boyhood and later a company vice president. "I don't remember that Henry was any different," Merrell recalled. He seemed a little surprised that anyone would expect Ford to be visibly affected.

As for Ford's own recollection of the event, he brushed it off. "I guess I might have been a little scared," he said. "I don't remember."

Henry Ford II's courage was fed in large part by his acceptance of that massive responsibility, the name Ford. His grandfather's impetus was the perfection of a dream. After beating Winton in his first race, he permitted his former backers to put up new money and organize the Henry Ford Company. But he hadn't changed; work came before money. This was a man who forgot to cash his paycheck when he was making $90 a month, and who left millions lying around in open accounts when he was a billionaire. As much as any artist or composer, Ford wanted to make his dream an opus, rather than a fast buck.

His backers hadn't changed, either. They put money first, and their insistence that he get a product on the market, ready or not, got under his skin. He dropped out, taking his name with him, but leaving a car he had designed and built in 1902. The company hung the name Cadillac on it.

Years later, when Henry Ford II needed an organization man, the proven corporate genius Ernest Breech came in through his own warmhearted response to a nice young man's problems and the open invitation to make a fortune. In 1902, Ford's Breech was James Couzens. Tough-minded and ambitious, Couzens backed into the job. He was the underpaid office manager of a wheeler-dealer in coal named Alexander Y. Malcomson. Ford drew $7000 from Malcomson to design and build another car, but it was Couzens who helped him work out a production program. The mercurial dreamer and the hard-nosed pragmatist made an excellent combination. While Ford and his little circle of excellent technicians developed a product, Couzens developed plans for a company that would permit each to do what he did best.

By purchasing the major components of the car from outside suppliers working with Ford's specifications, Ford would be rid of manufacturing headaches and free to create and design, and Couzens could run the store. John and Horace Dodge agreed to build the better part of the automobile in their highly regarded machine shop. But the Dodge boys, hard working, hard drinking, and pugnacious—they hadn't put on their white hats yet—demanded $10,000 cash in advance and $10,000 worth of stock on credit. Ford and Malcomson divided 51 per cent of the stock, 255 shares each at $100 per share, for which they put up no money other than the $7000 Malcomson had advanced Ford. That was, of course, $7000 more than Ford put in. Malcomson brought in his uncle, his cousin, his bookkeeper, and the two lawyers who drew up the contract. After that, money was hard to raise, for in his two previous ventures Ford had skimmed the cream off Detroit capital and proved himself eccentric and difficult. For a few days there were great hopes of

a merger with the Daisy Air Rifle Company, but the stockholders—Daisy's, not Ford's—shot them down. Nevertheless,
Daisy's president, Charles H. Bennett, personally invested $5000
in notes.

Couzens, the most frantic would-be investor, put up his life
savings of $400 and pried his sister loose from $100, half of all
she had. He knocked himself out getting a $500 bonus from
Malcomson, and borrowed $1500 at high interest from Mal-
comson's uncle, John S. Gray. The major cash investor at
$10,500, Gray was named president. Malcomson was secretary.
But it was understood that the two salaried officers, Vice President Ford at $3600 a year, Treasurer Couzens at $2500, would
do all the work.

The bright new company started out with $28,000 in cash,
$21,000 in notes. The cash dwindled to $223.65 before the
company, on the 30th day of its existence, sold its first car direct at the full list price of $850 cash. By the first anniversary
of the company, June 16, 1904, the directors had voted themselves dividends totaling $98,000. Some still hadn't paid for their
stock.

The car responsible for such success in a decade that saw
hundreds of other automotive companies begin and end was
the first Model A. It had a two-cylinder, 8-horsepower engine,
larger and better than those found in other small cars, with
unique features like cylinders that went up and down instead of
sideways. But it also had a few imperfections. The brakes were
bad, but this problem was nullified in part by a kind of built-in
governor: the engine would boil over if you got anywhere near
the top speed of 30 miles an hour. If you forgot to retard the
spark when cranking it, it retaliated by breaking your arm.

Henry put in long hours improving the car. He flitted from
one group of workers to another, slapping backs, playing pranks,
getting the most out of his people in his own way. He called
them all by their first names; they called him Henry, or Hank.

Couzens stuck with grumpy tenacity to his desk for equally long hours doing the financial housekeeping and working out better ways to produce and market the car. The two working directors resented the interference of those who had contributed nothing but money. After the first directors' meeting, in a conversation with Couzens, Ford referred to the others scornfully as "those fellows."

Malcomson's faction insisted on bringing out larger cars to sell for more money and more profit per car. Ford and his coterie had to satisfy them, taking time away from the light models they believed in. The company brought out first the ponderous Model B, followed by the six-cylinder Model K, the elephantine Edsel of its day. Ford hated the six. "I've got no use for a motor that has more spark plugs than a cow has teats," he said.

He was so disgusted that he accepted the opportunity to sell out. Ford people today don't realize how close they came to working for General Motors. The authorized versions of the episode have it that Ford demanded $8 million in cash, which he knew could not be raised. But that ain't the way I heard it, and I heard it from the wife of the man who made the offer.

While Ford had been building his company through diligent labor in the machine shops, a bouncy little operator named William Crapo Durant was working the same side of the street with an entrepreneurial approach. Billy Durant—his wife called him Willie—had made several millions as a buggy manufacturer and had retired at the age of 40 to play the stock market. When a hometown friend who'd been suckered into taking over a bankrupt automobile company sent out a cry for help, Willie came in and took over. All the company had was a car created by and named after a Polish mechanic whose primary interest was marine engines; the first order of business was to find a substitute for the unpronounceable Polish name. Thinking it over, however, Durant decided that the more people argued about

70

how to pronounce it, the more free publicity the car would get. He kept the name, Buick.

Durant, unlike Ford, was perfectly willing to use Wall Street money, and he got J. P. Morgan and Company to agree to put up $500,000 to form International Motors Company to bring out a line of cars. But when the ebullient Willie made the rash prediction that someday there would be more automobiles on the streets than horses, one of the Morgan executives told him he'd better stop talking like a fool, and Willie got mad and walked out. He financed the company himself, after angrily crossing International out of the name and substituting General.

People learned to pronounce General Motors' product well enough to buy it, and Willie, encouraged by his success, sought to add the Ford car to his budding little company. When Henry Ford came to New York, Durant made him an offer. Ford's stomach was acting up—he didn't go for that rich food on the dining car—and he had such a bad attack of lumbago that he was lying on the floor. In his misery, he agreed to sell out for $8 million, $2 million cash. Durant shopped around, found that he couldn't raise the money from any source other than Morgan, and he'd be damned if he'd go back there. Ford eventually got up off the floor and remained uncoupled with Buick.

Durant continued to play games with names, incidentally. When the Ford was famous, Durant decided to bring out a competitor. Buick's best known racing driver was a colorful French mechanic with handlebar moustaches named Louis Chevrolet. Durant happened to learn that the name meant "little mountain goat." The combination of Chevrolet, his hard-to-pronounce name, and the translation was too colorful to resist. Before Chevrolet, the car, was well underway, however, Chevrolet, the man, was fired for smoking in the boss's office.

In spite of Malcomson, lumbago, and queasy stomach, Ford continued to reach further toward his dream, a car that would be inexpensive to buy and inexpensive to run, yet me-

71

chanically reliable and sufficiently tough to take the pounding of the rocky wagon roads. The car would not be a toy for the wealthy, as most were at that time, but an effective means of transportation. It would actually enable people who lived outside of cities to get around the countryside without a horse. It was an improbable dream, but he had it.

Furthermore, he saw that if automobiles were manufactured all alike, like matches or pins, they could be turned out in larger numbers at less cost. From this evolved another theory, so obvious today that its inchoate stage has been almost forgotten, that producing cars more inexpensively would make them available to more people who would then buy more cars which would require better roads which would create more customers who would buy more cars which would make it possible to further reduce costs which would . . . It doesn't sound like such a whopping big innovation now, but if it had been that obvious in the beginning of the twentieth century, then maybe someone other than an ex-farm mechanic would have thought of it, fought for it, and brought it to reality.

Couzens bought the dream. He coupled his business acumen with Ford's needle-in-the-rear type of humor to play the best practical joke yet. Malcomson was the victim. Ford and Couzens organized the Ford Manufacturing Company to build parts for the lighter car—and froze Malcomson out. After the expected hassle, Malcomson and his group sold out. Ford took 330 shares, Couzens 85. Ford, who often danced a little jig when he was happy and chortled when someone stepped on a banana peel, probably did both. Couzens may have smiled. The remaining stockholders were content to have Ford and Couzens make money for them in their own way.

It might seem a little unfair to compare grumpy Jim Couzens with cocky Ernie Breech, but the two men played strangely parallel roles in the Ford Motor Company. Couzens, while holding down two jobs for a total income of $12 a week, had somehow managed to learn double entry bookkeeping. He had reorganized one of Malcomson's new companies and had straightened out Malcomson's own enterprises when Henry Ford appeared in his life. He must have liked Ford; everybody else did. But surely his primary concern was the potential of the company. He succeeded, far beyond any expectations he might logically have been assumed to have; he also enabled Henry Ford to achieve far greater wealth. You could substitute the name James Couzens in an earnest remark Earl Newsom, the public relations man, once made to me. "There would be no Ford Motor Company today," Newsom said, and he was in a position to know, "if it hadn't been for Ernie Breech."

Breech, the son of an Ozark mountain blacksmith, was successful in almost every venture he undertook, from trapping and selling rabbits in his grammar school days to reorganizing Trans World Airlines in his sixties. He was a hard worker, like Couzens, but a cheerful one. He, too, held two jobs, and at the same time became not only a certified public accountant, but a pioneer in the new and then arcane industrial tool of cost analysis. Newsom referred to Breech, affectionately, as "a cocky little squirt," and an episode early in Breech's career bears out the description. When Breech was 23, he applied for the position of controller for a large Chicago company. Two days after the interview he called up to find out if he had gotten the job. He was told the company had filled it. He promptly went to the company's offices to find out why in the world they had hired someone else when he was available. It turned out the company had been trying to find him; when he'd called they'd misunderstood his name.

When Breech started with General Motors, his ascent, thanks to his study of the GM system of cost analysis, was swift. He was an officer of the company at 32, vice president at 42. Assigned to the Bendix division of General Motors, then losing $250,000 a month, he overhauled each one of the scattered plants, set up controls and management to hold them together, and the next year showed a profit of more than $5 million. Though he was performing the duties of chief operating officer, in fact he had far less actual authority. His success must be attributed therefore to his managerial ability, tact, and leadership as well as to his highly developed expertise in cost finding. He was rewarded with the presidency of Bendix in name as well as fact. Under his direction the company performed so well during the war years that in 1946, when Breech was 49, people at GM were figuring him for the presidency of Chevrolet, and perhaps the Top Job itself. That's when 28-year-old Henry Ford II showed up to ask him to step down to executive vice president of a foundering company. Breech listened politely but you don't jump off the stairway to the stars into a swamp, and he gently turned down the opportunity. But Ford came back, and for a reason mountain people understand, that nice people help nice people, Breech agreed to take a look at the Ford books.

"Well, that did it," he said later. "The company was really in a mess. Not only did it need help, it had to have help or the Big Three would surely become the Surviving Two." The company, he recalled on another occasion, "faced the postwar market with rundown plants, obsolete products, almost nonexistent financial control, an inadequate engineering staff, and just sufficient cash to meet daily operating requirements."

Never had he been offered such a challenge. He discussed it with his wife, Thelma, a warmhearted country girl he'd met in high school. "Here's a young man only one year older than our oldest son," he said. "He needs help. It's a great challenge and if I don't accept it I shall always regret it."

The Breeches were a happy couple, secure and friendly. Earl Newsom told me of being invited to their home in Florida for a Sunday morning breakfast of Thelma's famous popovers. He'd gone down for a one-day conference on Saturday, had taken only one suit, and it was a wet rag from the damp climate.

"When I walked in, Thelma took one look at me, let out a shriek, and cried, 'Ernie, come in here and get Earl's suit and press it. It looks awful.' Ernie came in, growled that she could press the suit and he'd take over the popovers. So she did and he did."

When Breech asked his wife what he should do about the Ford proposition, she replied, "It's up to you, Ernie." He took the job. It was the big business story of the year. Naturally, somebody had to couple the homonyms, Breech in the breach; it happened to be *Newsweek*.

In spite of Breech's own statements as to why he went to Ford, in spite of my complete acceptance of his friends' assurances that he is indeed a sympathetic guy who likes a challenge, I'm afraid I was not completely satisfied with the explanation. As president of a major GM division, Breech certainly enjoyed financial rewards superior to the straight, taxable salary-and-bonus arrangement Ford initially offered. Even though Ford sweetened the proposition with a block of 30,000 shares of Ford stock at $40 a share, Breech, after seeing the shape the factory was in, refused the offer. ("Just think of what I missed!" he said later.)

So it seemed to me there had to be some inducement other than a challenge and a taxable income for Breech to give up his future with General Motors. Not that Breech is any greedier than anyone else in the motor city hierarchy; it really isn't the money so much as the principle of the thing. When you finish identifying all those birds, you want your merit badge. And so I kept sniffing around in my ungentlemanly fashion to find out just what Breech picked up through his association with the Ford Motor Company. The book on Breech was no help; it mentioned only salary. Neither was Henry Ford II. He told me only that he expressed a willingness to let Breech work things out for himself but that nothing definite was mentioned.

"I was pretty sure he could figure something out and that

75

was okay with me," he said. "However, I think his main reason for coming in was to see what he could do with the shambles. He's a warm, friendly guy. I owe him a lot. So does the company."

I had more sense than to approach Breech on this delicate matter without ammunition, and when I did approach him with ammunition he said that it was all a matter of court record and he didn't want to discuss it.

In my conversations with Ford people, some of them former, I was frequently asked if I had heard of Dearborn Motors. I had, of course. In 1938, Henry Ford I had incorporated features developed by a Scotch–Irish inventor named Henry George Ferguson into the Ford tractor. Ford and Ferguson joined forces in a gentleman's agreement to produce and distribute the Ford–Ferguson. When Henry Ford II took over the company he found the tractor operation to be one of its sickest divisions. One of his early and forceful actions was to terminate the agreement with both Ferguson and the distributor. A worrisome suit developed which dragged on for years with enormous legal costs. In the meantime the distribution was taken over by a corporation called Dearborn Motors.

It wasn't until I talked with Jack Davis, former Ford sales manager, that I got the full story of Dearborn Motors. Ford needed a new distributor for the tractor. Jack Davis suggested the formation of a distributing organization to Breech, and, Davis told me, "he jumped at it." Davis took the plan for Dearborn Motors to Ford, who okayed it. (Ford Motor Company was then entirely owned by the Ford family, of course.) Dearborn Motors began operations in January, 1947, six months after Breech arrived.

Davis listed the participants and their percentages for me on the kitchen table in his Virginia farmhouse. Breech was allotted the lion's share, 20 per cent. Next came Davis with 12 per cent. ("I was flattered to be included at all, let alone receive the second highest participation," he said. "Next highest was 10 per cent." "Maybe you got that extra 2 per cent for thinking up the whole thing," I suggested. "You could be right," he said.) Four men, all top executives Breech brought in, received 10 per cent. They were William T. Gossett, the company attorney; Lewis D. Crusoe, finance and management; Harold T. Youngren, engineering, and Delmar S. Harder, manufacturing. I had wondered how men of such high caliber had been enticed to join Ford, but Breech assured me that Dearborn Motors had nothing to do with it. Four men received 6 per cent. They were Bugas, Mead L. Bricker, long-time Ford executive, Ernest C. Kanzler, Ford's uncle and close adviser, and Albert J. Browning, whom Breech brought in to head up purchasing. Herman L. Moekle, a Ford veteran elevated to the post of treasurer, received 4 per cent.

Davis recalls that he purchased his 12 per cent of the shares for $25,000, and that the total put up was a little more than $200,000. Dearborn Motors added $25 to the price of each tractor. In three months Dearborn Motors had paid back its original investors. It continued doing good business, paying good dividends, until 1952 when the Ferguson suit was finally settled. The Ford Motor Company then bought Dearborn Motors from its stockholders for $11 million net. That is, Ford assumed all the liabilities of the company.

So now the original stockholders had $11 million. If they put the money in their pockets, of course, they'd have to pay out a good portion in taxes. They met to determine what to do with it.

Davis and Gossett were sitting together at the end of the table. "What about a finance company for people buying tractors?" Davis suggested. "Farmers need financing just like anybody else, and from all the Model T's I've sold them I can vouch for the fact that they are good credit risks."

Almost immediately Gossett called down the table, "Say,

I think Jack has the answer here." The Dearborn Finance Company was approved on the spot. It also, of course, had no direct connection with Ford Motor Company. Davis's estimate of the situation proved correct. When the Dearborn Finance Corporation was liquidated in 1956, the Aurora Holding Company was created to provide a repository for the money. Aurora invested in a portfolio of securities of which the market value on April 30, 1958, was just over $37 million. At that time Mr. and Mrs. Breech had a 17 per cent interest in Aurora or a net worth of $6 million on an original investment of about $40,000—which had been earned within three months. Aurora's holdings formed the nucleus of the One William Street Fund, Incorporated, a diversified investment company located at 1 William Street, New York. Its directors included Breech, Bugas, Crusoe, Gossett, and Harder. In 1964, Lehman Brothers, investment adviser to the fund, issued a second prospectus showing total net assets of more than $253 million.

Davis told me that he and his wife each put up half of his $25,000 allocation. She shared some of her earnings with the children before her death. Davis, however, kept a clear record of his $12,500 investment, which was 6 per cent of the total. When he talked to me in the spring of 1968, his original investment had grown into 270,000 shares of One William, worth, at that time, about $4,752,000. He estimated that he had drawn about a million in income subject to capital-gains tax, or about $750,000 after taxes. Without a detailed examination of his records, he could not estimate the dividends earned by Dearborn Motors and Dearborn Finance.

With this kind of financial security you don't need money, and Davis has been able to pick up other financial tidbits—hotels, skiing clubs, a subdivision and shopping center. The easiest way to find out how much a man is worth is to ask him, and fortunately, Davis was not coy.

"Oh, about 10 million dollars," he said. "Maybe 15. It's

hard to estimate this kind of thing because it all depends on what you could get if you had to sell. I don't have to sell."

As an example of what you can do when you have money, he mentioned one of his minor real estate transactions. He had an opportunity to buy some land in Bloomfield Hills and develop it. He, Breech and two other individuals signed their names for $125,000 each, he said. "I don't think Ernie was real sure what he was signing," Davis said. "It only took him about two seconds and then he forgot about it. He didn't have to put up a nickel cash. The thing has paid off about $175,000 apiece." That's a fair amount of spending money for signing your name.

I don't mean to imply here that any of these people were insincere when they said that their major motivations in joining Ford were his own personal appeal and the challenge in rebuilding a moribund concern. But the million-dollar merit badges over the years have been pleasant rewards for kindness to a nice young man. Later, when stock options were made available to company officers in accordance with their rank, Breech was granted options worth about $1,900,000. After Ford stock had split and reached a high of $60, these options would have grown in value to more than 10 million dollars.

Whatever Breech earned from Ford, he was worth it. Talking about the high salaries paid in the industry Davis used Breech as an example. "A man like Ernie could earn his annual salary in one decision," he said. "He brought in the system that saved the Ford Motor Company."

4

IN THE HISTORY of the automobile, more than 4100 makes of cars have been manufactured and sold. The few still available have survived only through extraordinary and timely combinations of circumstances and individuals. In the case of the Ford, the most successful of all, the combination of Henry Ford and Jim Couzens was singularly fortunate. At the time of the break between Ford and Malcomson, based strictly on the current trend toward larger cars, Malcomson had been right and Ford wrong. The difference was that Ford didn't give a damn about the current trend. Even then, when an automobile cost more than a house and lot, Ford went about the plant telling his mechanics that some day they would be able to drive their own cars.

One of the men to whom Ford confided this crazy idea was a pattern maker, Charles E. Sorensen. Sorensen was stunned, then agreed that it was a magnificent idea.

Sometimes I wonder about that magnificent idea. A couple of days after I read about it in Sorensen's memoirs I was talking with a knowledgeable and articulate executive named Ford Finfgeld in his suite in the Rouge complex. Suddenly Finfgeld looked at his watch and said, "Oh, my God, you'd better get out of here. It's almost time for the shift to change."

I ran to my car, but I didn't make it. It was like trying to get out of a football stadium after a big game, with thousands of Ford workers honking and squeezing and bluffing and cutting in front of me. Magnificent idea, my foot.

But even Henry Ford's dreams had some limitations. About the same time he talked to Sorensen he mentioned to another employee that the automobile would encourage neighborliness not only among American communities, but among all the people of the world. "We won't have any more strikes or wars."

When he was able to devote all of his energy to one light car, Ford warmed up on the Model N, and then, in 1908, brought out the Model T. How can anyone today describe the impact on the world of this ungainly contraption, 7 feet high with false doors and a crank? Ugly and simple as it was, when the tin lizzie came out it was more than modern, it was the car of the future. A European steel alloy Ford had stumbled on and developed made its tough, light weight possible. The flywheel magneto, a Ford invention, enabled the car to generate its own electricity for ignition, thus doing away with the crude batteries of the time. Its planetary transmission (parts of which were cut out in wood by Charlie Sorensen so that Ford could work with three-dimensional objects instead of with blueprints) enabled women and children to drive it, though maybe not crank it. Push a pedal down with your left foot, pull the gas lever down with your right forefinger, and off you lurched. It had the world's most efficient gasoline gauge, a black stick. If you wanted to know whether you had enough gas to get you to

the next country store you got out, lifted off the front seat, thus
exposing the gas tank on which you sat, removed the cap, and
stuck in the black stick. If it came out dry, you needed gas.
Many a time, stranded on a lonely road, I've wished my fancy
gauge had been as accurate.

Deliberately designed for the impossible roads of 1908,
the Model T, by encouraging travel, forced the improvement
of those roads. It anticipated two-lane highways and oncoming
traffic; its new left-hand drive made it easier to see if another
car was approaching before passing the one ahead. With farm
adaptations and reliable motor, it overcame the aversion of the
farmer to anything that scared a horse, and began the process
of bringing the rural population into the mainstream of the
nation. It cost no more than the first inefficient Model A, $850,
and, after years of constant improvement, hit a low of $260,
ready to roll. Fifteen million were sold, and many are still
around. The flivver stimulated songs, poems, jokes, cartoons,
articles, and books. It covered the world. Fortunes were made
by entrepreneurs who made more than 5000 accessories for it—
racing bodies ($70), cleated wheels and four-wheel drive for
farming, gasoline guages and speedometers, locks of all kinds.
Old-timers in Greene County, Virginia, still remember me primarily as the son of the man who had the first Model T in the
county. It was the first car of any kind; nothing else would take
Greene County roads. I wish I had it now; a pre-World War I
Model T is worth more than a new Mark III, and I could still
buy parts for it from Sears Roebuck.

The day the Model T came out the directors voted themselves another dividend of $100,000, and repeated a month or
so later to make the total dividends paid in the company's first
five years just over a million dollars. They also split their stock,
20 for 1. The next year they gave themselves $1,800,000 more.
That one share of stock bought under tearful protest by Cou-

zens's sister was now 20 shares, and she had received $28,000 in dividends in five years. Few white-collar people came close to $5000 a year for a 60-hour week at that time.

Ford and Couzens got a raise to $75,000 a year. But still most of the earnings were plowed back into the business, particularly for new plants and tools.

The first advertisement for the Model T appeared on a Friday; Saturday morning's mail brought in 1000 advance orders. The office staff wasn't large enough to open the envelopes, much less to process the orders. As for dealers, they were mostly proprietors of bicycle shops and hardware stores. Henry Ford had foreseen the importance of the dealer to the entire operation —for it was to the dealer you went when the car boiled over or broke your arm—and so had insisted upon local men of high quality to handle his product. But there weren't enough of them, and they had only the most primitive, completely centralized direction. Ford couldn't care less about the organization of anything not on wheels, and in keeping with his firm policy of developing his own experts, he plucked an ex-convict (embezzlement) out of the office force and made him sales manager. Norval Hawkins put together a sales organization of which the basic principles are still in use today.

Henry Ford was enthusiastic about international trade and had already encouraged operations in Canada and the British Isles. A Ford was sold in England in 1903. Although France supposedly had a jump on America in automobiles, Model T's were soon rattling around French cities. The first automobile sold in Turkey was a Ford; Model T's were everywhere.

All this time Ford distribution was operating under a severe legal handicap. Back in 1879, George B. Selden, a Rochester attorney, had the forethought, if not the gall, to file for a patent for the entire concept of a horseless carriage; it was granted in 1895. It sounds crazy, like patenting books or television, but he got away with it for years. The major companies, including Olds, Packard, and Cadillac, decided they'd rather negotiate than fight, and organized the Association of Licensed Automobile Manufacturers. It collected Selden's royalty of one and one-fourth percent of the retail price of every car sold in America. Today this would amount to about $300 million a year.

Even before the Ford Motor Company was really underway, Ford refused to pay this tribute. One of the greatest coat holders in history, he had Couzens tell the ALAM representative: "Selden can take his patent and go to hell with it!" When informed that the Selden crowd would put him out of business, Ford himself stood up, pointed a finger, and said, "Let them try it."

They did try it. Suits were filed. The ALAM ran newspaper advertisements warning that "any person making, selling or using" unlicensed automobiles "will be liable to prosecution. . . ." When the ad was first shown to Ford and Couzens they were in their shirtsleeves loading a shipment of cars. They went right on with their work.

Though Ford prepared to fight the suit and answered the ads with equally forceful ones of his own, the threat naturally inhibited both potential dealers and customers. The intense and complicated battle went on for years, both in the courts and in the newspapers. In 1909, the court upheld the Selden patent. Ford appealed and ran more full page advertisements. Americans like people who buck the establishment, and in some ways the fight helped more than it hurt. The total bill came to at least a million dollars, and if he had lost the appeal he might have been wiped out. But he didn't lose. The case was settled in his favor in 1911 and the resulting elation was nationwide.

Whipping the ALAM strengthened Ford's innate iconoclasm. He was one against the conventional world, the hippie of industrialism. From the time Henry I defied his father and left the farm to the Presidential campaign of 1968, when his three grandsons supported three different candidates, every Ford has been an independent cuss. Even Edsel carried within him a visceral revolt and on occasion accomplished his own projects, like the highly styled Lincoln Zephyr and the classic Continental. And Henry Ford II's Maverick was aptly named.

Henry Ford II made a gesture toward conventionalism when he and Breech finally brought the company into the Automobile Manufacturers Association in 1956. He lived with the association's policies for a time but then he, too, showed the Ford aversion to complying with regulations a Ford considers stupid. In 1957, he supported the AMA decision to get all major manufacturers out of high-performance activity, or racing. For the next few years he watched with increasing frustration while other cars, particularly Pontiac, participated on a sub rosa basis. Bunkie Knudsen, who as head of Pontiac inherited a dull chunk of iron, restyled the car, souped it up, won races with it, and brought it from eighth place in the industry to number three. Ford held the number one place in 1957 and 1959, but as the models became more and more like vegetables, it sold less and less of them. The economical but colorless Falcon did well during the national reaction against the chrome gas guzzlers of the Fifties, but economy waves don't last long and the Falcon began to droop. The Falcon was McNamara's bird, and, as automotive writer Charlie Barnard put it, "He wore granny glasses and put out a granny car."

When the Ford frustration finally broke, the reaction splattered all over Dearborn. The company was going back into racing, and to hell with the AMA. The happiest man in the organization was Lee Iacocca, who'd been leap-frogged to vice president at the age of 36. Though he had engineering degrees from Lehigh and Princeton, Iacocca was a throwback to the original type of Ford executive: he could spout caustic criticism and back it up with remedial performance. He knew that young people thought the Ford a fuddy duddy and he said so. "Nobody ever called me shy," he barked at me rather unnecessarily, glaring past his hawklike nose with dark glittering eyes. Iacocca looks more like a falcon than the Falcon, but the bird-of-prey impression he gives is not really hostile, just intense.

Iacocca knew young people and he knew racing buffs. Youth wants sporty looking cars. As for racing buffs, automobile racing is second only to horse racing as the most popular spectator sport in the country, and the crowd doesn't go to bet. Nor do the fans get there on horseback; they associate their cars with those they see roaring around the track. Furthermore, the people you see at the big races make good money with which they buy good cars equipped with expensive accessories.

One of these racing buffs is Henry Ford II. He subscribes to all the racing magazines and goes to races himself when he can. He was wide open to Iacocca's rapid fire sales pitch that racing helps marketing. But his decision to get Ford back on the tracks required a green light for both money and effort. It's not easy to turn a manufacturing philosophy from producing sturdy black Falcons to engineering high-performance components, and Ford assigned his best men to the job. It takes more than money to win races; you've got to have intense enthusiasm as well as the ultimate in engineering talents and facilities. Even with this combination, the length of time it took to produce winners tested Henry Ford's patience. He tried a short cut, the purchase of the then king of *gran turismo* racing, the great Ferrari, but Enzo Ferrari, the 65-year-old Italian manufacturing genius, backed off on the deal at the last second. The best explanation is that he was smothered by the swarm of American organization men with their briefcases full of codicils and conditions written in incomprehensible legal jargon. All Ford said, when I asked him why the deal fell through, was, "Somebody sent a boy."

If Ford couldn't buy Ferrari, he had to beat Ferrari. Le Mans is the center court of sports prototype racing, and though

Ford failed there in '64 and '65, Fords knocked the big red Ferrari right out of the racing picture in '66 and '67. Ford was there with Cristina, jammed in the uncomfortable box during most of the 24-hour run, both years. In '66 he was grand marshal. Victory in 1969 gave Ford a four-year winning streak.

In stock car racing, the big thing in America, the Ford showing in the first year of the comeback was miserable, but in 1963, Fords took the first five places at Daytona Beach. By 1969 Ford could field the most impressive driving team in the world. In the Riverside 500 in February, Ford took the first three places with Richard Petty, A. J. Foyt, and Parnelli Jones at the wheels. Dan Gurney was also in there with a Mercury. Later that month Lee Roy Yarbrough won the Daytona 500, setting a new record of 157.950 miles per hour. A month later Ford put the new Boss engine under the hood, and started a new cycle.

In the 450,000 drag races in America each year, Fords have won their share. The Ford people still scream that they were robbed in the biggest single American event, the Indianapolis 500, in 1963, but they won it in '65. By 1970, Ford was active, successfully so, in six major racing categories: stock car, drag, sedan, Indianapolis, Grand Prix and sports car. Each has a large following, not necessarily the same; each gets excellent coverage in the news media, including television, and the influence on race followers is direct. Ford sales figures prove it. The aura of competitiveness and speed spills over onto other potential customers. Further, if you've never seen a race in your life and never expect to take your car out of a 35-mile-an-hour zone, you still benefit by the improvement in performance and endurance that spreads throughout the entire line of any manufacturer who wins.

In drag racing, for example, you hold your accelerator on the floor while jamming into the next gear. When Ford first returned to dragging, second gear kept breaking down; it couldn't take the punishment. The entire transmission was re-engineered, and the entire line—and Ford customers—benefited. It wouldn't have happened this way if Henry Ford II, like his grandfather, hadn't been willing to buck the establishment.

In 1911, people backed the winner as much as they do today, and the defeat of the Selden monopoly brought in not only dealers and customers who had previously been leery about a nonlicensed automobile, but those who admired the Ford courage and success. Ford built 21,000 Model T's in 1910, 54,000 in 1911, 82,000 in 1912, 199,000 in 1913—and the number kept increasing.

By this time Ford had all he could do to produce enough cars without considering frills and options. Choice of color was discontinued. As Ford told Sorensen, "They can have any color they want as long as it's black." In 1916 you could buy five models, from the $345 runabout to the $640 sedan, but not one option. You took it or left it.

The escalation both required and resulted from a new plant and new production methods. No one could deny the superiority of Ford machinery and its maintenance during the company's first third of a century. New production methods comprised the ultimate in the precomputer era of the industrial revolution, the assembly line.

I'm not going to go round and round here with the industrial archeologists as to whether Ford's assembly line was an absolute innovation. The first caveman to push a half-skinned carcass at his mate for her to finish up probably started the whole thing. And if the caveman didn't, an industrial consultant named Frederick W. Taylor deserves credit for the germ of the idea. But it was developed and perfected by several production experts working with and inspired by Ford. The line as we know it today incorporates the same basic principles as those developed at Highland Park with the encouragement, inspiration, and personal know-how of Henry Ford during the years prior to World War I. You can see the action today, and it's fascinating, at assembly plants in Atlanta, Chicago, Dallas, Dearborn, Kansas City, Lorain, Los Angeles, Louisville, Mahwah, Metuchen, Norfolk, St. Louis, San José, St. Paul, Wayne, and Wixom in the United States as well as in Canada at Oakville and St. Thomas, Argentina at Buenos Aires, Australia at Brisbane, Broadmeadows and Sydney, Brazil at São Paulo, England at Dagenham, Halewood, and Langley, Germany at Cologne, Chile at Santiago, Belgium at Genk, Mexico at Mexico City, South Africa at Port Elizabeth, Ireland at Cork, New Zealand at Lower Hutt, Holland at Amsterdam, Peru at Lima, Portugal at Azambuja, the Philippines at Manila, Venezuela at Caracas, and Singapore.

The words Henry Ford and assembly line are inextricably entwined in industrial history. At one time, assembling an automobile or one of its complex components was comparable to a child building an elaborate model with his Erector set, with the set itself in the next room and most of the parts not fitting. That was the way it was in the beginning, when much of the hardware was handmade. With the design and purchase of excellent machinery, it became possible to turn out millions of parts each identical to the others. That not only made it possible to put together something, say a magneto, without constantly selecting and twisting and filing things until they fit, but led to the next step, a moving belt. One man, instead of assembling the whole magneto, would start it with one operation, and then it would move on to the next man. Twenty-nine men took a crack at it before it was finished. One day it took one man 20 minutes to assemble one magneto; the day after the conveyor belt was put in, the time was cut to 13 minutes 10 seconds per magneto per man. Refinement of the process brought the time down to 5 minutes: one man could do the work of four.

When they first attempted to assemble an entire car by the assembly line method, they put a frame on skids and pulled it from one end of the building to the other with a rope. A group of men walked along with it, grabbing parts from pre-placed piles as they went along. The next refinement was to station different men, or teams, by the equipment, and drag the chassis past them. In this crude second-generation method, the frame had to stop while the men performed their assigned operations. To allow for the fact that some operations took longer than others, the interval between each production was increased or decreased. As the process was refined, the number of man hours per car was cut from 15½ to 1½.

Fascinating as an assembly line is to watch, what you see now is only a fraction of the entire process. Today the assembly line is set by automation and computerization, in both of which Ford was the industrial pioneer. Say you want a red Mustang convertible with about a dozen items of optional equipment from high-performance engine to whitewalls. As your chassis comes down the 700-foot lane at 22.2 feet per minute (a car rolls off every 54 seconds), each item you ordered is delivered by automated control to the precise spot where it will be installed at the precise moment. But all those items have to come from somewhere, which means that there are other assembly lines putting together components, and other operations all the way back to blasting out the iron ore. Look at the moving line, consider the countless unseen operations that make it possible, and marvel. But remember that Henry Ford I brought a Model T off the line every 1.6 minutes before Henry Ford II was born, when the only computers were in people's heads.

Henry I got a great kick out of all his smoothly functioning, gleaming machinery. But the organization and paperwork that went with the consequent increase in procurement, production, and sales bugged him to the same degree. Norval Hawkins in his days as an efficiency expert particularly got in Ford's hair, though some of Hawkins' contributions met with the boss's approval. Ford was tremendously impressed with Hawkins' experiments with shipping. At that time, the only way to get a car to a dealer was by railroad, three Model T's to a boxcar. For weeks Hawkins packed and unpacked boxcars with knocked-down vehicles. When he had completed the three-dimensional jigsaw puzzle to his satisfaction, he could get parts for twenty or more automobiles into each boxcar. The automobile industry's first off-premises assembly plant, at Kansas City, was the result.

But Ford only liked what he could see, like engines packed in boxcars. Hawkins bustled around the plant with pads and sharpened pencils, and started control procedures that enraged Henry I. One day Ford sent for a part to show a visitor, and when it arrived he was told he had to sign for it. He promptly went to Hawkins' office, grabbed all the papers having to do with materiel flow, took them outside, poured gasoline on them, and set them on fire. When Hawkins still didn't get the message and persevered with other types of routing slips, Ford took Sorensen to Hawkins' office and the two dumped the contents of all the drawers on the floor and stirred them up into a paper stew with their feet.

Henry Ford II, thanks in part to the tutelage of corporate master Ernie Breech, earned a reputation for paperwork. But traces of the old man's gut feel and insistence on three-dimensional visualization often come through. Ford I liked to see Sorensen's wooden gears; Ford II likes to see new models in clay, full size and in color. Stacks of folders containing detailed performance reports on the top level executives cross his desk, but he still likes to get out and see the faces and hear the voices of the men he can make or break, and who can make or break the company.

Gene Bordinat, the loquacious vice president in charge of design, commented on Henry Ford II's interest in cars as cars and people as people. "He knows personally every man in the top three echelons of my department, which means about 40 people in this relatively small division. At one management review session he brought up something about one of my men that I didn't know. It was sufficient cause to get rid of him."

Bordinat is bluntly frank about his role. It's to design cars that will sell. But before selling a car to the public, he has to sell it to Henry Ford II.

Bordinat was an eager collaborator with Lee Iacocca in the early Sixties in the effort to supplant Ford's fuddy-duddy image with a youthful one. Iacocca had the marketing people make extensive studies. They showed that the products of the World War II baby boom were coming of buying age, and judging by increased college enrollment, these young people would be sophisticated buyers. More families were buying second cars, and the wives who ran car pools and did errands wanted those second cars to be small and maneuverable as well as stylish and attractive. The survey even included a special study on collegiate opinions of bucket seats, which are patently not conducive to the furtherance of active romance. Forty-two per cent of the students preferred bucket seats on the first date, when they were out to impress the girl, but after starting to make time, 85 per cent wanted no part of them.

Even with his detailed information, Iacocca knew it was going to be difficult to sell Henry Ford II on a completely new model. Ford had just okayed an expensive program for the new intermediate Fairlane. Iacocca needed help for the selling job and Bordinat was happy to work on the design for a new model. In the meantime Iacocca injected some facts and figures on the financial potential of a new line in conversations with the boss. When the model was ready, Iacocca lured Ford to the design center, and he and Bordinat started moving Ford toward it. Suddenly Ford exploded.

"I know what you're trying to do," he said sharply, "and I don't want to be bothered with it." He turned and walked away from the car without ever taking a look at it.

Iacocca and Bordinat were both crushed. "Mister Ford

93

never spoke to me that way before or since," Iacocca told me. Reliving the experience was still unpleasant. "We learned later, though, that he was just coming down with mononucleosis. He would never have spoken that way if he had been well."

Chevrolet had been pursuing the same market. It had tried to follow the early success of the Falcon with the Corvair, but the little car with the rear engine did not achieve the same popularity. Then, Bordinat says, a Chevrolet ad man cooked up a clever scheme. "Call one a Monza, pep up the trim a little bit, put sport insignia—crossed flags—on the side, and pretend it's a sports car. Sports car, hell. They couldn't put any size engine in it, and it couldn't get out of its own damn way. But it took. People bought it."

Bordinat and his designers had previously tried every conceivable trick to jazz up the Falcon, but it had built-in limitations. It was too high, the hood was too short, it wouldn't take the biggest engine. It had been designed in the late Fifties when Henry Ford was caught between two finance men, Breech as chairman of the board and McNamara as group vice president of cars and trucks. A prosperous and outspoken dealer, looking back on that period, said, "They had too many cost-analysis specialists holding down expenditures for every stupid nut and bolt."

A few years later, with Breech and McNamara gone, Iacocca pouring out ideas, and J. Edward Lundy describing his finance department as "gung-ho," Ford, now chairman of the board, told one of his chief lieutenants: "The next time we build a car around here that won't accept the big engines we manufacture I want you to tell me the name of the *former* engineer responsible."

Unable to modify the original Falcon further, Bordinat had to make a fresh start. He knew all the features that make a car look sporty—long hood, short rear deck, low body, curving lines over the rear wheels giving the impression of a grasshopper about to spring. With Iacocca's encouragement, his department continued working on designs incorporating these features, but they still had to sell the chairman of the board on approving the idea—and the expenditure.

One day Bordinat got an idea. He lined up every Ford model in the yard outside the building. He obtained every Chevrolet model and arranged them so that each one faced its Ford counterpart. Then Bordinat enticed Ford, now fully recovered and chipper, over to the design center. He casually walked him down the gantlet between the two rows of cars. Opposite the Monza there was nothing, a blank space in the line of Fords.

That hole was as dramatic a visual aid to Henry Ford II as Charlie Sorensen's wood carvings had been to his grandfather. Ford gave the go-ahead to fill the gap. Iacocca and Bordinat already knew generally what they wanted. An unprecedented crash program was inaugurated, with seven design sections given just two weeks to produce clay models. One stood out. Ford authorized its production: he personally authorizes *every* model. In 22 months, an extremely short time in which to bring out a completely new model, the car was introduced to the public. It was the Mustang. In its first year on the market, 418,812 Mustangs were sold; it reached the one-million mark in less than two years. The Mustang was the hottest car in automotive history. It had been rejected by Henry Ford in theory but he approved a car to fill a hole he could see.

A couple of years later Iacocca had another idea. Looking over a picture book of every car produced in the world, his eye fell in succession on the Rolls-Royce and the old Continental of the early Forties. The two pictures remained in his mind overnight. The next morning he had to go to Canada for a meeting, but the mental pictures went with him. Then the pictures fused: the long thrusting hood of the Rolls and the short deck of the old Continental. He left the meeting, put in a call to Bordinat, and described what he visualized. Bordinat, who turns on with equal rapidity, immediately went to work on the idea.

While he was waiting, Iacocca did some hard business-thinking on the market potential for a car of the size and cost he had in mind. Some of the executives with whom he discussed the idea expressed a negative viewpoint. It was expensive, they said. Who wants it? "Over a million people in the United States make $25,000 a year or over," Iacocca said. "That's who wants it."

But that was not the approach he used on Henry Ford II. He waited until Bordinat had come up with the finished concept.

"Ford is a gut poker guy," Iacocca explained. "He's not some faceless chairman of the board, he's Henry Ford. Nobody else can make that statement in the automobile business. Once we have a concept that looks good, we go to the boss. And if he has that gut poker feel about the product, nobody in the business can move as fast as we do to get it out."

Ford looked at the new model for only a few seconds. "Gee," he said, "I'd like to drive home in that."

Iacocca gave him some figures, but he knew that the car was approved. It was introduced in the spring of 1968, the new Continental Mark III. Usually the price of a model is not settled until the last moment, but long before this car reached the production stage, I was told its price—exactly $20 lower than the Cadillac Eldorado. It was brought out as a patent competitor of the Eldorado, and in its first year it outsold the Eldorado substantially.

Its acceptance by the public was as dramatic in its way as the Mustang's. Production was limited, advance orders were heavy, and many customers waited months for delivery. I know of one instance in which a lucky purchaser bought one at full price including automatic temperature control at $563 extra, drove it long enough to impress the daylights out of his peer group, and sold it at a used car auction for a $200 profit. One of the editors of an automotive magazine dressed up in an outlandish costume and started out on a weekend without a nickel or a credit card in his pocket, but behind the wheel of the Mark III. He didn't need cash to live it up. Gas stations, motels, and restaurants extended immediate credit and some even offered to advance cash. I don't want a Mark III because I'd live in constant terror of getting a scratch on it, but when one goes by I look to see who's driving it, which is why he bought it.

As for its economics, the company isn't talking. Due to its limited market, it can't sell millions like the Mustang. But it is no secret in automobile manufacture that once you've made enough models to pay for the initial investment, the profit per unit on even a low-priced car is pretty good. On a medium-priced car it's more so, and on the Mark III or Eldorado it's best of all. If you're one of the 400,000 Ford stockholders, this profit is probably okay with you. The reason General Motors consistently shows a higher percentage of profit is because of its heavier penetration into the higher-priced field.

If the base price of the Mark III were appreciably less you probably wouldn't want one anyway; part of its appeal lies in its demonstration to your neighbors that you can afford it. One of the unfortunate advertising bloopers of the economy period at Ford's was the short-lived Mercury slogan, "Only $50 more than a Ford." You ought to hear Lee Iacocca get off on *that*. "Who the hell wants a so-called luxury car that only costs $50 more than a Ford?" he shouted at me.

Though Iacocca is more vociferous than Henry Ford II— he's more vociferous than *anybody*—he reflects the boss's thinking or he wouldn't have that huge office on the 12th floor. Henry Ford II is also interested in increasing profits, and feels a sincere responsibility to his stockholders. He wants Ford to be bigger and bigger and bigger, and one way to accomplish this goal is to spend money in capital improvements. In the ancillary corporations abroad the holdings of the Ford Motor Company represent far more than a mere majority interest. This gives the company flexibility in operations. Ford is interested in growth.

His grandfather, however, carried the capital-improvement principle to the extreme. Money was not something to be doled out to the few remaining stockholders, whom he publicly called parasites, but to be used to improve the product by making it available to more people and to develop and build new tools with which to put more people to work. Jack Davis, who knew him from 1919 on, commented that the old man had the farmer's economic philosophy. If a farmer has fertile land, well-kept buildings, and excellent farm tools, from big tractors to little hoes, he considers himself well off regardless of his bank account.

Still a hayseed, Ford was actually embarrassed by the profits aggregating like the manure pile of a big dairy farm. He said his profits were awful—that was the word he used, *awful* —and he began figuring out ways to cut them down. One obvious method of making less money is to cut prices, and he continually did so, but still the profits went up. One day, with a backlog of orders, he grabbed a pencil and lopped off about 20 per cent of the retail price of each car. In early 1914, he announced a kind of customer profit-sharing plan. If people bought more than 300,000 Model T's, he'd return $50 to every purchaser. Sales hit 308,000 and there went $15 million. But as his experts were constantly designing machinery to manufacture basic parts more efficiently, lower production costs cancelled out the reductions.

A less obvious method of siphoning off profits, at least in the new automotive industry in the early 1900's, was to increase wages and improve working conditions of the men who built the cars. In the early days there was no reason for Ford to pay his workers more than anybody else did; he knew them all and kept them working their hearts out through his own personality and direct leadership. As the working force grew larger, he could not continue this chummy camaraderie, and Sorensen gradually assumed more authority.

Sorensen was a true martinet. Humble bootlicker to the man over him, he was harsh and arrogant with those under him. He worked like a dog himself, all day every day six days a week and most nights and Sundays, and he expected the hourly workers to knock themselves out for at least the normal 60-hour work week. New members of the work force didn't see much of Henry but they got a bellyful of Sorensen. And Ford found, to his bewilderment, that he was no longer universally loved.

One day when he and young Edsel were walking through the plant, he caught a look of unconcealed hatred from one of the men whom Sorensen had probably just finished chewing out. Ford wanted to do something about his unpopularity, and unable to woo the affection of 13,000 employees, he set out to buy it. The company had an embarrassment of profits and Sorensen had just completed a set of figures demonstrating the savings in production costs that plant improvements would bring about. Ford called a meeting of his little coterie one Sunday morning in January and stood Sorensen at a blackboard with a piece of chalk. Sorensen wrote his projected figures for materials and overhead on the board, and then the current wage of $2 a day. Ford told him to increase the minimum to $2.50 and see how it would work out if put into effect throughout the plant. With the new wages added in the total still did not approach the selling cost of the product.

"Put down $3, Charlie," Ford said, and Sorensen obediently chalked up the figure on the board. "Try $3.25," Ford said, like a bidder at an auction. The others began to protest but to no avail. He kept calling out numbers and Sorensen kept writing them down, then extrapolating the figures to the entire work force. Goaded by the protests, Ford kept going until the figure reached $5. Then he went to the blackboard, picked up an eraser and wiped off the figures.

"It's all settled," he said. "Five dollars a day minimum pay and at once."

The work day was also reduced to 8 hours, but it was the $5 minimum which shook the world. The announcement, on January 5, 1914, knocked the worsening international situation out of the headlines both in North America and in Europe— and put Ford in them. Before then he had been just another successful businessman; *The New York Times Index* for 1913 did not mention his name and he wasn't in *Who's Who*. In one day he became a household word. Public reaction was mixed. The *Wall Street Journal* disapproved; the $5 day was both unsound and unethical. Adolph S. Ochs, publisher of *The New York Times,* appeared in the city room asking, "He's crazy, isn't he? Don't you think he's gone crazy?" He didn't have to identify whom he was talking about. Everybody knew. The big industrialists thought Ford was not merely crazy, but downright dangerous. To pay an ordinary worker $5 a day would wreck the country. But views of the ordinary worker, who in many parts of the United States, not to mention the rest of the world, wasn't getting even $2 a day, were understandably a little different. Men poured into Detroit by coach and boxcar, bicycle and on foot.

That one announcement directly changed the lives of thousands. I happen to know of two personally. One, Vincent Ogar, was a Polish peasant immigrant shoveling coal on the docks of Duluth. He put down his shovel and headed for Detroit. Ogar had not learned to read and write in the old country—who could afford a book?—but his Ford paycheck enabled his son Thaddeus to get a college education and become news editor for the United Automobile Workers.

Another, Philip Sadowsky, was an Alabama farm boy when he heard the news. He, too, made his way to Detroit, and eventually became the multimillionaire land developer who transformed a series of chunks of coral into the paradise that is now the Florida Keys.

A strong case has been set forward by socioeconomists that Ford's $5 day exerted heavy influence on the continuation of capitalism in most of the productive world. Ford did not go broke; his company prospered, and his principle of paying a worker more than enough to live on gradually infiltrated industry. With food in his belly, his own roof over his head, a car in the garage, and a son in college, who needed Karl Marx?

Ford was 50 years old when he put in the $5 day. Henry Ford II was the same age when he started his campaign for job opportunities for the hard-core unemployed. I was with him when he addressed the midwestern regional meeting of the National Alliance of Businessmen on the subject, and drove to the Chicago airport with him and Ted Mecke following that speech. I hoped that he would reveal how he had come to understand the frustrations of those battling for existence in the jungle of Detroit's riot-torn inner city, but he did not.

The black Continental stopped for a red light, and our conversation, such as it was, stopped with it. Then I began a different tack. "Here you are trying to find jobs for 500,000 hard-core unemployed," I said, "and you've already hired five thousand or so yourself. Did you know that when your grandfather was your age he started the whole thing by hiring just one Negro?"

A small glimmer of interest flickered in his blue eyes. "Really?" he said.

"Yeah. The fellow's name was William Perry, and he and your grandfather used to cut wood together. Your grandfather said something about partnership being two men on either end of a cross-cut saw. Apparently he didn't care about the color of the man on the other end of the saw as long as he put his weight on it."

The light changed, we were off, and so was Ford. He began talking about his grandfather, and there was great pride in his voice. He told me how the old man had remained vigorous and athletic until the closing years of his life, and how he had insisted on getting up and walking around the day after an appendectomy. "They do it all the time now but they didn't then." He talked about how his grandfather had built a light-weight railroad train in the early Twenties, and an airplane not long after. And then we got around to the coincidence of the Fords at fifty.

Grandfather Ford put in the history-making $5 day after a morning's discussion of two or three hours; his grandson put in the history-making employment program after an afternoon's discussion of an hour or so. Henry I, the mechanic, made his decision from large figures chalked up on a blackboard; Henry II, the midcentury executive, worked with memos.

It was at lunchtime, October 11, 1967, that Levi Jackson handed Ford his three-page, double-spaced memorandum recommending new approaches in hiring methods which "could benefit not only the company but could do an effective job in aiding the inner city residents." It was a ten-point program, but the main point was that the company should go to the people and that artificial employment barriers—education, tests, police records—should be eliminated. Though he himself had little in common with the ghetto denizen, Jackson had come to realize some of the inherent problems of this large but basically unknown and unrecorded segment of the population of almost every large city. Here live people with no established homes, people who do not exist on any census. Many are illiterate, some do not know who their parents were, or who their children are. Soon, Jackson knew, the currently strike-closed company would reopen, and it would need thousands of new workers. Those uncounted thousands in the ghetto needed jobs, but current hiring practices virtually eliminated them. How could they be expected to come to the company personnel centers to apply for jobs which they knew they could not get? Many would not be able to pass the standard tests of verbal and arithmetical skills, tests of abilities not needed by many categories of un-skilled workers, nor would they all be able to produce clean police records even though they might never have been charged with any crime. Anyone picked up on suspicion in periodic roundups finds his name on the police blotter.

Jackson proposed that the company go to the inner city, lure the workers it needed from the ranks of the forgotten, waive the tests, and even advance those hired money to get to work with and eat on before the first paycheck came through. He expanded on his memo in a conference with Ford three hours after he placed the memo in his hand. The chairman bought the program that day.

The strike ended eleven days later, and by that time the details had been worked out. The company advertised for workers through the usual media, and continued its hiring op-erations at the usual personnel centers. But the other step had no precedent in industrial relations: the announcement that jobs paying more than $3 an hour were open, that no tests would be given and that persons with police records would be considered. The word was spread throughout the inner city by one hundred company recruiters.

Ford set the tone of the new program. "If they want jobs, we'll get them jobs," he said. "Equal employment opportunity requires more than the elimination of deliberate racial discrimi-nation. Opportunity is not equal when people who would make good employees are not hired because they do not know of openings, because they lack the self-confidence to apply, or because formal hiring criteria screen out potentially good employees as well as potentially poor ones. . . . Management should be willing to go directly into the city, to seek out the unemployed, to make sure that hiring standards are not unnecessarily or unrealistically restrictive."

Gertrude Samuels of *The New York Times Magazine* reported a typical day in one of the inner city recruiting centers. Laurence J. Washington, a Negro personnel executive who had started out at Ford at 75 cents an hour in 1939, directed the operations. He laid the new policy on the line: he didn't want supermen. He wanted men who'd get to work on time and put in a full day, every day, with plenty of overtime.

One of the men seeking work lived with his wife and two children with twelve other families in a two-story house. Years before he had served time for breaking and entering, and since then he had been able to get only part-time work. "Take me! I need a job!" he cried, and Washington took him and gave him that job, right then and there. Under the old system, followed by most of the major Detroit industries, he would not have been given the job in the first place because of his record; and even if he had had no record, he would have undergone weeks of processing. He would have had to go to the employment office to make application, then wait perhaps a week while the company checked him out. He might never again hear from the company, and if he did, it would be a notice to come on a certain day to take a written multiple choice test. After another week, he'd be notified if he passed—not if he failed—and would then have to take a full physical examination which could nullify all previous effort. Word gets around in the ghetto, and as a result of this system even some of those who had a good chance of making the grade were too proud or too impatient to apply.

Even with the new system, signing on of a man did not guarantee a full-time faithful worker. Some of the new employees didn't even show up; some of them because they couldn't read even enough to know which bus to take to work. Most of the problems of the new workers, however, were natural outgrowths of their simply not knowing how to work. For a man who's never had a steady job in his life ten hours a day in a foundry can be agony, mental as well as physical. The company had to do more than give its new worker a job and show him how to do it. Foremen and supervisors had to baby the new men along. Many of the supervisory personnel, who'd worked their own way up the ladder through hard work and ambition, had no taste for holding a grown man's hand and pleading with him to stick it out a little longer. Turnover was heavy.

Henry Ford has one marvelous quality with which many other big shots are singularly unendowed. That's candor. He was completely frank about the turnover among the newly hired workers.

"It's running about forty per cent," he said. "With a lot of these guys we laid an egg." He grinned. "We got other problems, too. Hell, some of them were selling dope on the property. We caught some people stealing. We had fights—some of 'em even fought the foremen. Some of 'em showed up blind drunk and on Mondays a lot of 'em didn't show up at all."

Normally it's the cynical journalist who refers to a glass as half-empty while the fellow he's interviewing calls it half-full. With Ford the situation was reversed. "Well," I said, "if you had forty per cent quit, that means you've got sixty per cent who stay. That's sixty per cent of people who desperately needed jobs who still have 'em."

"That's right," he said, pleased that I had interpreted it that way. "That's why this whole program is so important. If they weren't working they'd be scrounging for a buck here or there, or on relief. Maybe both. Relief carries with it no dignity, no pride. These men can hold their heads up. People talk about the matriarchal society of the Negro. Well, this is the way to break it down, through paychecks."

Later I discovered that Ford was overly deprecating his own program. Studying the employment records of the Rouge plant with Ford Finfgeld, general services manager, I saw that the turnover was not forty per cent, but thirty-seven, and that the figure applied only to one department, the foundry. "That's always been a high-turnover operation," Finfgeld said. Looking at the records of other plants, we found that none came close to 37 per cent. Most showed a turnover of about 15 per cent, which was about the same as the normal rate.

You can look at the disciplinary problem from two angles, too. Before the new group came in, the disobedience rate had been climbing steadily. In one plant picked at random there were six reported cases in 1963, 127 in 1967 before the strike. That's a factor of twenty plus.

Disregard for authority is calamitous to any establishment, and industry executives are particularly perturbed by it. The industrial worker has got to do what his foreman tells him to do (he is protected against outrageous or vindictive orders by both company policy and the union) or production suffers. No matter how deep the problems of the long-time unemployable, he still can't be allowed to go around beating up foremen. So the company attacked the problem from both ends. They educated the foremen on the complete unpredictability of the new employees. After years of frustration a man who didn't learn to read his third grade primer, much less Horatio Alger, can hardly be expected to become a model employee the minute he gets a job. But if he's worth going to all that trouble to hire he's worth going to more trouble to keep on the job, and the foreman has to take that trouble.

Another way to prevent trouble from starting is to ensure that it will be stopped promptly and dealt with firmly if it does, which means plant police. Fully conscious of the schism between the ghetto denizen and the white cop, Ford administrative personnel discussed the advisability of adding more Negroes to

106

the plant guards. The advantages were obvious, but so was the question—would the Negro guard discipline other blacks according to company rules? The question was dismissed; Negroes were recruited for the guard force, and they worked out fine.

"Practically all Ford executives realized that hiring the hard-core unemployed is something we must do," Finfgeld said. "We're proud to be associated with a company led by a man who is showing the way to a solution of one of America's greatest problems. A few may have had some reservations, but not after the Blue Letter came out. A Blue Letter is something we take pretty seriously around here. We got the message loud and clear."

The following letter was sent out to 10,000 members of supervision in all Ford plants in North America.

> Equal opportunity is one of Ford Motor Company's oldest, firmest and most basic policies. The purpose of this letter is to call on each of you to give that policy your full and active support, and to put it into practice in new ways and with a new sense of urgency.
>
> Our goal is to do all we realistically can to give people who have been held back by prejudice and poverty a chance to earn a decent life. This goal is entirely consistent with our responsibility to conduct our business soundly and profitably. We cannot provide wider employment opportunities by hiring more people than we need or by keeping people who cannot learn to do their jobs or work with other people. There are, however, many things we can do.
>
> —We can make sure that our requirements for hiring, training and promotion do not exclude able people for irrelevant reasons.
>
> —We can continue to improve our internal training programs and provide leadership and support to public and private community programs to seek out and develop latent abilities that may be productively employed in business and industry.

—We can lend a helping hand in adjusting to the work and the work place, and treat all employees with the dignity and understanding every man owes every other.

—By helping people to help themselves, we can help to cure a social cancer that threatens the vitality and peace of the communities where we do business, to reduce the costs of welfare and crime and the taxes we all pay, and to enlarge the markets for our products.

The company's Detroit inner-city hiring program is one example of the new approach I am calling for. Its aim is not only to offer employment opportunities, but actively to invite the interest of people who would not normally come to us—not to screen *out* doubtful applicants but to screen *in* if possible— and not merely to hire, but to help them make the grade after they are hired.

I hope that this innovative spirit will be reflected in our personnel policies at every level, and in every other aspect of our business. Opportunities to become a successful Ford dealer or supplier, for example, must be as open and as equal as the opportunities to become a successful employee. And, when we are considering locations for new facilities, we should consider the inner-city as well as the suburbs.

I ask each of you to be continuously alert in your own areas for conditions that could obstruct equal opportunity, and to make or suggest changes in the practices that are responsible. I ask each of you to receive suggestions with an open mind, to put good ideas into prompt effect, and to pass them on to others.

New approaches will bring new problems, but I know we have the management ability to solve them. Our company and our country will face far greater problems if we and other employers fail to do what we can to help disadvantaged people overcome the barriers that keep them from sharing in the abundance of the American economy.

The achievement of genuinely equal opportunity is the most urgent task our nation faces. Ford Motor Company is pledged to provide equal opportunity in its own operations, but

that commitment can be only as good as the personal performance of each of us. I therefore ask you to accept a full share of
the responsibility for making Ford Motor Company an equal
opportunity business in every sense of the term.

(Signed)

HENRY FORD II

The response in the Philco-Ford plant in Philadelphia
was particularly effective. One of the early recruits was a high
school drop-out named James M. Mercer. He was eager to
work. After his training program he was not assigned to the
plant, but back to the streets—as a recruiter. He understood
the mentality of the long-time unemployed; not long before he
had been one. Still it took time to gain the confidence of those
in the direst need of what he had to offer. Finally, however, he
was able to say, proudly, "Now they are all coming after me."

The founder of the company made his plant into an industrial guinea pig and the success of his experiment not only
changed industry, but hastened the social and economic progress
of the world. Since his grandson sent his recruiters into the
inner city of Detroit and found capable workers there, other
major companies have followed his example. General Motors
and Chrysler quickly availed themselves of the new source of
production workers, and the Big Three's plants all over the
country followed the Detroit example. Other broad-based industries joined in, and trade associations climbed on the hard-
core bandwagon.

Neither of the two men for their times, Fords I and II,
seemed to realize fully the consequence of their employee programs. Certainly the patriarch did not anticipate the impact
of the $5 day. Nobody realized that his announcement would
bring hordes of job hunters knocking at the gates. Ten thousand
men showed up the next morning. During the week the out-of-
town job seekers poured in, and on the following Monday
people were standing outside the plant before dawn in near zero

weather. Some were women coming in to beg for jobs for their husbands. Even the nicest people become monsters in a mob and they began pushing, shoving, fighting, and throwing things. Even intelligent people lose their senses when frightened, and somebody ordered the plant's fire hoses broken out. The icy water froze on the thinly clad, desperate job-hunters almost as it landed.

This senseless action had one by-product. The sight of people freezing made a liberal philanthropist out of the penny-pinching James Couzens. In later years he contributed millions to good causes, especially a foundation to help crippled children, became mayor of Detroit, and died a Republican senator supporting the New Deal.

Almost from the start, and continually throughout the years, Ford was accused of putting in the wage increase not for humanitarian reasons, but in order to get more work out of his employees. He never denied the benefit to him as an employer; he bragged about it, for the wage increase did pay off in incentive, productivity, and in a sharp drop in absenteeism and turnover. William R. Knudsen told of observing incredulously the productivity of a man on the Ford assembly line. Knudsen couldn't figure out how the worker accomplished so much, and finally asked him directly. "Henry give me double, I give him double," the man explained.

The wage increase encouraged an enlightened personnel man, John R. Lee, to implement his own idealistic principles. With Henry Ford's approval he improved working conditions in the plant and set up a sociological department to extend the beneficial influence into the homes of the workers. When I commented favorably on this program to Henry Ford II, he reacted with the usual embarrassment of a supposedly tough guy accused of being human. "Aw," he mumbled, "it was just paternalism."

Paternalistic or not, in Detroit in 1914 it represented a courageous step forward. At that time, when members of the Old World's huddled masses yearning to be free arrived in Detroit confused and unable to speak the language, they were met by a member of their ethnic group who found them lodgings and introduced them around to the neighborhood merchants. What the newcomers didn't know was that their interpreter was a professional vulture who got his cut on every purchase they made. Ted Ogar remembers when his mother had a separate book for every merchant—butcher, baker, greengrocer, dry grocer, shoe store, clothing store—in which the seller himself wrote the amount of the items purchased and the amount paid following pay day. The merchant arrived at his figures by deciding what he could unload and what he thought the traffic would bear. Selling goods was a sideline; the profit was in cheating. But still the newcomers had never had it so good and they spent money lavishly, buying Sunday suits and living it up Saturday night. To pay the exorbitant rents and food bills, their wives took in boarders and the women worked longer than the men. They prepared huge breakfasts in the morning, cleaned house, made the shopping rounds each day, prepared full-course dinners and suppers, cleaning up after each, and wound up the day's work by dragging the men out of the bars at night.

Henry Ford went along with Lee's effort to improve the domestic life of his employees. Anybody who didn't live according to his own simple but comfortable habits didn't live right, and anything that wasn't right Henry Ford set out to change.

"We want to make men in this factory as well as automobiles," he told his minister, Dean Samuel Marquis. "I believe that I can do the world no greater service than to create more work for more men at larger pay. I can foresee the time when we will have a hundred thousand men—and more—employed in this industry, and I want the whole organization dominated by a just, generous and humane policy."

Marquis was so convinced by Ford's sincerity that he left the church and became head of the company's sociological department. He and his staff went into the homes of workers and showed them how to live more efficiently. They encouraged home ownership.

City judges commented on the benefits to the entire community from the financial and social betterment of Ford families. The chief of police noted the decrease in the number of Ford workers picked up for Saturday night brawls, and the improved housing conditions which resulted in "many thousands of men becoming better and more dependable citizens."

Ford employees developed a reputation for helping each other, thereby driving several parasites out of business. Some of the members of Marquis's staff went a little far—there were few trained social workers—and some people, like the Ogars, who had fled officialdom in the old country, resented investigators poking in their closets. But overall it was a happy time for Ford workers.

The authority for all this, incidentally, was Marquis himself, who gave full credit to Henry Ford though he wrote the account of it after he, like just about everybody else connected with Henry Ford, had parted company with him under strained conditions. Marquis, although the victim of Ford's alternating current, nice today and nasty tomorrow, was still able to write about him with both affection and admiration. Nevertheless, when his book *Henry Ford, an Interpretation*, came out in 1923, its few critical passages were considered by many to be blasphemous. Ford's disciples condemned it and an effort was made to buy up all copies.

Henry Ford, an Interpretation triggers the question: What transformed Henry Ford? How did the man who built a billion-dollar empire out of dedication, ideals, and personal charm turn into an industrial despot? From the millions of words written about him I've picked up some indications, but no definite answers.

Ford's good qualities were by no means submerged completely. As Marquis commented, "There are in him lights so high and shadows so deep, that I cannot get the whole of him in the proper focus at the same time."

Though everybody has good and bad points, in Ford the contrast was pronounced. "Phenomenal strength of mind in one direction is offset by lamentable weakness in another," Marquis wrote. "Astounding knowledge of and insight into business affairs along certain lines stand out against a boasted ignorance in other matters. Sensational achievements are mingled with equally sensational failures. Faith in his employees and at times unlimited generosity towards them are clouded on occasion by what seems to be an utter indifference to the fate and feelings of men in his employ. There seems to be no middle ground in his makeup. . . . He has in him the makings of a great man, the parts lying about in more or less disorder. If only Henry Ford were properly assembled! If only he would do in himself that which he has done in his factory!"

Let's go on with Marquis a little bit more, for his is the most thoughtful summation of Ford as a person that I have read.

"Henry Ford possesses the most elusive personality of any man I have ever known. The baffling thing in him is the puzzling mixture of opposing natures. There are rages in him and endless conflicts between ideals, emotions and impulses unlike as day and night—a conflict that at times makes one feel that two personalities are striving within him for mastery, with neither able to win a final decision over the other." These changes in moods and attitudes were generally accompanied by outward changes in physical appearance. "Today he stands

113

erect, lithe, agile, full of life, happy as a child . . . out of his eyes there looks the soul of a genius, a dreamer, an idealist . . . but tomorrow he may be the opposite. He will have the appearance of a man shrunken by a long illness . . . his face is deeply lined . . . the affable gentle manner has disappeared. There's a light in the eyes that reveals a fire burning within altogether unlike that which burned there yesterday. He has the appearance of a man utterly weary and exhausted, and yet driven on by a relentless and tireless spirit. Back of an apparent physical frailty there evidently lies concealed a boundless supply of nervous energy."

This physical change was so marked that other executives recognized it, and ran for cover.

5

THE MAJOR PERIOD of Henry I's metamorphosis seems to have been the half-dozen years following his international emergence in 1914. The rube mechanic turned hero-industrialist had no preparation for his fame. He, his wife, and son lived quietly in an ordinary house on an ordinary street one week, the next they had to have a police escort to get through the crowds to their front door. He couldn't take a walk in his own neighborhood. Even in sophisticated New York a mob pursued him in the streets and the hotel had to place a guard in front of his suite. Everybody wanted money from him; one time he was with a group of clergymen and each one sought a donation. It took three people, working all day, just to open letters from people recounting their tragic misfortunes and asking for money. At first Ford had a sampling investigated; most of the case histories turned out to be imaginative. People tried the most elaborate schemes and subtle approaches to share his wealth. The intended victim could hardly fail to become suspicious of every proposition.

Ford had the human frailty of liking to see his name in the paper, spelled right. At first he turned up enough publicity all by himself to satisfy anybody, but eventually, as a mass production man, he got professional help from a series of ghostwriters and editors.

The Peace Ship episode, which required tremendous courage even for a man of whim, began as a crusade and ended in his ridicule. He became involved in two lengthy lawsuits in both of which he was inquisitioned by sharp lawyers and learned that journalists looking for a front-page object of ridicule can make a great deal out of little. One of the lawsuits he brought on himself when he sued the *Chicago Tribune* for libel. Some of his testimony was ridiculous, as the battalion of reporters assigned to the case were happy to quote, but some of the reporting was unfair. Asked, for example, if he knew who Benedict Arnold was, he replied, "He is a writer, I think." The remark was gleefully reported. Note, however, the use of the present tense. A man named Arnold was at that moment doing some writing about Ford.

Ford was the defendant in the other case. Contemptuous of the stockholders, and determined to continue his policy of making transportation available to more people at less cost, he cut off dividends in order to make his greatest expansion along the River Rouge in Dearborn, where the enormous complex functions today. The Dodge brothers, who by then were building their own automobile, subsidized in large part by their Ford dividends, brought suit on behalf of the stockholders. The testimony in the case was interesting. Ford said he was enlarging his facilities, "to make money and use it, give employment, build factories, and send out the car where the people could use it . . . and incidentally to make money."

116

"Incidentally?"

"That's right. Business is a service, not a bonanza."

Ford lost the case and had to pay out more than $19 million to the stockholders. He, of course, got 58 per cent of it, or $11 million. He was also enjoined from proceeding with the Rouge plant, but it would take more than a court order to keep Henry Ford from building the Rouge. Anyway, he'd had it with the stockholders. He took his family, which included Edsel, Edsel's wife, and their baby boy, Henry II, to southern California and practically disappeared. After a while he emerged to give an interview to the *Los Angeles Examiner* in which he announced the plans for a new company to build a better and cheaper car. The stockholders went into a panic. Ford delegated an agent to go around getting options on the rest of the stock. Scared to death that Ford would proceed with his threat, they sold out for a lower price than they would have gotten under normal conditions. Ford bought them all out at $12,500 a share, $13,000 a share to Couzens and his sister. It wasn't too bad a deal for the stockholders; considering the 20 to 1 split, a $100 investment brought a quarter of a million dollars. Ford had to borrow the $100 million plus, but he was so happy he danced a jig around the room.

He was now the sole owner of a company worth a half billion dollars, and which was to double in value within a decade. But this was one victory during those bitter years, and to gain it he had to borrow money. Ford did not like to be indebted to anyone, particularly bankers.

These were also the years of World War I, and Ford had an intense hatred for the blood and destruction of war. He rushed the production of tractors in response to the pleadings of the English, and delivered 7000, for they would produce food. But he resisted American war contracts. When he was finally inveigled into building Liberty engines and subchasers —in the building in which Mustangs and Cougars are now assembled—he stated that he would return every cent of profit he made on war work to the government. It took about six years of unraveling red tape to determine his profits and by that time he was so fed up with bureaucracy that he reneged on the promise. The sum was less than a million dollars, and the war had cost him many times that in curtailed production of automobiles.

Far more painful and infuriating was the criticism of Edsel's failure to put on a uniform. Edsel himself, though married and a father, was willing to enlist, but both government and company officials assured him that he could do a far greater service for his country in war production. Soldiers, sailors, marines, and their wives and families did not share this view.

Edsel's marriage, in 1916, was another blow to his father. His father had not had much time for his only child when he was building automobiles day and night. Though Edsel would have benefited greatly by a college education, he followed his father's wishes and went directly into the company after high school. On his twenty-first birthday Ford took his son to the bank and showed him his present, one million dollars in gold. The Fords had built Fairlane, their mansion on the Rouge, and had included within it elaborate quarters for their son, plus a large game room and indoor heated pool for his use.

Edsel's departure from his parents' roof was particularly distressing to his father. Eleanor Lowthian Clay was a lovely and gracious girl and a member of an old, established Detroit family representing both wealth and society. Her uncle was J. L. Hudson, founder of the Detroit department store. But her social status was a liability as far as her father-in-law was concerned for Henry Ford had no use for the country club set. Edsel and his bride chose to live on the social east side of Detroit near their friends rather than in unfashionable Dearborn. Though he and his wife were never social butterflies, they were interested in culture, the arts, philanthropy, and civic works, for all of which his father showed a lack of enthusiasm. And to make father–son matters still worse, Edsel was more interested in the financial and design facets of the company than in manufacture and assembly. Henry's coarse treatment of his only son began shortly after the marriage, sporadically at first, but with increasing intensity. Edsel responded to the abuse with paternal loyalty all his life.

Jack Davis consistently described Edsel as having an inherent sweetness. Even the harsh Charlie Sorensen, in his memoirs, referred to Edsel Ford as "a gentleman in the finest, fullest meaning of the word. He was gentle, considerate of others, unsparing of himself—and he was a *man.*"

Another blow to Henry Ford's pride resulted from his unsuccessful political campaign. He was a strong supporter of Woodrow Wilson. The Democratic party, in danger of losing its Senatorial majority, saw that Henry Ford would be its only hope in Republican Michigan. Ford agreed to serve if elected, but not to campaign for office. Though he liked to prattle on in conversation, he was tongue-tied before an audience and flatly refused to make a speech. He was a ghostly candidate, but nevertheless a popular one. His name was seen on half the vehicles on the road and he was popular with farmers, labor, and prohibitionists. He won the Democratic nomination against little opposition. The Republicans put up a formidable candidate in Truman H. Newberry, member of a prominent Detroit family and former Secretary of the Navy. He had none of Ford's reticence and staged a hard-fought, dirty campaign in which Edsel's deferment was a major issue. Ford still didn't open his mouth, but even then the Newberry forces had to buy the election. Ford's backers produced evidence of corruption, excessive expenditures, and voting irregularities, and Newberry resigned from the Senate. But Newberry's resignation was no victory for Ford; it was the Republican Jim Couzens who was appointed to take his seat, not the Democrat Ford.

119

A grass roots Ford-for-President movement developed in the early Twenties but one political experience was apparently enough. After a conference with President Calvin Coolidge in the White House, he announced his support for the incumbent in the 1924 elections and the grass roots movement died.

In the postwar depression, Ford sales dropped as did those of all other automobile companies, and the note on the money he borrowed to pay off his stockholders came due. An emissary from a New York bank arrived in Detroit with a plan for refinancing. Ford listened politely until the banker announced that his group would want to put their man in as treasurer as part of the deal. Ford considered the proposition insulting and had Charlie Sorensen hand the visitor his briefcase and escort him to the door. He had always been distrustful of financiers, now he was contemptuous. Why a treasurer? If they'd had any sense they'd have suggested an engineer.

Ford took care of the loan in his own way. He unloaded it on the dealers. At that time you couldn't give away cars. The factory was closed, but it had a large inventory of parts on hand, and so Ford called in his workers, assembled thousands of cars, and shipped them and the leftover parts out to the dealers. It was then standard industry practice for dealers to pay cash for both parts and cars on arrival. They either had to accept the shipments or lose their franchises. Many of them had to take out loans from their own banks to buy cars they couldn't sell. The Fordophobic niece of a dealer told me with angry tears that the overload of stock broke her uncle and caused his suicide. Most dealers, however, seemed to survive.

During this industrial climacteric which apparently began during the war years, several of Ford's oldest friends and finest executives, men who had organized and operated the business for him, left the company. Marquis himself, and the considerate John Lee, his predecessor in the sociological department, were invited out. Couzens had already quit after a direct disagreement with Ford. C. H. Wills, who had contributed so much mechanically that Ford had shared with him 10 per cent of all his earnings as well as the pleasures of hunting, fishing, and picnicking and long conversations on the betterment of mankind, was bought off with a lump sum.

For the decapitation of the others, however, Sorensen was the hatchet man, a job in which he became most proficient. Norval Hawkins took his sales expertise to General Motors. When William H. Knudsen, who had supervised the planning and construction of Ford assembly plants in America and Europe, was cut down by his fellow Dane, Hawkins opened the GM doors to him. It was Knudsen who first as head of Chevrolet and then of GM led both to dominance over Ford. His son Bunkie came along later with Pontiac to cause more anguish in Dearborn. But the rivalry was impersonal, for Bunkie told me that his father always had the highest regard for Mr. Ford. Like so many other victims of those days, he blamed the executioner Sorensen, rather than prosecutor, jury and judge, Henry the One.

Couzens, of course, was too big a man for even Sorensen's pranks and the story is that he quit through choice. The question is, did he have any choice about the choice? The Couzens-Ford bout started over an antiwar editorial in a Ford publication when World War I was just underway. Couzens, Canadian-born and an avowed Anglophile, changed the editorial and Ford changed it back. Couzens threatened to quit. The next thing he knew he was walking to the door. He wasn't needed anymore. Ford had learned how to run the company.

So, about 45 years later, had Henry Ford II. Greater Detroit is actually a small and gossipy community, as far as the automotive industry is concerned. One rumor, in active circulation since 1960, is that Jim Couzens and Ernie Breech both got the same Fordian treatment, with, in Breech's case, a few corporate refinements.

The theories advanced by the dark-suited executives around the tables of the mezzanine dining room in the glass house at Dearborn are based on several known factors: the consummate corporate expertise of Breech, and his vociferous compulsion to display it; the mental capacity of Henry Ford II, attested to by Breech himself, to learn and retain this expertise; Breech's primary interest in organization and financial control; Ford's overwhelming passion for the automobile, or, in Detroitese, the gas in his veins.

A common proposition derived from these premises, bandied about the industry from the assembly line to Grosse Pointe cocktail parties, is that Ford soaked up all that Breech could teach and arranged to take over sole occupancy of Mount Olympus. There are indications that the saturation point was reached during the planning for the 1962 line of Fords. The car guy wanted a smashing new line; the corporation man, with characteristic fiscal caution, did not. This, according to some executives, triggered the resignation of Breech as chairman of the board on July 13, 1960, and the immediate election to that position of Henry Ford II, who also retained the presidency. Two years and three months later the Fairlane, a new size a step up from the Falcon, went on sale.

The resignation of Breech was of course the big news of the month in industrial circles, but none of the reporters on the automotive beat could give the authoritative answer as to whether Breech jumped or was pushed. In my telephone conversations with Breech, he emphasized the splendid relationship Ford and he had shared.

"In 14 and a half years I had nothing but support from Henry Ford," he said. He told me of a social occasion in which Ford had sought out Mrs. Breech and talked with her for some time of his appreciation of her husband's great contributions to the company. People who know him say that Breech ate this kind of stuff up.

Only once during my phone talks with Breech did he depart from his panegyric, and that was when he growled, "Lately he's beginning to act more and more like his grandfather." He refused to elaborate, but what I think he had in mind was Ford's support of President Lyndon B. Johnson and the Great Society. In another conversation with me Breech expressed his opinion that a man of the prominence of Henry Ford should not make political statements. His reasoning was that the name Henry Ford has a captive audience and its bearer should not take advantage of it. This viewpoint is hardly shared by either Henry Ford.

I inquired about the circumstances of his resignation by letter, referring specifically to the version involving the 1962 Ford. He replied: "I had hoped when I went to the Ford Motor Company that conditions would be such that I could retire when I was 60 years of age. I so told Henry Ford II. I reviewed the situation with him at that time, and stayed on a year-to-year basis until I was sixty-three. So my retirement was a gradual and natural development. There was no misunderstanding whatever about any '62 model."

In J. M. Hickerson's authorized book on Breech with the indicative title *Ernie Breech: The Story of His Remarkable Career at General Motors, Ford and TWA*, no reason is given for the resignation. Surely, aged 63 and a multimillionaire, he had no reason to continue working. Yet shortly after terminating his full-time position with the Ford Motor Company, he went into another arduous situation with Trans World Airlines where he performed his usual superb job in the face of extreme difficulties, one of which was named Howard Hughes. His was hardly the usual type of retirement.

I asked Mister Ford himself about it. We were sitting in his plane at the time, and he was looking out over the green mountains of Pennsylvania. He turned his head and looked at me with those baby blue eyes. "I really don't know what

123

motivated him to leave," he said. "I certainly didn't want him to, and I asked him to stay, but he seemed to have already made up his mind. He consented to stay on as chairman of the finance committee and he still has an office in the plant."

So I took my questions to the man who was privy to the inner workings of the Ford Motor Company under both Fords named Henry. This was Jack Davis, who had gone to work at Ford's in 1919 after leaving the Navy, and had served as general sales manager during two separate periods under each Ford. He had become internationally respected in his field. You don't reach his eminence in sales without having a sense of psychology, highly developed powers of observation, creative ideas, and the ability to express them. Bouncy and vigorous, Davis appeared to be in his early sixties when I talked with him in 1968, rather than 74 with a medical history of ulcers and three coronaries. He loved to relive the exciting years of his life with Ford. Loyal to and respectful of the grandfather, almost worshipful of Edsel, and fond of the grandson, he nevertheless saw both Henry Fords for what they were, fascinating individuals with marks on their halos. And as a multimillionaire and former amateur boxer who never lost his scrappiness, Davis wasn't afraid to say what he thought about anybody.

He had been almost as interested in Ernie Breech as he had in the Fords. He and Breech had often talked about young Henry during the renaissance of the company. "I'd do anything to help that young man," Davis said Breech told him many times. They both looked upon Henry as a son.

Davis and I were sitting in the kitchen of his farmhouse in Virginia. He'd bought it for $75,000 several years before, and had been offered $355,000 for it, but he didn't consider the offer. Money is only money, but the house was something to cling to after the death of his wife. He was spending a week or so there every spring and fall. The local lady who came in to clean up during his brief visits had left a huge deep-dish apple pie, and Davis and I bustled about the kitchen boiling water and making instant coffee. His eyes twinkled as he recalled the Ford–Breech interplay of which he had been a bemused spectator. As Breech had brought the company out of its decrepitude and into rightful prominence Davis watched him become more expansive, more delighted with the importance and publicity of his office. Davis had waited patiently for the second act of the drama to unfold.

"I'd been through this before with The Old Man," he explained. "I've seen Mr. Ford let somebody get puffed up with his own importance, then cut him down to size. I wanted to see if Henry Ford was still Henry Ford. At first it was 'Henry and I think this,' 'Ernie and I think that.' Then it became more and more Henry and I, less and less Ernie and I."

Davis held up two fingers close together. "At first they were Siamese twins, just like this." Then he slowly separated his fingers, like a V. "Then they weren't twins anymore. Henry began bringing up things suddenly at board meetings, things that weren't on the agenda. Ernie presided at the meetings as chairman of the board, and he'd have his agenda all neatly typed up in front of him. All of a sudden Henry would throw in a subject that wasn't on the agenda. Ernie wasn't used to that type of thing. It took him off guard. He was presiding, sure, but he couldn't tell Henry Ford II to shut up. Then one time in the late Fifties at a managers' council at the Greenbrier—you know, in West Virginia—we were discussing the continuance of certain committees. It was an administrative procedure. We were discussing the question around the table, with Ernie presiding, of course, and all of a sudden Henry broke in. 'Well, this is what I'm gonna do,' he said, and went on to tell us just exactly what it was *he* was going to do. It shook everybody up at the meeting.

"During this time I was watching a young fellow we had, Jack Reith, pretty closely. He was brilliant and energetic, but I suspected that he was going too far too fast. He was beginning to get carried away with his own importance. Reith should be of great value to the company, but he was permitting himself to destroy his own effectiveness. It might be possible to straighten him out, but it would take a superb handler of personnel like Ernie Breech to do it. Henry couldn't do it, he's too damn impatient with people. But Ernie's a warmhearted guy. I talked to Ernie about it, in confidence, I thought. The next thing I knew Henry called me in. 'Why did you go see Breech about Reith?' he said. 'Come to me when you've got a problem.' I could hardly tell him that he wasn't the right man for the job. So nobody talked to Reith, and he never did settle down. He got too big for the company. It was a tragic thing, and I still think I was right. Breech's masterful touch might have saved that boy.

"Well, Ernie resigned. Henry paid tribute to him publicly and they remained good friends. Henry wrote a glowing introduction for his book. I wouldn't be a bit surprised if he didn't mean every word of it. That's the hallmark of Henry Ford, whether he's Henry Ford I or Henry Ford II. Breech once said publicly, 'Henry doesn't need me anymore.' Now what does that mean? Anybody in corporate management knows what that means. It means, 'He doesn't consult me anymore.' It means, 'He's bypassing me for major decisions.' It means, 'He's in and I'm out.' That's what it means."

Two other men who were around during that period agreed with Davis. Theodore O. Yntema, an economist who had joined the company as vice president of finance in 1949 after an academic career and had retired in 1965, told me that he and other executives could see the shift in power taking place.

"Henry never puts on airs," Yntema says. "He doesn't have to and he doesn't understand why anybody else does."

Earl Newsom, whose public relations firm handled Ford for several years and later helped Breech with his encore at TWA, was too tactful, as well as too genuinely fond of both

126

parties, to volunteer information. But when I asked him point-blank if Davis's summation was correct, he said, a little sadly, "I think this is so."

In 1915, Henry Ford could afford to lose Jim Couzens only because of the mechanical superiority of the product. Henry Ford II could afford to lose Ernie Breech because he himself had become a superb master of both finance and administration as well as a car guy. "The system we use is supposed to run itself," he told me, referring to the Ford organization plan he installed eight years after Breech's departure. "That's why we went to all the trouble to set it up."

Both Couzens and Breech became men of enormous wealth through their contributions to the respective Henry Fords. Couzens was thrown an extra bone in the form of an extra $500 per share for his stock, but that was it. Breech, whether he was pushed or whether he jumped, received the ultimate gesture of graciousness from Henry II. A Ford ship was named after him. At the ceremony he was close to tears. Money is only money, but the *Ernest R. Breech* is a floating monument.

6

PERHAPS IN 1921 it appeared to Henry Ford that not even the Ford Motor Company was big enough to hold the two Danish geniuses of production, Knudsen and Sorensen, but letting Knudsen go has to remain one of the old man's classic mistakes. In early February, 1968, the industrial world was hit with the biggest business news of the year: Henry Ford's grandson had brought in Bill Knudsen's son as president of Ford Motor Company. You can usually tell the importance of an industrial event by the jokes which immediately spring up about it. I must have heard two dozen the first week: "Did you hear about the new car Ford is bringing out? It's called the Vendetta." Or, "Want to buy a slightly used Cadillac cheap?"

Semon E. Knudsen was executive vice president of General Motors, its fourth-ranking officer, when Henry Ford II brought him to Dearborn. Several automotive workers called it the biggest job change in the auto industry since Knudsen's father left Ford. Bunkie Knudsen had been with General Motors for 30 years, and had served as head of both Pontiac and Chevrolet. Through inheritance and his own efforts he was a multimillionaire. His General Motors stock alone was worth more than $3 million. The vendetta joke stemmed from his supposed pique at losing the presidency of General Motors to Edward M. Cole, when James M. Roche stepped up to chairman of the board. The betting had been about even between the two. Cole had had seniority, but Knudsen was believed to have had the blessing of the retiring chairman of the board. Anyway, exactly three months after Cole became president of GM, Knudsen became president of Ford.

The announcement was made by Henry Ford II at a huge press conference with Knudsen present. For the next week or two he was interviewed constantly while he was working all hours to learn what was going on at the Ford factory. Ted Mecke, who usually comes in about eight, found Knudsen's light burning on his squawk box every morning when he came in. Knudsen was there and wanted to talk with him. Curious, Mecke came in one morning at 7:45. The light was on. The next morning he came in at 7:30; the light was on. He gave it the final all-out effort and arrived at 7 on the button. The light was on, and Knudsen was in. Mecke decided he'd carried his experiment far enough.

When I figured Knudsen had settled down a bit, I went in and had a quiet talk with him. I wanted to know just how Mister Ford had gone about hiring a millionaire with a salary and bonus of about $500,000 away from his biggest competitor.

Knudsen is a man of striking appearance; he looks like a president. He has a strong, tanned face, with high cheekbones and a theatrical shock of wiry hair, white on top and black around the ears. He was wearing a black silk suit, a shirt of very fine blue stripes on white with white collar and a light blue figured tie, Windsor knot. His cuff links were almost as big as Gene Bordinat's. He seemed right at home behind his big desk in the corner office overlooking the fields of Dearborn. (Putting him in that office had required moving two vice presidents and the vice chairman of the board.)

Knudsen talked of his father with respect and affection; his own nickname Bunkie, a World War I sobriquet short for bunkmate, was given him by his father, symbolic of their close relationship. When Bunkie was 14 his father told him to stop by the plant and pick up his new Chevrolet. The boy hurried down —and found the car unassembled in a thousand pieces. He put it together and wound up with both a new car and an even more valuable educational experience.

The new Ford president was proud of his father's association with the elder Henry Ford. "Mr. Ford always called Dad William," he recalled. "I remember that he called Dad on his sixtieth birthday. I don't believe my father left Ford with any bitterness. It was a basic disagreement. He objected to several features of the Model T: the three-pedal transmission, false door, the general aspect of the car and the general unprogressive attitude of the company."

I said that I had read that Bunkie was a car guy, and he said, "Sure, I like automobiles. I like this business. I guess I was born with a competitive nature; I'm aggressive. I admire courage and that's what it takes to be successful in the automobile industry."

Did he leave GM because his nose was out of joint? "I'm not bitter—I can't afford to be. You can't do anything if you're motivated by bitterness. I haven't told the whole story because, frankly, anybody who didn't know me and didn't have confidence in my honesty would think I was making the whole thing up. It goes back to when I made some suggestions concerning GM's Euclid operation. I wanted to make some changes and they turned me down. Why were they paying me good money if they wouldn't accept my recommendations? I talked with my wife about it. Should I be a good corporation man? Take orders whether I agreed with them or not? Take their money and keep my mouth shut? I told her, 'I don't care how much they pay me, I'm going to be unhappy if I can't contribute.' She said, 'Then why don't you quit?' And I said, 'I think I will.'

"I called Roche the next day, Thursday, and told him I'd decided to resign. He asked me to wait at least until I saw him—we had an appointment the following Tuesday—and though my mind was made up I promised not to do anything until after I saw him. Friday night the phone rang at home and I answered it and somebody said, 'This is Henry Ford.' I have a friend—Ted Mecke knows him too—who has a habit of calling up people and pretending he's the first name that pops into his mind, and I almost cracked back at him. But I didn't, thank God, because it *was* Mister Ford. He said that someone had told him a story and he wanted to know if it was correct. I said it depended on what the story was. He said he'd better not tell me over the phone and asked if we could get together. I said, 'Do you want me to come to your office?' He said, well, he guessed that wouldn't be such a good idea. 'Your house?' He said no to that, too, because Mrs. Ford had some house guests and they were talking Italian all over the place. 'Well, then, how about my house?' He said that would be fine and would I be home tomorrow morning. I said yes and he said how about ten o'clock and I said I'd look forward to seeing him.

"Well, next morning, about five minutes to ten I happened to look out the front and here comes an Olds up the drive. Oh, oh, I thought, I'm really in a pickle. Here comes somebody from GM. But it stopped and out stepped Mister Ford. All alone in an Olds.

"Now I guess I'd better fill in some background here. About three or four years ago he had asked if I would come

132

with Ford, and I'd said I was happy with GM. So when he came in now, he sat down and told me that he'd been at a cocktail party and a doctor had told him that it was unfortunate he hadn't asked me to come with him now instead of three or four years ago. He wanted to know if there was anything behind that story. At that time nobody knew my plans except me, my wife, and Roche. Mister Ford did not know. Anyway, I told him I had an appointment with Roche on Tuesday and I couldn't act until then. When I saw Roche on Tuesday he thought I was crazy. He kept asking me, 'What are you going to do?' I agreed to stay on through January, but I called Mister Ford. He came out again Friday night and we had a long discussion about what my duties would be. I left the salary and money arrangements completely up to him. When he told me what he had worked out I was satisfied."

I'd have been satisfied too. Placed in Salary Grade 28, sharing that eminence only with the chairman of the board, he received a stipulated salary of not less than $200,000. In his first year on the job—actually eleven months—he also received the same bonus as Ford, $400,000. In addition, 15,000 shares of Ford stock with a value of $750,000 were transferred to the new president under an arrangement approved by the U.S. Treasury which enabled him to defer the taxes on the stock for at least nine years and to spread the payments over a period of five years. Regardless of the value of the stock at payoff time, taxes are based on their worth in 1968.

As for his GM stock, he set up a system similar to that used to avoid conflict of interest by industrialists going into public service. Some of his stock was placed in a charitable fund, some was sold through a broker in an orderly procedure and the rest was placed in trust beyond his control.

I discussed my conversation with Knudsen with my interpreter of the Detroit scene, Jack Davis, and he filled in a few bits and pieces. According to the gossip in Bloomfield Hills, the

133

relationship between Cole and Knudsen had been closer to out-right enmity than mere rivalry. Davis hastened to explain that this is no reflection on either of the two men.

The automobile industry, like any other, is composed of determined and ambitious people. In his conversation with me, Knudsen used the word aggressive three times. In order to get to the top in industry it is necessary to climb over those who don't. But you don't have to stab a man in the back before you climb over him. It is possible to play by the rules and still have your company-owned Continental, Cadillac, or Imperial.

It is not true in industry that nice guys finish last. I spent a lot of time with a good many of the top executives at Ford's, and I haven't met one yet I disliked. I think they are basically honest and decent human beings. On the other hand, soft guys never finish first. Not one top executive would be where he is if he had not blown the whistle on somebody, maybe somebody's father, who wasn't getting his job done. It's a constant process of weeding out, and the people who go the highest do the most weeding. So it's possible that the higher you go the larger the number of people who have reason to hate your guts.

When I mentioned to Davis that Ford had driven up Knudsen's driveway in an Oldsmobile, Davis's eyes lit up. One of his boys had just scored the winning touchdown in the Super Bowl. "Oh, that's Henry," he chortled. "Oh, boy, that's just like Henry, driving up in an Olds! That's maneuvering!"

He could tell by the expression on my face that I didn't get the significance. "You see," he explained, "if Henry had used a chauffeur-driven Continental, or even if he'd driven himself in a Ford product, he might as well have sent a brass band on ahead. Anybody watching would have known by the license number that it was a Ford company car."

"But where would he get the Olds from?" I asked.

"Oh, we've got plenty of Olds. We buy all makes of cars to look at them. No trouble getting an Olds."

"Then it would have the company license on it."

"Yes, but say you're watching Bunkie's house. If a Ford drives up you take the license number. With an Olds you don't bother. GM cars are coming in all the time. Henry figured all this out. I can see him doing it." Davis chortled again. "That's my boy!"

After all this intrigue, I wondered audibly about Knudsen's casual remark that he had left all the details about compensation up to Ford. Davis dismissed that with the expression that I was getting used to. "To these people money doesn't mean anything. It's not how much you pay or receive, it's how you play the game."

It was during this conversation with Davis that I asked what had caused the change in Henry Ford I from the dedicated humanitarian of 1915 to the scheming splenetic of the Twenties on. He suggested as one of the factors the reaction to his anti-Semitic campaign—and pointed out that Ford's anti-Semitism had its business aspects. "It was his major concern there for a long period. It was all published in his paper, the *Dearborn Independent*, you know. Some have claimed that the company coerced the dealers into buying the *Independent*, that they had to take their quota of papers just like they had to take their quota of automobiles. We had many Jewish dealers and they used to throw the things in the trash without even untying the bundles. They weren't the only ones. There were a lot of other dealers who were disgusted with the whole thing. That campaign haunted us in sales long after it was all over. When I was exiled to Southern California years later, I found that Ford products weren't permitted on the lots of some Hollywood studios because of the old man's anti-Semitism. Overcoming that situation was one of my greatest challenges when I was out there.

"Anyway, the whole thing blew up in his face and he had to admit he was wrong. I'll give him credit for that—when he apologized, he apologized all the way. But it took a lot out of him. He couldn't understand why the Jews didn't appreciate what he was trying to do for them. Oh, he was so inconsistent!

"He really gave those of us in the sales department a hard time. He carried on a crusade against cigarettes, and alienated everybody in the tobacco business. We had a hell of a time selling Fords in the whole tobacco belt from Virginia through the Carolinas. He expressed his Prohibitionist views with such vehemence that he alienated another group of potential customers—breweries wouldn't buy our trucks. During the Thirties when the old man was fighting labor, many union members, and there were millions, would not touch a Ford product. Years later, when Henry was beginning to come on strong as president, I reminded him of how his grandfather had turned large blocs of people away from us. I said that if there was any advice I could give him as sales manager, it was not to get involved with any issue that divided the American people, because if he did he'd lose a large segment of the population."

Davis paused and pointed his finger at me. "The next thing I knew Henry was coming out publicly in support of Lyndon Johnson. Just like the old man, Henry doesn't give a damn! He's so independent, so sold on his own interpretation of what's right and what's wrong, so confident in his own judgment that he just goes ahead and says and does what he thinks is right. You know what? I admire him for it."

As Henry the One caromed from one project to the other, somebody had to run the store. So when organization man Couzens went out, production man Sorensen came in. Sorensen, who was proud of his designation in the industry as "Mr. Ford's man," magnified two images of his leader: perfection in manufacturing and imperfection in his relations with his employees.

Davis knew Sorensen well. For a period of several years they were both regulars at the round table in the engineering building where Ford ate lunch with the top six or eight men in the company. Davis would synchronize his watch each morning with official company time, so that he could arrive, with the others, a few minutes before 1:00 P.M.

At one o'clock, never more than two minutes after, W. J. Cameron, editor and interpreter, would enter, followed by Ford. Ford would go around the table shaking hands, then take his accustomed seat. Sorensen sat on his left, Edsel on his right, and Davis on Edsel's right. Sometimes Ford would start the conversation on anything that struck his fancy. ("It might occasionally be about sales, but never about profits," Davis said.) If Ford said nothing for two minutes, then Sorensen, the number two man, would open the conversation.

Sorensen was an extremely handsome man, tall and blond, self-confident almost to the point of arrogance. If Ford was the example of the Puritan Ethic, then Sorensen was the epitome. He drove himself beyond his own limits—he blacked out several times during the World War II production years—and he expected everyone in the plant to follow his example. In one narrow sense he had a counterpart in later years in Robert McNamara. "McNamara was never a good judge of personnel," one of the current Ford executives told me, "because he expected everyone else to be as brilliant as he is."

Sorensen strode through the plant, cracking his whip. Supervisory personnel, including superintendents, were not permitted to have offices and desks, or to waste time keeping unessential records. Their job was to drive the men under them like drill sergeants. Ambitious men in the plant, seeing Sorensen's progress, patterned themselves after him.

When his little operation had first begun to get big enough to need department heads, even technical experts, Ford had turned to his own bunch of cronies. When he had first become interested in vanadium steel, for example, he was told he should bring in a metallurgist. Instead Ford pointed to a man whom he had hired as a sweeper, and said, "There's a good man, make him a metallurgist." As the metallurgical department grew in

137

size and importance, its head, the former sweeper, grew with it. Other departments followed the same pattern of filling jobs from the ranks: Sorensen himself had started as a $3-a-day pattern maker.

Under Sorensen's leadership, plant leaders clawed, scratched, and hammered their way to the top. Nearly every foreman could whip every man under him, and did so if the occasion arose. Ted Ogar remembers the dread in his house on Saturday night when his father's foreman made his rounds of the block. One family would give him a Polish sausage, another a quart of homemade wine, another cash. The apprehension was greater if the foreman began his route on the other side of the street; by the time he got to the Ogars', he'd be drunk and nasty. One Saturday night he made advances to Ogar's mother, and that was where his father drew the line. He knocked the foreman down the stairs, and himself out of a job.

Neither Ford nor Sorensen was interested in paperwork. Production was measured strictly by the hardware coming off the line. Ford had no interest in financial controls. "One morning I was in the treasurer's office," Davis recalls, "and Mr. Ford came in and asked him, 'How much money have we got?' At that time we kept cash deposits in several banks and the treasurer made a quick addition and said, '$375 million.' Ford nodded and said, 'Get Charlie on the phone.'

"When Sorensen came on, Ford said, 'Charlie? Go ahead with that blast furnace,' and hung up. That was an expenditure in millions based entirely on the fact that we had the money on hand. Cost, technical details, amortization, even whether we could buy it cheaper than we could make it, all that was meaningless. He had the money and that was the extent of his reasoning. He went on the pay-as-you-go system. If he had the money to do something, he did it. If he didn't, he didn't."

Ford considered the bookkeeping and accounting processes through which money coming in was transformed into cash on hand unnecessary folderol. From the days when he and Sorensen messed up Hawkins's routing slips, he had no use for paperwork.

His son, Edsel, who inherited his father's searching mind and the determination to do things better, expanded his father's machinery-restricted vista to modern methods of management. His appreciation of financial controls was one of the causes of friction between them. Ford admired production men who knocked workers down, speeded things up, and turned out more hardware. Edsel, through association with Detroit's financial leaders, understood the beneficial aspects of knowing where the money was going. In the bridge between the Puritan Ethic of his father and his father's generation and the Social Ethic of his son's, Edsel leaned more to the future than the past. As a gentleman, he was more a leader than a whip cracker. He could see the pragmatic advantages of harmony and cooperation, rather than disruption and fear. His father had contempt for these soft ideas.

One episode sums up the growing schism between father and son. The sales force was occupying crowded quarters in the administration building. The accounting department, located on the fourth floor, was also cramped for space. During a period when Ford was off on one of his junkets, Davis convinced Edsel of the necessity for new quarters for the sales force, as well as for the accounting department. Plans for a new building were drawn, bids received and the contract let, and work began. Ford returned and, with Sorensen, visited Edsel's office. He looked out the window and saw the excavation.

"What's going on there?" he asked.

Edsel proudly described the new building, pointing out that it would provide space sorely needed for the expanding company. "Space for who?" his father demanded.

Davis, who was present, recalls that Edsel made a major error at that point. "The building was designed primarily for the sales force, and sales the old man could understand," Davis said. "We had to sell the product. Other departments were going to use the building too. But Edsel, for some reason, began with the accountants. The old man didn't wait to hear any more. He said, 'Come on, Charlie,' and they left."

When Davis came in the next morning he found members of the accounting department milling around the building in perplexity. The fourth floor was barren. During the night a crew of maintenance men had come in and had stripped the floor completely. Desks, chairs, file cabinets, even rugs and telephones had been removed. No one was on hand to say what had happened, where the accountants should go or what they should do. Eventually some of the men learned from the administrative office that the entire department had been wiped out. Men and women, many of whom had been with the company for years, found that overnight their duties had been abolished and their employment terminated.

Later that morning, Henry Ford came into Davis's office, and Davis went with him to see Edsel. Ford looked at his son and said, with a grin, "Edsel, if you really need more room you'll find plenty of it on the fourth floor."

Plans for the building were abandoned and the hole filled in. Edsel accepted the episode quietly. He arranged for the accountants to be rehired and scattered throughout other company buildings in an inefficient and expensive subterfuge. His father had proved his point, and had his Schadenfreude.

Early in the Twenties, Edsel quietly began recommending to his father that a more modern car should supplant the dated ugliness of the Model T. Many of the women of America—unlike his mother, who followed the presuffragette concept that woman's place in the household was to cook and keep quiet—were beginning to have some say in the purchase of the family car, and the Model T, even with its cut-glass vases, was hardly appealing to the feminine eye. Improvements in streets and highways obviated in many areas the Model T's durable but unimaginative simplicity. Knudsen at Chevrolet was bringing out a more aesthetically appealing car at a comparable price, and it was eating into the Ford market.

But though Edsel was now president of the company, the old man owned it, and he stubbornly refused to liquidate his baby. Charlie Sorensen, in his memoirs, said that it was the Model T that drove a wedge between father and son, and that Edsel's desire for a change was one of the reasons Ford resisted its discontinuance. The conflict became so bitter, Sorensen said, that Ford called him in one day and told him to send Edsel to California. "I'll send for him when I want to see him again." Sorensen, who professed a loyalty to Edsel unrecognized by other observers, said he deliberately procrastinated until the storm blew over.

In the case of Ernest Kanzler, however, Edsel's confederate in the flivver fight and his personal friend (they married sisters), the storm did not blow over, but whisked him right out of the company. Kanzler, brilliant, legally trained and with sound fiscal ideas, was successful in bringing some semblance of organization into the factory. But he went too far. He signed an official memorandum recommending the termination of the T and brought on himself the Henry Ford Treatment. Ford began a campaign of belittlement by snide comments and rude interruptions. Kanzler was not Ford's son, and he couldn't take it. He left.

Edsel stayed on under continued harassment and continued to make recommendations for improvements in the product. On one occasion, he was recommending to a large group of executives a hydraulic braking system to replace the less efficient mechanical brakes when the old man suddenly turned on him and rasped, "Edsel, you shut up!"

Why did he take it? Two reasons. One, he was a loyal son. He loved his father. Two, he was a Ford, with that awful burden on his shoulders. Suppose he had quit the company, as he was financially able to do. Imagine the headlines. He felt he couldn't damage the company.

Edsel Ford developed ulcers, but he never brought his problems home with him. His sons assured me that there was never any indication that he was under strain at the plant until the very end.

"When all these things come to light, there's not a question in my mind that they did go on," Billy Ford told me, "but it comes as kind of a revelation to me. I didn't know that there were any great problems, management problems or whatever, going on out here in the plant. My father, as far as I was concerned, disappeared in the morning and came back at night. He and my grandfather were running a company and that was it. Maybe I was too young to understand. At any rate, it continues to amaze me. It just didn't make a full impact."

Billy, the fun-loving, happy-go-lucky Ford, remembers his grandfather only as a wonderful, exciting adventure. They'd walk over the fields together and often they'd take a drive, Billy sitting on Granddaddy's lap and steering.

Benson, more serious and quiet than his younger brother, said that he could recall no feeling of resentment against their grandfather on the part of any of the four young Fords. "I don't think I knew there was any friction between my father and grandfather. They kept it to themselves and never talked about it at home. I don't think I realized it—I knew there was something, but I didn't realize what it was. My father would call up Granddaddy every night. He'd come home from work and call him. I've heard about the trouble since, but really not too much. Mother kept it to herself, too. I don't know about Henry. I don't think we've ever gone over it."

Henry II told me he had no recollection as a boy or a youth of his father's unhappiness. And he has never spoken to me of his grandfather without pride in his voice.

The fact that the Fords still have affection and respect for both their grandfather and their father is due to Edsel's inherent decency. He could easily have poisoned the minds of his children against their grandfather simply by speaking the truth, but he didn't. He kept their home life warm and loving. When I asked Benson what he called his father, Dad or Pop or whatever, he chuckled and said, "Well, we called him Daddy and Father, but mostly we called him Paul. I don't know why. I think it had something to do with the Paul and Jerry cartoons. I don't know who started it or how it started, but it stuck. We never called Granddaddy anything but Granddaddy."

Certainly, even during the worst of times, the Edsel Fords suffered no material losses. Edsel maintained lavish homes, in Michigan, Florida, and Seal Harbor, Maine. As far as the kids were concerned, there were too many houses. "Our friends were in Detroit," Billy said. "We all went away to school and college and when we came home we wanted to come home. That Maine bit was a drag."

The Michigan home was a 60-room mansion on Gaukler Pointe in Grosse Pointe Shores. The cottage at Seal Harbor cost 3 million dollars. In Florida, home was the *Onika*, a 125-foot houseboat anchored in Hobe Sound. Edsel also had an 88-foot auxiliary schooner.

Edsel had an entire line of automobiles to play with. Though Henry Ford had acquired Lincoln, his major love was the car which bore his name, and so Edsel was permitted to do pretty much as he pleased with the luxury product. The Zephyr, a highly styled streamlined car far in advance of its time, was Edsel's, not his father's. Jack Davis, who had the job of selling it, told me that the automobile looked beautiful but did not function well.

"The design was all right," Davis recalled, "but they had made some very serious mistakes in the tooling. It was just too rough. Edsel was helpless in getting the complete cooperation, the complete sympathy that he should have had from all the toolmakers and draftsmen and engineers on down the line. Because they knew that wasn't Mr. Ford's car. It was Edsel's project."

Another Edsel project was the classic Continental, the one that came out in 1939. It started out as just one car, hand built to Edsel's taste. People liked it, talked about it, and Edsel got permission from his father to put a few in production—provided it didn't disturb the assembly lines.

Talking about that first Continental, Davis said, "Edsel enjoyed it so much. He had one project he could work with and enjoy." Davis's voice lowered and his expression became tender when he talked of Edsel. Davis had had his ulcers, too, and depression and headaches brought on by life with the unpredictable overlord. His empathy with Edsel was still discernible after a quarter of a century.

Ownership of the original Continental became a kind of cult. Of the 5000 built between 1940 and 1948, excluding the war years, over half were still running when its third generation, the Mark III, came out in 1968. No other American car has ever had such a survival rate. The Continental fanatics do not believe the words of more objective experts. As Charlie Barnard put it in *True,* "Some people called these the most beautiful cars man has ever made. Others, more interested in how automobiles performed than how they looked, called the sainted Continental a dog on wheels." For, as in the case of the Zephyr, Edsel did not get the full cooperation of the production men.

I don't want to give the impression that Henry Ford's relationship with Edsel was constantly belligerent. Nothing about Henry Ford I was constantly anything. A designer who had an appointment with Edsel at the engineering laboratory was kept waiting for several hours. Finally Edsel and his father came in, their arms around each other's shoulders, talking earnestly.

Edsel apologized to his visitor and took him back to a small shop to show why he had forgotten the appointment. Father and son had been building a baby carriage for Edsel's daughter, Josephine.

7

IT WAS WHILE the relationship between Henry Ford and his only son was worsening that the one-man industrial empire reached its zenith and then descended to its nadir. No single industrialist ever sat on so extensive a pyramid as did Henry Ford in the Twenties. During the period of American participation in World War I, production of the Model T was curtailed to a degree, but never halted. In 1919 monthly production climbed to a high of 86,000 and in two years exceeded 100,000. In November, 1922, the assembly lines turned out 240,000 cars. The River Rouge complex was growing. As you drive along M-39 through Dearborn today, you have to look twice as you cross the Rouge to see it; where I come from we call a stream that size a creek. Just a mile downstream is evidence of what man and money can do to nature. There the creek is a harbor, with Ford's oreboats, big as ocean liners, docked along the wharves.

I've driven all over the Rouge, walked over it, taken my family through it, and I still get lost in it. I've been in parts of the country where the piles of coal along the docks would be called mountains. Today, guided tours go through the entire complex. You can stand and watch while an immense block of orange-hot steel is bumped and banged and squeezed by gigantic presses until it becomes several long narrow strips. You can see iron ore, brought in by the great Ford oreboats from the Ford mines in Michigan and Minnesota, transformed to steel in the basic oxygen furnaces with heat supplied by coal from the Ford mines in Kentucky and continue on through the stamping mills and foundries to the finished Mustang coming off the assembly line. Eight miles of glass float out of the mill every day. The generators turn out enough electricity to serve cities the size of Kansas City or Dallas; the 85 miles of track and the 19 locomotives comprise the largest private railroad in the world. Should the food in the company restaurants disagree with anyone there are 120 doctors and nurses available.

Though it has been modernized in every way, it is still basically the same complex it was when the old man built it in the Twenties. The Rouge plant is but a compact fraction of Ford holdings over the world, but it symbolizes the empire. To ensure a constant flow of the raw materials necessary for this insatiable monster, and because he didn't want to depend on anybody else for anything, Ford began buying up the world. He bought a third of a million acres in the Iron Mountain section of Michigan for timber and ore. He bought three large coal mines and then three groups of mines, all of them in Kentucky and West Virginia.

Henry Ford I's behavior as a coal mine owner is another example of the paradoxical nature of the man. He went along with Sorensen's policy of terror and strain in the Dearborn plant. He himself had people fired in underhanded ways. But he became personally concerned over what he heard about working conditions in the mines and so insisted on going down into one himself. Even today mine safety is a political football; disasters occur regularly and as for physical and emotional comfort, well, would *you* go down in a coal mine? In the early Twenties misery and danger were much worse, yet Ford *did* go down in the mine. In his sixties, he inched himself along the damp, shallow passageways a mile underground the way the miners did, lying on his back and pushing himself backward with the heels of his feet and hands.

On his return to the surface, black, wet, and rubbed raw, he immediately set about making Ford mines better places for Ford miners. He consulted with miners and mine engineers. And he was concerned not only with the tunnels far underground but with the miserable hovels in the mountain coves to which the miners returned at the end of the long day.

A month later he made another trip down in the mines. "Let's see how much we have to slide on our tails *this* time," he said. Below ground he found larger passageways, shored up by sturdy timbers; on the surface, house repairs were well underway. The pay of Ford miners was double that of the workers in neighboring mines and both living and working conditions were greatly improved.

When he became infuriated by transportation delays in getting his coal to Dearborn, Ford paid $5 million for a bankrupt and worn-out railroad which ran from the Ohio River to Detroit. Sophisticated railroaders laughed at the acquisition and predicted that Ford would find running a railroad a different proposition from turning out a tin lizzie. But with a former mechanic as his deputy, he proved that he could run a railroad, too. He put improvements into every phase of rail transportation from equipment to working conditions. In the days of soft-coal-burning locomotives, he had roundhouse walls painted *white* and washed daily. That took care of the dingy appearance associated with railroads. He increased his employees' wages—and reduced working time—to such an extent that he had to get special dispensation from the Railroad Brotherhoods.

He loved to ride on the pile of coal behind the engine. Edsel liked to run the train. (Edsel got carried away while at the controls of a specially built lightweight car and jumped the tracks, damn near killing all the passengers including his father.) Ford greatly improved the efficiency of the railroad but after a few years he got tired of fighting government regulations, and sold it for $36 million in cash. It had earned back its purchase price and improvement costs.

Dissatisfied with the quality of glass his purchasing agents were getting, Ford built a glass mill, adapted it to a system one of his men suggested, and became one of the world's largest glass producers.

One of Ford's most ambitious acquisitions grew out of a British plan after World War I to control the quantity and cost of natural rubber. Ford decided he'd grow his own rubber. He bought 2,500,000 acres of jungle in Brazil, called it Fordlandia, and started a rubber plantation. Disease killed off the trees and World War II hastened the development of synthetic rubber; after the war, Fordlandia was sold to the Brazilian government. The company did get some rubber and hardwood out of the plantation, but the project was a failure.

Just as raw materials came in from all over the world, so the finished products returned. Through Ford of Canada, the Model T penetrated into the outlying parts of the United Kingdom, with assembly plants in Australia, New Zealand, and South Africa. Through the English operation Ford set up plants first in Manchester, then Dagenham, and then started a tractor plant in Cork.

The Cork plant was typical of the way Ford combined ideals with business. Against the recommendation of his English advisers, who preferred Ulster, Ford placed the plant in southern Ireland because that area suffered from greater emigration. Ford wanted to keep people happy, and at home. Part of Ford's deal with the city of Cork was his promise to employ 2000 workers. But partly because of the postwar depression, the plant employed only 1600 men. The Cork city fathers, in an action reported throughout the world, threatened to cancel the lease if 400 additional people were not immediately put to work. Ford thereupon announced that he would close the plant down if the city didn't get off his back, and immediately stopped new construction and laid off 500 men—who sought unemployment relief from the city. He had no more trouble with Cork.

An assembly plant was built in Copenhagen to provide northern Europe with Model T's, and there were others in France, Spain, and Italy. In Latin America, assembly plants were built in Argentina, Brazil, and Mexico.

The Soviet Union imported 25,000 tractors during this period, and used the Fordson as a model to build an inferior duplicate called the Putilowitz. The tractor itself and the factory's mass production methods—Fordizatsia—brought benefits to the farmer and the industrial worker and made Ford one of the best-known names in Russia. Later, several teams of Ford production experts visited the Soviet Union to help set up two automobile plants; the capitalist teachers and Communist students enjoyed excellent relations.

Henry Ford was as busy with his outside projects as he was making automobiles. One of his most ambitious ideas was to take over the now defunct wartime project to utilize the power of the Tennessee River, on which the government had spent $100 million, and build what would be in effect a forerunner of the Tennessee Valley Authority. His proposal bogged down in politics. He devoted a great deal of time to publishing his *Dearborn Independent*, which carried a variety of fact and opinion other than that telling Jews they ought to be Gentiles. He also devoted a lot of time to lawsuits, two of which grew out of his bigoted polemics.

Ford was interested in commercial radio. Station WWI, which went on the air in 1921, developed out of his experiments in wireless communication between factory, mines and ships. He got out of radio when the government, through the forerunner of the Federal Communications Commission, got into it.

Henry Ford's decade in the aviation industry started in the early Twenties with an experimental monoplane built by William B. Stout. Stout used metal instead of canvas. Ford became interested in this new approach and went into the aircraft business. On Dearborn land that had been marked for housing, he built what was then the finest commercial airport in the world. You could see the name Ford, spelled out in white gravel, from two miles up. He was involved in one of the earliest commercial airlines, flying between Detroit and Cleveland in a Ford plane.

After four years of experimentation, Ford in 1926 decided to go with an all-metal, tri-motor monoplane and announced that he would build this model exclusively: only a few multi-engine planes were then in existence. Ford's first flight was in the *Spirit of St. Louis* with Charles A. Lindbergh as pilot, shortly after Lindbergh flew the Atlantic alone. After that Ford flew often, but with only one pilot, Shearman LeRoy Manning, a friend of Lindbergh's. Soon Roy Manning was also a friend of Ford's. They were both interested in timepieces. They discussed and tinkered with watches by the hour, sometimes aloft.

Manning flew Ford all over the United States and in Europe. At Ford's insistence, he wore a derby instead of helmet and goggles. But Ford was not his only passenger. At the Dearborn field, where the Ford no-smoking rule was in effect,

Manning used to take other employees up long enough for them to catch a quick cigarette.

The Ford tri-motor was snapped up by commercial airlines. In 1929 Ford built and sold 86 planes, but then the Wall Street crash curtailed the aviation market. To keep production going Ford permitted the Air Corps to talk him into building an experimental plane for the military. Apparently, he was under the impression that it was to be the prototype for air ambulances, of which he approved, not for combat planes, of which he did not. Roy Manning knew better: it was a bomber, with five gun mounts. Manning took the plane up at Wright Field in an unofficial test and told a friend that it was faster than any bomber he had ever seen.

In the official test flight at Dearborn, Roy Manning put the big plane into a full power dive and pulled out of it without mishap. Then he flew a measured 3-mile course just 200 feet off the ground. At the conclusion of the run he put the plane into a steep climbing turn. A wing tore off. The plane crashed. Roy Manning never had a chance.

Henry Ford wept. He knew the truth about the plane now. His tears of grief may have been mixed with tears of rage. "We made a plane to kill people and see who we killed!" he said.

It was September, 1931. Ford built no more planes for the Air Corps until World War II. Company records show that only three planes were sold the following year and that production stopped in July. The official story is that the depression caused the company to get out of aviation. With Henry Ford, however, it is possible to believe anything, even that the death of one good friend was the final factor in his decision. After all, who saw him cry any other time?

A total of 130 tri-motors had been built. Regardless of his reason, the discontinuance of aircraft production was surely one of Ford's greatest errors. His foot had been as far in the aviation door as that of Douglas or Boeing. Even after the tremendous output of planes during wars and commercial boom, several of the sturdy old tri-motors kept flying.

In spite of all the activities in which Ford was involved in 1927, he was still able to direct the planning, design, and production of a completely new car in a period of less than a year. For when he was finally convinced that his beloved Model T was passé, he threw himself into the production of the far more sophisticated and luxurious Model A with all the enthusiasm and vitality he had poured into all its predecessors. Though approaching 64, he worked far into the early morning hours day after day. The company had no proving grounds, and Ford tested the car himself, overloading it and bumping it over rough terrain. Though the new engine weighed no more than that of the Model T, it wound up enough horsepower to pass everything on the road. The Model A required 5600 new parts. Hundreds of skilled tool and die makers were hired; one of them was a young high school student named Walter Reuther who became one of the highest paid artisans in the plant. "We were located in the old Highland Park plant," he told me, "and no one could ask for finer work conditions. The work space was meticulously arranged. I was a conscientious worker and I gave it all I had. It was a delicate and difficult job, working with a thousandth of an inch tolerance. At the same time, I used my employment there for my own self purpose. I completed high school and went on to college while working for Ford's."

While Ford was planning and engineering the new car, manufacture of the old Model T was terminated and thousands of production workers were laid off. Detroit suffered a crisis trying to feed them, but Ford didn't seem to care. (Edsel contributed heavily to welfare programs.) Potential customers put off buying cars until the new Ford was ready. The national economy was affected. But when production began, with more outside suppliers going full blast than had been needed for the Model T, the stock market jumped. When the Model A was first shown, police had to be called out in several cities to handle the crowds. In England special trains were added to take the curious into London to see it. In the first two weeks after it went on display 400,000 people put down cash deposits with their advance orders. With all its improvements the lowest-priced model sold for slightly more than its Model T counterpart, and for a hundred dollars less than its rival, the Chevrolet. In 1929, the Model A's biggest year, Ford's personal income was almost $14 million; Edsel received over $8 million.

Two years later, at the age of 68, Ford again exceeded himself. He knew the sturdy little four-cylinder engine was no longer powerful enough, and as one of his bugaboos was the six-cylinder engine, he had nowhere to go but to the eight. His flathead V-8 remained in production for 20 years. It brought back sports car racing, and eventually led to the stock car racing so popular today. The year after they were introduced, Ford V-8's took the first seven places in the Elgin Road Race.

With the production of the Model A, automotive operations in Highland Park were phased out, and the company moved into the Rouge. Sorensen and his chief assistant, P. E. Martin, were now in complete command. They eliminated practically all supervisory personnel from the Highland Park– Model T days in a purge of near-Stalinist proportions.

Walter Reuther recalls that one day he was sitting at his comfortably efficient bench at Highland Park and the next day he was standing up at the Rouge. "You can't work with these fine tolerances standing up," he said. "You need to be firmly planted. But that wasn't the big difference. Those two places were different as day and night. Highland Park was civilized, but the Rouge was a jungle. The humanitarianism that Henry Ford had shown so dramatically in his early days just didn't exist anymore. Sorensen and Pete Martin were in charge of production and that's all they cared about. I don't think they were sociologically aware that the harshness and speedups for which they were responsible, combined with the terror and brutality for which they weren't, actually interfered with production. The Rouge was a jungle because of one man, Harry Bennett. His gangsters ran that company. Harry Bennett was a mean man, a neurotic man, a man with a gangster mentality. It was absolutely fantastic that a man like that could reach the position he did with a great company like Ford. If you read it in a book or saw it in a movie, you just wouldn't believe it. But I was there, and I believe it because I've still got the scars."

People who knew Bennett and his relationship to Henry Ford and to the factory use words like fantastic and incredible when talking about him, and he was one man to whom these overworked words can be judiciously applied.

A former sailor, and a fighter under the name of Sailor Reese, Bennett was taken to see Henry Ford in 1916 by Arthur Brisbane, the columnist, after Brisbane admired his action in a street fight. Ford hired him and kept him on, apparently observing him, until, through an elaborate ruse, Bennett was assigned to the Rouge. He knocked down the first man he saw, and from then on he was in. His job was to serve as Henry Ford's eyes and ears in the Rouge, and no one can fault him in his accomplishment of this mission. He built up a spy network that penetrated not only every corner of the factory, but into the Detroit and New York underworld as well. He paid off the most notorious gangsters with both undercover payments and open, legal franchises. Chester La Mare, a Detroit gang leader who was later liquidated, was given the fruit and vegetable concession in the Rouge, and Joe Adonis, a Brooklyn overlord of crime, was granted a haul-away franchise at the New Jersey assembly plant. Through his underworld contacts Bennett convinced Ford that he could prevent the kidnapping of Ford's grandchildren. He even faked several incidents which increased his boss's fear of kidnapping, thus making Bennett's protective presence all the more necessary.

156

Another Ford phobia was that all Wall Street bankers, particularly the Jewish segment, were conspiring to get control of the company. Bennett kept this fear alive by launching rumors of plots and counterplots which would eventually reach Ford's ears.

Bennett was unquestionably a man of great physical courage, or put another way, a man completely without fear. Though only 5′7″ and 160 pounds, he kept himself in excellent physical shape and took on anybody. He swung on Jack Davis in Ford's presence. Davis recalled, chuckling, that Ford scuttled out of the room in a hurry. (One thing both Davis and Bennett agreed about was that Ford liked to start a fight but didn't want to see the blood.) Bennett actually decked the production head at Willow Run. These were important men in the company; how many others Bennett took on is inestimable. He related in his memoirs that he took off his coat and challenged Edsel, but that Edsel refused to fight. It's possible.

He walked fearlessly if foolishly into the middle of a mob during a hunger march and was knocked down by a brick just before police opened fire. One of the four men killed in the fracas, a leader of the Young Communist League, actually fell on him; if Bennett hadn't been knocked down he might have stopped the bullet. Bennett used the misadventure to good advantage, daubing himself with mercurochrome and then making a carnadine appearance in Ford's office.

Bennett's bravery, as well as his Machiavellian talent for intrigue, had a tremendous impact on Ford. Bennett's bravado stood out in marked contrast to the quiet moral courage of Edsel. Observers close to Ford have reported, and Davis has assured me personally, that Ford was convinced his only son was too soft, too gentle. Bennett virtually admitted that his prime target was Edsel. He said in his book, "He was a nervous man; when he got angry he threw up. He was just a scared boy as long as I knew him. Mr. Ford blamed himself for this. He

157

had always overprotected Edsel." As for himself, Bennett revealed his own motivation in the opening sentence of his book, *We Never Called Him Henry*: "During the 30 years I worked for Henry Ford I became his most intimate companion, closer to him even than his only son."

Bennett and Ford frequently drove around the plant together, and Ford dropped in at Bennett's office regularly to chat with him for long periods of time. Ford often picked Bennett up and drove him to work in the morning, and he called Bennett at 9:30 every night. They went out on the target range together, and shot up boxes of ammunition. Bennett had a target in his office and plinked away at it with a pellet gun. He also kept a .45 automatic in his desk drawer and once shot a cigar out of the mouth of a visitor. ("Take that cigar out of your mouth when you come in here." "Aw, it ain't lit." BAM!) Bennett reported that Ford used to borrow the gun and shoot it into the ceiling to frighten the occupant of the office above.

The man upstairs happened to be William C. Cowling, sales manager before Davis. Ford didn't like Cowling; he was a big talker but a poor organizer. But rather than fire him, or transfer him to some other position in which he could have been effective, Ford and Bennett used him as the butt of one of their sadistic little jokes.

Ford executives could have their personal cars repaired at minimal cost, and Cowling brought his in for some minor job. Ford and Bennett personally supervised the operation, and added their time to the labor charges which of course resulted in an exorbitant bill. Cowling was embarrassed out of the company.

An engineer named Frank Kulick provided even greater entertainment for the Mutt-and-Jeff pair. When Kulick was discharged in the Rouge purge, he went to see Ford to get his job back. Ford, all charm and smiles, told him that of course it had all been a mistake, and to report to Sorensen. Hardly had the door closed behind Kulick than Ford, as he did on so many occasions, called Sorensen and told him to do the dirty work. Sorensen, tough but not sadistic, passed the fun on to Bennett who assigned Kulick to a tricky engine repair job which required a great deal of both time and expertise. Bennett took the finished job out to test it. Insisting that he could still hear a strange noise in the engine, he inveigled Kulick into lying down on the running board with his ear close to the engine so that he could hear it too. Bennett stepped on the gas, skidded around a corner, threw Kulick off, and kept going. Kulick, scratched and bruised, got the hint.

Edsel Ford attempted to intercede in the Bennett–Davis hassle. Davis, who became general sales manager after Cowling's departure, had felt himself secure; one time Ford had put his arm around his shoulder and said, "Jack, I don't know what we'd do around here without you." But against Davis's wishes, Bennett put one of his men, Harry Mack, in the sales department. Davis was hosting a dinner meeting of his branch managers one night when Mack barged in with six drinking companions and broke up the gathering. Davis left, but one of the men on his staff, a former tackle for the Chicago Bears, hit Mack and knocked him through a showcase. Bennett told Ford that Davis had planned the whole thing to get Mack. Davis appealed to Ford who agreed to listen to him but in Bennett's office. He was standing between the two when Bennett started to give his account.

"I interrupted," Davis told me, "and said, 'Harry, you're a liar! Just a goddamned liar.' I was furious. Harry jumped up and said, 'No one is going to call me a liar and get away with it.' And he raised his arm and the old man scooted under it and out the little door back of Harry's desk. After he was gone Harry never did anything. I said, 'Why don't you hit me?' We didn't fight but I did call him a liar in front of the old man. It was some satisfaction."

Davis immediately reported the incident to Edsel. "Jack," Davis recalled Edsel saying, "this is a very serious situation. I completely agree with you, and I want to support you but I just can't fight any longer with Father. If I continue to support you in this matter I don't think I can hold on much longer." Davis volunteered to step down, but Edsel said, "Father doesn't want you to or expect you to. We talked a good deal about it last evening and we both think that if you would go to the West Coast and literally keep out of Harry's hair, maybe things will quiet down, be better for me, be better for Father and better for everyone. But I want to add this, you'll be back as soon as I can get everything squared away and get rid of Bennett. I don't think the time is too long before we'll be able to do just that."

Davis was given the 11 western states at his same salary, plus bonus. Ford personally signed the salary authorization. "This was hurting Edsel," Davis said. "He did this because he knew it was the only thing to do, but he really felt as though he preferred to just step out and forget it all."

Walter Reuther also told me of Edsel's concern. They had talked about the situation in Washington during the war years. "I believe fully and completely," Reuther said, "that Edsel Ford was a decent human being and a man who hated with every drop of blood in his body what he knew was going on there at the plant. I know he knew it because he talked about it. I told him what was going on, but I didn't have to because he already knew. He hated it, but he was completely without power to do anything about it. He was helpless. His soul bled. Being an unwilling part of this brutality had a great deal to do with his death. He was a decent man and he cared. I felt sorry for him. I still do."

Although Bennett's spies covered the plant, he denied in his memoirs that he had Edsel's home under observation. He claimed that Henry Ford himself, however, had a spy in Edsel's home. And he told of driving Ford to Edsel's house when the family was away, and waiting outside while the old man went in and smashed up his son's supply of liquor.

Though Edsel's own family did not know of his problems with his father, his mother, according to Sorensen, knew enough to resent Bennett. One day Sorensen happened to mention to Clara Ford the target practice that went on in Bennett's basement room, and, he reported, she cried out indignantly, "Who is this man Bennett who has so much control over my husband and is ruining my son's health?" She then burst into tears.

In his book, *My Forty Years with Ford*, Sorensen said he could not tell Clara Ford that it was Ford who controlled Bennett. Well, if Bennett did not have control, he sure had leverage and the shrewdness to play on the old man's prejudices and rages. Sorensen also said that Ford had no close friends. But if a close friend is a man whose company you enjoy, to whose toadying you are blind and on whom you depend, then Ford had a friend. His name was Bennett. The only way to get to Ford was through him. Attempting to contact the old man directly was foolhardy, for Ford's secretary reported such efforts immediately to Bennett and then the only avenue would be closed.

Bennett's influence extended into both purchasing of supplies and distribution of products. If you wanted to do business with the company, you saw Bennett. He could make or break you, either way. He himself did all right, too. He had a castle with two towers near Ann Arbor, an elaborate home on Grosse Isle with secret passageways, a cottage on the shores of Lake St. Clair, a camp on the Huron River, and a ranch in California.

Unfortunately for people who like allegories with all-evil witches and one-hundred-per-cent pure fairies, this ain't that kind of book. If Henry Ford does not quite meet Arthurian standards, and if the strength of his grandson Henry does not stem from the same source as Galahad's, then neither was Harry Bennett as thoroughly wicked as Modred.

A lot of people liked Harry Bennett. My guide on my ramblings through the Ford factory was a friendly master of the self-preservative art of remaining obscure named Clayton Sheldon. Clayt had been a popular high school athlete in East Tawas, Michigan, with dreams of college, when his father died in the middle of his senior year. He was able to finish high school but then he had to go to work. He knew that Bennett had a summer camp nearby and would drop in at a local bar for a drink now and again, and he also knew that Bennett liked athletes. One night when Bennett was in the bar, Clayt put on his basketball sweater—the senior class had chipped in to buy it for him—and entered the bar just as Bennett reached the mellow stage. Bennett caught the resplendent colors of East Tawas and struck up a conversation. Within half an hour Clayt had a note to the personnel department, and he has been at Ford ever since.

Bennett enabled him to get a working schedule that would interfere neither with classes nor with basketball practice at the University of Detroit. A little later, when Clayt's mother became concerned over his full load, he told Bennett the sad news that he was going to have to drop basketball. Bennett was disappointed too, but agreed that the mother's wishes should come first.

"A lot of us never saw Bennett's bad side," Clayt said. "God knows how many college graduates and professional men —doctors and dentists and lawyers—there are in the state of Michigan thanks to Harry Bennett. College students were given easy jobs, like night watchmen, night drivers, with time to study. He paid the tuition for a lot of guys. In the summer the football players showed up. Every afternoon they'd all disappear at

162

the same time, and report back two or three hours later fresh and clean straight from the shower."

Thanks to the Ford payroll and summer workouts, the University of Michigan had great football teams during that period, so great that the coach, Harry Kipke, was sacrificed in the name of academic purity. In retribution, Harry Bennett used his extensive political pull to get Kipke on the Board of Regents of the University. "Mr. Ford and I" built him a house, gave him two boats and a couple of supplier accounts. This meant that, inasmuch as the company bought only through Kipke, the companies involved paid him his commission.

Bennett liked boxers and wrestlers as well as college athletes, and many of them, particularly the big tough ones, wound up on the payroll. Ford had long shown an interest in the redemption of ex-convicts, and had given many of them a second chance. Bennett continued the policy, with adaptations. He encouraged the thugs and hoodlums to continue their line of work in the plant. He also sought out tough cops and hired them. With this material he built up a small army of goons who kept the workers under complete control. Anyone doing anything naughty, like talking union, was beaten to a pulp and fired for starting a fight.

In spite of Bennett's activities, Sorensen's speedup, and the industrial and domestic turmoil, Henry Ford remained one of America's most popular personalities during the Twenties and Thirties. For one thing, he was marvelous copy. Major papers and news services kept staffers in Detroit assigned solely to Ford. He was constantly bubbling with ideas, and if at times his conversation was totally incomprehensible, W. J. Cameron was on hand to interpret.

Martin Hayden, editor of the *Detroit News*, gave me a delightful example of Ford's press relations. Ford had steadfastly refused to go along with the National Recovery Act of

163

the New Deal. The reason was obvious: the NRA was a merger of four of Ford's black beasts—Wall Street, the New Deal, the Jews, and Labor—for the purpose of taking over the company. Ford was finally persuaded to meet with President Roosevelt in the White House. Martin's father, Jay G. Hayden of the *Detroit News*, and Clifford Prevost of the *Free Press* met Ford at the White House following his morning session—unsatisfactory, of course—with Roosevelt, and rode with him in his Pullman compartment to New York. Cameron was also along. During the entire trip Ford talked of nothing but his visit with Roosevelt, and both reporters assiduously made notes, although neither of them knew what in the hell the old man was talking about.

When they arrived at Pennsylvania Station, Ford saw a long flight of stairs and swiftly ran up it and down the other side. "Haven't had any exercise all day," he explained. Prevost was on deadline and had to write his story immediately. Ford disappeared. That left Hayden with Cameron, and the two sat down together to decipher the notes. Hayden would read a couple of sentences and Cameron would explain what they meant. Frequently Ford's actual words and Cameron's interpretations bore absolutely no relationship to each other. Hayden based his story on Cameron's version, quoting him at length but attributing the quotes to Ford.

Next day Ford read both stories, in which Prevost used Ford's actual words, and Hayden used Cameron's. Ford immediately banned Prevost from the plant, on the grounds that he had garbled the story completely and put words into Ford's mouth that he had never said. As proof, Ford held up the *News* story. "Jay Hayden quoted me just right," he said.

Cameron paid a stiff price for serving as Ford's mouthpiece, especially on the anti-Jewish polemics. He was not only no anti-Semite, but also as a member of a small group known as the British Israelites who claim descent from the lost tribes of

Israel, he considered himself to be one. For almost twenty years thereafter he was stuck with the job of sitting in on Ford's interviews, translating Ford's incoherent ramblings with the prefatory remark, "What Mr. Ford means is. . . ." It's no wonder that he became an awful drunk. Ford, in all his glorious inconsistency, still relied on him although he knew full well Cameron's dependence on the bottle. "I like him," he explained to Davis.

During the period of the Ford Sunday Evening Hour I was just getting interested in classical music, and a group of us pre-war newspaper reporters who couldn't afford phonograph records or concerts used to get together on Sunday evenings for the weekly radio broadcast of the Detroit Symphony Orchestra. At the halfway point of each program, W. J. Cameron would come on with a platitudinous homily which we would always cut off. On rare occasions, however, we would be spared his banalities and get an unexpected lagniappe of music instead. We never knew why or when, for the extra piece was never announced in advance. Many years after, I learned from someone who had several friends in the Detroit Symphony during that time the reason for the musical bonus and Cameron's unexplained absences. He was drunk. Every week the orchestra rehearsed a special piece to be performed just in case. Cameron had to be in a comatose condition, incidentally, to be cancelled, for if he could stagger to the mike he could deliver his little piece perfectly.

I mentioned this to Jack Davis while we were talking about Cameron, and it triggered another reminiscence. Somebody got the novel idea of having the president of another automobile company appear on the Ford hour with Cameron. The guest, it seems, suffered from the same malady as the host, and Davis accompanied both of them to New York, from which the concert emanated that week, to get them to the hall on time, sober. They were elusive, however, and shortly before the concert both had managed to become plastered in different bars. Davis, a good salesman himself, as well as a muscular one, collected them, poured them in front of the mike just in time and they came over the air clear and strong. Nobody would have had any idea that they were anything but sober businessmen.

8

FOLLOWING THE golden years of the Twenties, the Ford Motor Company was coasting down a steep hill toward disaster with both antiquated brakes and driver. The financial criteria and operating controls vital to the success of even a crossroads filling station were nonexistent in the Ford Motor Company, and the head of the company didn't care. Any decision made with respect to investment, product, design, and price was made by Henry Ford on a purely subjective basis, mostly hunch. His distaste for cost analysis bordered on the psychotic; he had built the greatest family-owned enterprise with emphasis on mechanical production and to hell with the pencil pushers. As he neared and then passed the age of three score and ten he reacted with phobic intensity to the new generation of innovators, the practitioners of the art of cost-finding whom General Motors was using to become the colossus of the industrial world.

About that time, George Keller, a professor at Yale, was writing the textbook that Henry II was later to study, in which he described the importance of the Great Man in the evolution of mores. He could have been writing directly of Henry Ford: "The really Great Man is endowed with a higher degree of sensitiveness, so that, seeing a little sooner and farther than his fellows into coming situations, he can size them up in advance of the rest. Thus is he able to lead a necessary readjustment. But, when all is said, his function has been no more than that of a guide to what had to come anyway." Henry Ford, Great Man, had indeed led in necessary readjustments, but he was leading no more. He was resisting leadership.

The senescence of the company went unnoticed by all but the other great men in ascendance. Robert Young, the far-sighted financier, told me that when he was treasurer of General Motors in the Twenties, the small group of corporate planners used to laugh at Ford and his operations. But the world did not. In 1924, the representative of a group of manufacturing interests had offered Ford a billion in cash for his stock in the company. Ford had said he'd rather have the company and something to do than money and nothing to do with it. But word of the offer got around and a billion dollars is an easy sum to remember.

Right after World War I, Ford was doing 60 per cent of the automotive business of the world, General Motors less than 12. But GM was climbing. It came out of the next war with 50 per cent of the business, while Chrysler, the newcomer, was up to 20 per cent. By the ultimate criterion of industrial success, profits, the Ford decline was even more striking. From 1929 to 1940, General Motors made close to $4 billion after taxes. Ford's earnings during that period are not as easy to calculate, because the company was run like a country store. At the end of the year somebody would tote up the cash on hand, and that was the profit. According to some financial analysts, using more complex and sophisticated means of measurement, the company really didn't make any money at all. Ernest Breech, on the basis of his personal knowledge of the company and his mastery of industrial finance, says that in the decade of 1931–40 Ford lost $8.5 million. But Breech-type figuring didn't mean anything to Ford. In 1937, for example, the factory wound up the year with $7 million more taken in than went out, and that to him was profit. Seven million dollars split among two families who already had every material comfort wasn't bad. On the other hand, this $7 million was made on a total of $848 million in sales, which means that the percentage of profit was less than 1 per cent.

As for the competition, Ford told a *Fortune* writer in 1933: "I don't care how many cars Chevrolet sold last year. I don't know how many they are selling this year. I don't know how many they may sell next year. And—I don't care."

Ford management, what there was of it, was chaotic. Henry Ford had no title, but the final say on everything. Edsel was president, without power. Sorensen was more or less the general manager, with Bennett's spies in his camp. Bennett, with the seemingly unimportant title of director of services, was number four man in the hierarchy—with the actual power to undercut the two men directly above him, and with great influence on the untitled top man himself. Furthermore, if Bennett issued an order, saying it came from Ford, who was going to argue with him? In effect, there was no organization, and consequently no planning. In the late Thirties Jack Davis, by then sales manager, saw clearly that the company needed a new car for Ford owners of moderately increasing affluence to step up to. Ford was producing customers for Oldsmobile, Pontiac, Buick, and Chrysler. The Zephyr had not served the purpose and the Lincoln was too many steps up. Davis proposed the new car first to Edsel, who heartily approved but suggested that

Davis would get further if he took the idea to Sorensen for presentation to Ford. Try to work up an organization chart for that.

Davis did as directed, and Sorensen then went to Ford—alone. Davis never knew what Sorensen said. It was never discussed at any meeting. Davis was never consulted about his own idea and did not even see the car he was to sell until it was in production. He then realized that it was nothing but an overgrown Ford with the name Mercury hung on it. He had planned to set up a thousand dealers to merchandise it, but after seeing the car he simply gave it to existing Ford dealers, saying here's another car for you. "I'm still surprised that the Mercury survived at all," he told me.

Contrast that procedure with the story of the Mustang.

This non-method of operating extended through every phase of company operations. Personnel was no better. As one company official put it, "A hundred men could hire you one day and a hundred others could fire you the next." To carry that one step further, any one of those two hundred could be fired the day after that, and some of them probably were.

This information has been gleaned only since Henry Ford II took over the company. Before that, as a business reporter commented, "Trying to find out what goes on in Ford is like trying to find out what goes on in Russia." Anybody who knew what was going on also knew better than to talk about it. Ford, the onetime humanist, had publicly stated that men worked for money and were kept in line through fear. For the labor force, this philosophy was policy, carried out to the letter by Sorensen and intensified right on down the line.

Yet Ford believed, in spite of his stated philosophy, that he was a kind and generous employer. He resented any attempt to unionize his workers: how could the union leaders improve the lot of the happy Ford family? So while Sorensen and his straw bosses drove the men mercilessly, Bennett's army of thugs kept them in line. The assembly line, designed both to increase production and to make work easier, became the chain to bind free men into virtual coffles. The speedup aged men prematurely; when they could no longer produce, they were discarded. Bennett's spies infiltrated the plant. The result was the occupational disease known as Forditis. Men had ulcers and the shakes. If they talked at all on the job, it was out of the sides of their mouths.

A sagacious union leader once told me, "We could never organize a plant if it weren't for the cooperation of management." He was referring to inadvertent cooperation, the harsh practices which organizers can promise to eradicate or alleviate. Bennett's labor policy invited unionism; he strove with bloody and effective means to keep the unions out. It was one of the most sickeningly brutal episodes in industrial history. Any suspicion of union sympathy brought retaliatory action from Bennett's men. Men were beaten up on the job, in their own homes and in their own neighborhoods. His brutality extended to Ford plants over the country.

Ford was not the only American company resisting the march of labor in the late Thirties. In the 1937 Memorial Day massacre at Republic Steel in Chicago, 10 people were killed and many injured. The Ford Motor Company's actions made it particularly vulnerable to the revulsion of a growing segment of Americans to union-busting brutality. The swing was to liberalism. The National Labor Relations Act, guaranteeing the right of labor to organize, reflected the trend. Bennett's activities were not only vicious, but, from a strictly business viewpoint, ill timed. Anything Ford did was news, and now the news was bad. The Black Legion and the Ku Klux Klan were active in the factory. Fritz Kuhn, Nazi leader of the German-American Bund, had once been on the Ford payroll. Ford accepted a decoration from the German government in 1938.

Newspaper reporters and automotive writers who had once

treated all Ford news in friendly fashion now became critical. Ford responded in the worst possible way: the company tried to keep reporters out. This is not the smart way to handle the press. Most journalists are dedicated to the professional mission of communicating truth, but we can be vindictive toward those who attempt to thwart us. Getting slugged in the head in answer to a question has deterred me on occasion from finishing up the interview, but when it came to writing the story there is no greater incentive to turn out a vicious diatribe than blood dripping on the typewriter keys. The spirit of righteous vengeance extends all the way up to the editors and publishers far removed from the firing line.

When leaders of the United Automobile Workers obtained a permit from the city of Dearborn to distribute handbills in front of the Rouge plant on May 26, 1937, reporters and photographers made arrangements to cover the event in full force. Bennett did too. UAW leaders, including Reuther and Richard Frankensteen, went to the pedestrian bridge over Miller Road to Gate 4. Among the men waiting for them were Bennett's boys, including professional boxers, wrestlers, and hoodlums. The guards moved in on the union men from either side of the overpass and trapped them there. Suddenly the guards pulled Frankensteen's coat back over his shoulders and while he was unable to protect himself with his arms others began hitting him in the face and body. They knocked him down, then kicked him in the head, kidneys, and testicles. Reuther was worked over, and dragged down the 36 iron steps. Another man's back was broken. The thugs then turned on the other union people, including several women. One girl, kicked in the stomach, vomited. Those who could still move retreated, dragging their wounded with them.

The reporters witnessed the entire event and photographers took pictures, but after the fight was over, the goon squad turned on the press. They tore the reporters' notes from their hands, grabbed and smashed the photographers' cameras. One photographer escaped. He ran to the edge of the overpass and dropped his camera into an open convertible, which sped away. In the camera was the complete photographic record of the assault, and the pictures were printed all over the world. After more than 30 years I still remember vividly the smile on Frankensteen's face looking at me from the pages of *Life* just before the goons went to work on him. (So does Ted Mecke, the one-time newspaperman who became Henry Ford II's vice president for public relations. He even remembers the date of the issue. As a symbol of the factory's enlightened attitude toward its workers, and also, I'm sure, as a reflection of his own innate decency, he had the ill-famed overpass and Gate 4, front door to the Rouge, redecorated in the motif of the modern Ford Motor Company as part of a new corporate identification program.)

The reporters buttressed their stories of the Battle of the Overpass with accounts of eyewitnesses, including a minister, and, after having been pushed around themselves, they pulled no punches once back in the safety of their offices. If anyone had not known what was going on at Ford's, they did then. In the face of the photographic evidence, Henry Ford denied the whole thing. Edsel Ford sought to negotiate with the union but had been told by his father to stay away and let Bennett handle the problem. He must have been almost as sick to his stomach as the girl who got kicked. Sorensen said that during this period Edsel determined to resign, but Sorensen talked him into staying. Edsel insisted on at least attempting to bring about union negotiations, but his father told him flatly, in a direct way, not to interfere. Most of the workers in the plant shared his discomfort more directly, for, after the physical defeat of the union, Bennett unleashed his full tactics of terror and brutality on the men.

There was one brief period of rapport between Ford and

the union, when Bennett apparently made a deal with Homer Martin, then UAW president. Reuther told me that during this period Martin opened up his briefcase and showed him $50,000 in cash and a .45 automatic. But Martin was thrown out of the union and the battle began again.

Ford could not win. The company was found guilty of numerous violations of federal law, and the Supreme Court upheld the convictions. The company lost out on government contracts. The CIO backed an all-out organizing drive with money and direction. When a handful of workers were fired, word spread through the plant and the strike was on.

Edsel returned from Florida and for once had some influence in keeping his father and Bennett from making outright fools of themselves. Bennett wrote later that the company could have won had it not been for Edsel's attitude. The company agreed to an election. Though Bennett and his aides worked for the more tractable AFL union now led by the turncoat Homer Martin, the UAW received 70 per cent of the votes. Only 2.7 per cent of the workers voted for no union at all.

Sorensen wrote that this "was crushing news to Henry Ford, perhaps the greatest disappointment he had in all his business experience. He had been certain that Ford workers would stand by him. This was the last straw. He never was the same after that."

The contract drawn up in 1941 was the most generous the UAW had received. It raised Ford wages above those of Chrysler and GM, and it provided for both a union shop and a check off. It reinstated some 4000 employees with back wages. The UAW's concession to Ford's generous deal was to drop or settle all the cases against Ford.

After Ford and UAW negotiators had drawn up the contract, Ford told Sorensen that he would not sign it. "Close the plant down if necessary." The next day Ford agreed to the contract *in toto*. When he heard the news Sorensen was dumb-

174

founded. Why the complete reversal? Only later, he wrote, did Ford give him the reason: it was Mrs. Ford. She told him that she had had enough riots and bloodshed and that she would leave him if he persisted in fighting the union. "Don't ever discredit the power of a woman," he told Sorensen.

Bennett's account was that the complete capitulation to the union in wages, union shop and check off was Henry Ford's own idea. He said that Ford did not realize his wages were lower than those paid by GM and Chrysler. As for the union shop and check off, his point was that if he gave the union everything its leaders wanted, then they would begin fighting among themselves.

Shortly after his capitulation to the union, Henry Ford suffered a second stroke. The first, which came three years before when he was 75, had brought a warning from his doctor to take things easy, but Ford had recuperated quickly and seemed to be as energetic as ever. After the second stroke, he deteriorated rapidly.

But Edsel was sicker. Ulcers were gnawing at his belly. To soothe them he drank milk, and the milk came from the Ford herd which his father had refused to inoculate against undulant fever. He caught the disease and suffered its high fever and intense pain. And cancer was developing in his bowels. He was a very sick man, but his father refused to believe it. His frequent hospitalization, his very appearance as he gauntly tried to carry on, increased the old man's hostility. There was nothing the matter with Edsel that his own chiropractor couldn't fix, Henry Ford said. According to Sorensen, the old man extended his hostility to Edsel's two older sons, and insisted that Sorensen get them out of the plant, send them far away. Sorensen reported that he refused to be a party to the exile, and Ford relented.

When I asked Henry Ford II about this, he said, "Aw, Sorensen's full of crap," and closed that topic of conversation.

For the next two years, Sorensen says, the irascible old man

175

hammered away at his son through Bennett, and in April of 1943 he landed the heaviest blow yet. Ford ordered Sorensen to change Edsel's attitude on several major points. Edsel was to cooperate with Bennett on all matters in general, labor discord in particular, to break up his relationship with his old friend Kanzler, and to "regain health by cooperating with Henry Ford." Sorensen was convinced that Bennett was responsible for the whole thing, but he had no choice but to pass on the father's wishes. Edsel said there was nothing left for him to do but to resign. Sorensen again dissuaded him. A month later Edsel was dead. Henry Ford was smitten with grief.

Five days later, at the age of 80, in the midst of a war, with huge military orders to fill, Henry Ford himself assumed the presidency of the company. He was not fit for the task. In effect he had no lieutenants, for the only man on whom he chose to lean was Bennett, more interested in personal power than in production. The War Production Board, of which Kanzler was a prominent member, and the Armed Services, particularly the Air Force, which was depending upon the production of B-24's at the Willow Run plant, were concerned to the point of desperation. But, starting from scratch, Willow Run in two years produced 8600 B-24 bombers. In August, 1943, Henry Ford II, a month away from his 26th birthday, was released from the Navy and sent into the plant.

He detested Bennett and stayed away from him. With the fresh eye of youth he could see that Sorensen's methods were abrasive and outdated. He went around the plant talking to people, learning. "I didn't even have a desk!" he told me. At the time his only assets were his name, which may have seemed of dubious value, and his personality, which was his real lever. For everyone seemed to like him. Not having a desk, or a definite assignment, was paradoxically helpful. "It left me free to roam around and find out a lot of things about production

176

that I didn't know, and it also gave me time to find out a lot of things about Bennett. When an important policy matter came up, Bennett would get into his car and disappear for a few hours. Then he'd come back and say, 'I've been to see Mr. Ford and he wants us to do it this way.' I'd check with my grandmother and find out that Bennett hadn't seen my grandfather on these occasions. In fact he hadn't seen my grandfather in months."

Henry *could* see his grandfather—"the front door was open, I could walk right in"—but it didn't seem to do him any good. "I won't hear a word against Harry!" his grandfather told him on one occasion.

It must have been frustrating, but he hung in there.

Getting thrown into a river is a hell of a way to learn how to swim, but some people do it. Henry stayed afloat. His first self-assigned mission was to find out who could do the work, and whom he could trust. One of these men was provided by, of all people, Harry Bennett. The FBI director in Detroit, a tall, Wyoming lawyer named John S. Bugas, had broken up a ring of spare-parts thieves operating within the plant. Bennett, who liked to collect headliners, asked Bugas to come to work for Ford. Bugas insisted that his duties be meaningful, and that his employment be approved by both Henry Fords. Sitting in his office, Bennett picked up his phone and called Henry Ford. The president and founder of the empire walked in and, while giving Bugas the impression he wasn't really aware of what was going on, approved his employment. Bennett then called in Henry Ford II, who also agreed.

Bugas's first duty was to sit in with Bennett on the negotiations with R. J. Thomas, president of the UAW. The union was asking for total raises amounting to some $50 million. Thomas, a jovial man, commented on Bennett's Florida tan. Bennett, furious, told Thomas that his personal life was none of the union's business, and screamed at him almost hysterically for several minutes. Then he abruptly cooled down, said, "Okay, you can have your damn raise," and the meeting was over.

Bugas had sat mute and amazed through the whole performance. So this was the way a company handed out $50 million. As he looked further into the operation, however, he found that episode typical. It was a company run on impulse. Coming from a strictly disciplined organization, he was shocked by the contrast. Bugas felt that his relationship with Ford was either going to be a complete fiasco, or an opportunity to help rebuild the company. He soon found out, however, that he had no real assignment; he was the assistant to the man without a title. One night he and his wife went into Detroit to have dinner with some old friends, and, when the hour grew late, spent the night at a hotel instead of going home. Immediately on appearing at work the next morning he was summoned to Bennett's office. Bennett began chewing him out for immorality.

"What in the hell are you talking about?" Bugas asked.

"I have an eyewitness report right here that you checked into the Book Cadillac Hotel with a redheaded woman last night," Bennett said.

Bugas was still furious when he told me about it 25 years later. He tracked down the man who had been spying on him and fired him. But from then on he had no effectiveness. "I was as isolated as a tuberculosis germ," he said. With nothing to do, he began doing it with Henry Ford II. Ford had found one man he could trust.

Thinking back over my interview with John Bugas I can see why their relationship deepened. My appointment had been made for me through the appropriate channels by the excellent public relations staff, and I had reported to Bugas's luxurious office exactly one minute before the time of the appointment. I knew that he had put in nine years with the FBI, and I've dealt with these types before. Bugas received me politely, if not warmly, gave me a firm handshake, and we sat down in the comfortable chairs around the oval table away from his desk. Tall, rangy and handsome, looking much younger than his 60 years, he made no response to the small talk I customarily use to grope my way into an interview. He just sat there looking at me like a frog.

I abandoned the small-talk procedure and started on a nuts and bolts presentation of what I knew about his role in the rebirth of the company and what information I needed from him. I had my tape recorder with me, of course, ready to go, but I didn't touch it. When it appears that an interview is going to be difficult, I don't increase my chances of failure by fooling around with gadgets. I was desperately trying to elicit some spark of interest from his expressionless eyes, when, suddenly, I found myself listening instead of talking.

The transition was so abrupt that I honestly don't remember what it was I said that caused it. Whatever it was, I think it proved that I had done my homework and was prepared to listen intelligently.

Bugas had been sizing me up. When he concluded that I was worth talking to, he did so. I think he used the same process, on a much grander scale, with Henry Ford II. When he decided that the future of the company, and his own future with it, lay in the developing capabilities of young Ford, he joined forces with him. Having made his decision, he could call upon his FBI experience in dealing with people to convince Ford of his trustworthiness and value.

One other observation from the Bugas interview. After telling me of an episode in which Ford chose to do his own dirty work rather than to delegate it to Bugas, he paused for a second, looked at me directly, and said, "That's the mark of the guy." The tone of his voice and the expression on his face marked this as one of the greatest tributes I had ever heard paid to Henry Ford II. At the time I didn't know that Bugas himself was

179

leaving the company, but he knew it. In retrospect, this encomium was also the mark of John Bugas.

Ernest Kanzler had told Henry of another man he could trust, Jack Davis. Kanzler approached Davis, but the former sales manager was happy in Los Angeles. His salary, personally initialed by Henry I, remained at $50,000 plus bonus. He was doing a good job of overcoming the reactions to the old man's prejudices. He wanted no part of the action in the home office. He had had his share of Harry Bennett. Henry himself went to Los Angeles, but again Davis refused. Henry did not give up. Once again, he made the long trip west and this time assured Davis that things were looking better.

"Come back and see for yourself," he said. "Stay around a month or so."

"Henry," Davis said, "I don't even want to do that if I'm going to be in contact with Harry again. I'd like to come back and work for you and be with you and help you. But not under present conditions."

"Well, Jack," Henry said, "I'll put it this way. If you get in any serious trouble with Bennett and you feel that you have to go, I'll go too."

Tears came into Davis's eyes. They came back 24 years later when he told me about it. He put out his hand and Henry grabbed it. "I'll come back," Davis said.

This was in July of 1944. Davis quickly sensed that Henry was gaining the confidence of his grandfather. "Mr. Ford was changing rapidly in his declining years," Davis told me. "He was leaning strongly on young Henry. He certainly was not treating him as he did Edsel."

Henry was also strengthening his position with a potential ally of tremendous influence, his grandmother. At first his mother, remembering what had happened to her husband, did not wish her son to become involved in the Ford jungle. Editor Martin Hayden told me that she had been heard to say more than once, "This company killed my husband and it's not going to kill my son." But when she saw her son's determination, she relented, and aided in winning Clara Ford to his side. "Women speak the same language," Jack Davis observed.

The drive for power had narrowed down to a contest between Bennett and young Henry. Sorensen had been dismissed in a most demeaning way; he had been fired by telephone on the old man's orders while he was in Florida, and the Jacksonville agency had been instructed to take his personal car away from him. The ax he had wielded on many good men had now fallen on his own neck.

After the departure of Sorensen there was no one on the second echelon to keep up production. One of Bennett's men, Ray Rausch, was in charge of the Rouge and, as one of the men who worked there put it, "the place was running wild." Supervisory personnel, used to knocking men around, could not adjust to the union's interest in working conditions, and the workers themselves, free at last, overreacted. Patriotism and hope kept the plant going.

Henry II unearthed another man of capability, an old timer named Mead Bricker in charge of production at Willow Run. During the summer, Henry was able to leave Dearborn long enough to make a tour of New England with Davis, in order to establish a new rapport with Ford dealers. He gained a reputation as, according to one of the dealers, "a grand young man with plenty on the ball."

Though hardly complacent about his progress, he was nevertheless unprepared for a sudden development which hit him like an elbow in the solar plexus. "One morning," Bugas said, "Henry came in my office more worked up, agitated, than I had ever seen him. He told me that he had just learned that his grandfather had had prepared, and had signed, a new will which would in effect give Bennett control of the company on the death of Mr. Ford. From the beginning I sincerely believed

181

that Henry felt that somehow or other he would take over this company. He was already formulating plans to make it bigger and better, to put it back in the position it had once occupied as one of the world's great industries. Here was a new frustration. In the impulsiveness of the moment he told me that he was going to quit, withdraw from the company completely, and sit down and write a letter to every dealer in the country announcing his decision. He was going to tear the whole place to pieces. It wasn't easy but I calmed him down and got him to wait until I could see what I could do. If I ever did one good thing in my life, it was keeping Henry Ford from going through with his threat."

At that time Henry himself was not quite sure of the nature of the document. We now know that it was a codicil to Henry Ford's will which, inspired by Bennett, would set up a board of trustees to manage the company for a period of ten years after his death. Bennett was prominent on the list of trustees, and assumed that he was to control the board. Neither Mrs. Edsel Ford nor any of her children was on the list. The purpose of the codicil was obviously to keep control of the company out of the hands of the grandchildren, primarily Henry II, until they reached greater maturity. It reflected the old man's hatred, whipped on by Bennett, of Ernest Kanzler, and his phobia that Kanzler would influence young Henry as he had influenced his father.

Bugas went to Bennett's office and, on behalf of Henry, demanded to know the nature of the document. "Bennett became very agitated," Bugas said. "He refused to discuss it. But the next morning he called me in his office. He pulled an envelope out of his pocket, took out of it a typewritten sheet of paper and a carbon, and showed it to me. It was the codicil to the will, all right—you already know what it said. I don't know whether it was actually signed by Mr. Ford or not, but there was a scrawl on it and the signatures of two witnesses. Bennett crumpled both up, put them on the floor, and dramatically struck a match and lit them. When the ashes were cold he scraped them up into an envelope and handed it to me. 'Take these to Henry,' he said."

Bugas just stood there watching the whole act incredulously. He'd practiced law before joining the FBI; he knew how illegal was this dramatic display. You just don't destroy a legal document signed by someone else, and you certainly don't destroy a document covering the disposition of a billion dollar company.

A day or two later Bugas went into his own office to find it completely stripped. He found that he had been moved, literally, into Harry Bennett's toilet. A thin partition had been erected dividing the toilet in half. The toilet and wash basin were on one side, a chair and a small desk for Bugas on the other. "I'd heard the expression of being relegated to somebody's outhouse before," Bugas said, "but this was the first time I'd actually seen it happen, and it happened to me. My first reaction was to get the hell out of there, but Jack Davis talked me into staying on."

The codicil was burned, and Henry had the ashes. But were there other documents floating around? What would prevent Bennett from influencing his grandfather to draw up another? Though there was some question as to whether the old man had actually signed the document—Bennett later claimed he hadn't—the realization of the possibility that had something happened to the feeble old man Bennett would have been legally empowered to run the company for ten years influenced the rest of the family to act immediately. Henry Ford II declined to tell me of the intrigue that went on, but his brother Billy Clay recalled it as not so much an official meeting as a series of telephone calls. Clara Ford increased her pressure on her husband to let Henry II take over. Eleanor Ford, who had remained in the background, now stepped in with the direst threat of all. "I shall sell my stock!" she told her father-in-law.

The thought of even a portion of the ownership of the company getting out of Ford hands was too much for the old man. He was a tired old bull, worn down and softened up. He agreed to let his grandson assume the presidency, but that was not enough for the determined young man. It was all or nothing.

"I want a completely free hand to make any changes I want to make," Henry demanded. Ford argued but Henry was adamant. The old man gave in.

Did he surrender with reluctance, the sword at his throat? Or was it with secret exultation, smug in the living proof that here was a Ford who met his specifications? We'll never know.

The stage was now set for the final dramatic scene. Bugas told me that Henry came in with the signed resignation of his grandfather, and the two discussed how the takeover should be handled. In spite of the signed paper, Harry Bennett was still a dangerous man who controlled other men high in the company.

"I could think of only two other men in the whole damn plant Henry could really trust," Bugas said. "They were Jack Davis and Mead Bricker. I proposed that the four of us get together away from the plant and plan the operation. Henry suggested that we meet in the Dearborn Inn, and I said, 'My God, no. Every room in that place is wired.' We decided on the Detroit Club, downtown. We didn't take any elaborate precautions, because we set the meeting up immediately."

For some time Davis and Bugas had been having lunch together at a small restaurant some distance from the Rouge, where they could meet without being observed and talk without being overheard. Davis, in talking about those days, said, "Henry knew how John felt, and he knew how I felt, and John and I knew we could trust each other, but Bricker was over in the Rouge with Bennett's man, Rausch. I don't know how Henry discovered Bricker was on his side."

Henry Ford with Barney Oldfield at the steering post of the 999 which Ford built at the age of 40 to beat the world speed record of 77.13 miles per hour. Barney Oldfield's name became synonymous with speed; Henry Ford's with the automobile.

Henry Ford II stands with his grandparents, Mr. and Mrs. Henry Ford, at Greenfield Village in Dearborn, Michigan, on May 2, 1946. Mr. and Mrs. Ford are seated in the 1896 Quadricycle—the first car Henry Ford built.

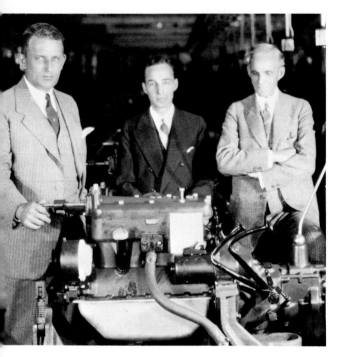

Charles Sorensen, Edsel Ford
and Henry Ford stand before
a Model A engine on a block
test on October 21, 1927.
Sorensen, a rugged executive,
always deferred to Henry
Ford, and provided the figures
that enabled Ford to introduce
the $5 a day minimum for
8 hours in 1914 (when $2 a
day for 9 hours was par).
The Wall Street Journal
disapproved; Adolph S. Ochs
of The New York Times
called it crazy. Ford was
not even in Who's Who!

Henry Ford liked camping trips with his close friends. On this forest outing in the
spring of 1928 are, from left, Harvey S. Firestone, Jr., Harvey S. Firestone, Thomas A.
Edison, John Burroughs, J. R. Watt, Ford, Chauncey D. Hakes and Samuel Ott.

The Ford works at Dagenham, near London, now half the size of the River Rouge plant in Dearborn, has achieved more export sales than any English industry. In 1969 the Dagenham, Essex, expansion plans made it the largest factory in Europe — a $43 million investment on top of a $48 million program in 1965. Here are Edsel Ford, Henry Ford II and Sir Percival (later Lord) Perry at the groundbreaking ceremony on May 16, 1929 — the beginning of international perspective for young Henry.

Henry Ford and Harry Bennett in Bennett's modest but fortresslike office at the peak of Bennett's power in the Ford Motor Company during the World War II period.

Henry Ford II, Edsel Ford and Henry Ford in about 1930. Grandfather Ford enjoyed bucolic pleasures, liked trees and birds and the simple life. His eldest grandson is urban-oriented, and reflects the generation that moved from Puritan Ethic to Social Ethic.

21-year-old Henry Ford II talks with his grandfather, Henry Ford, and father, Edsel Ford, at the New York World's Fair on May 3, 1939. Within five years Henry Ford II was head of the Ford Motor Company, his father dead, his grandfather ailing and soon to abdicate from supreme responsibility.

Henry Ford II talks with Walter Reuther on November 11, 1944, at an American Legion dedication. Since then Ford and Reuther have often been respectful opponents in union negotiations, but dedicated and friendly collaborators on civic and racial matters, locally and nationally.

The 10 men dubbed the Ford Whiz Kids form the front row of this photograph taken on June 28, 1946. They are, from left, Arjay Miller, F. C. (Jack) Reith, George Moore, James O. Wright, Charles B. (Tex) Thornton, W. R. Andreson, Charles E. Bosworth, Ben D. Mills, J. Edward Lundy and Robert S. McNamara. With Ernie Breech heading Henry Ford II's postwar management team the Ford Motor Company was saved from the catastrophe of deficits running $10 million a month—and the alumni of his emergency group went down in history as the smartest industrial crew in history. "Tex" Thornton went on to found Litton Industries, Robert S. McNamara was drafted soon after becoming Ford's president to be President Kennedy's secretary of defense; all attained fame and/or fortune.

TOP: *Time out for a major social event in 1961: the debut party of daughter Anne. Left to right: Mr. Ford, Anne (Now Mrs. Giancarlo Uzielli); Mrs. Ford (now Mrs. Deane G. Johnson); Charlotte (now Mrs. Stavros Niarchos); and young Edsel. Henry Ford II was the life of the party, leading the Meyer Davis band for Ella Fitzgerald, and staying with the young set until dawn.*

BOTTOM: *Ford Motor Company's giant River Rouge manufacturing complex located in Dearborn, Michigan, is the largest concentration of closely knit factories in the world. The Rouge is the only plant on the continent where iron ore, limestone and coal are unloaded on the docks, smelted into iron, converted into steel, and, within a matter of days, transformed into engines, frames, bodies and parts and, finally, completed automobiles.*

Portrait of America's best-known industrial dynasty: Benson Ford and William Clay Ford are seated with Henry Ford II standing behind them on May 27, 1959. Pictured behind the Ford brothers are their father, Edsel, and their grandfather, Henry.

A combination of industrial genius. Henry Ford II (right), president and chairman of the board of Ford Motor Company, and Ernest R. Breech pose on July 15, 1960, with a 1960 Falcon in front of the Ford Central Office Building in Dearborn, Michigan. Just two days earlier Breech had resigned as chairman of the board and Ford had been elected. Breech remained a director and was named chairman of the finance committee. Ernie Breech is the acknowledged hero of the recovery of the Ford Motor Company when young Henry Ford II took over at the end of World War II.

Henry Ford II with his close friend Whitney Young, Jr., head of the National Urban League. They have worked together on racial problems, especially the training and employment of the hard-core unemployed in the ghetto areas. On a Time Inc. tour of prominent Americans to Iron Curtain countries Ford carried Young's baggage off the bus to the consternation of their Communist hosts, who had thought Young must be Ford's valet.

*Henry Ford II and his wife
Cristina, whom he married in
1965, returning from a 32-day
European honeymoon. Ford's
daughters, Anne and
Charlotte, joined the couple
in Switzerland and found
their new stepmother
irresistible.*

*The Fords attend the opening of the Metropolitan Opera at
Lincoln Center in New York in 1966. Cristina bicycles
around Grosse Pointe Farms in Michigan, urges her husband
to exercise, and is totally immersed in his work, his causes
and in time out for travel and play.*

Henry Ford II looks over Ford Mark IV prototype on June 10, 1967, at Le Mans. Henry Ford II, like his grandfather, is a racing buff, and studies the engineering of high-performance components for such competition. He was grand marshal at Le Mans in 1966; and he and his wife, Cristina, remained jammed in their crowded box throughout most of the 24-hour run in 1967.

At the dedication of the new Ford Foundation building in New York, Henry Ford II made a speech in the spectacular enclosed garden which is a feature of the building. At far right is McGeorge Bundy, director of the Foundation.

Cleveland's Mayor Carl Stokes talks with Ford Motor Company Board Chairman Henry Ford II at the opening meeting of the National Alliance of Businessmen in Washington. Mayor Stokes had been a dropout. The challenge of finding jobs for the hard-core unemployed, including dropouts, so inspired Ford that he cancelled an African safari holiday and instead attended NAB sessions in a number of American cities.

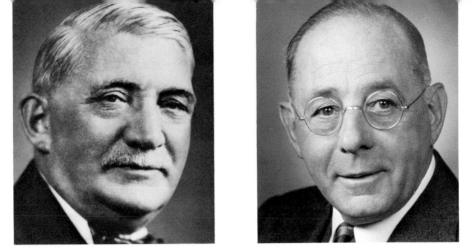

LEFT: *The late William S. Knudsen (a three-star general during the war) who left Ford for General Motors.* RIGHT: *Sidney J. Weinberg, member of Ford Motor Company's board of directors and financial adviser to the Ford family in the organization of the Ford Foundation. A self-made East Side boy, he was known in downtown New York as "Mr. Wall Street."*

Semon E. Knudsen (universally known as "Bunkie") who left General Motors to become President of the Ford Motor Company in 1968, with Henry Ford II.

The meeting began warily, while they waited for the waiter to take their order, bring them their drinks, then go away. When they were alone, Henry said abruptly, "I've asked you men to come here because I have confidence in you. I want you to help me rebuild the Ford Motor Company."

It was a holy moment. No man could speak. Bricker, described to me as a "big, marvelous man," had been hired as a machinist back in the early tractor days, had worked his way up through sheer ability to a position of power and then had been put down by Bennett. Davis had been with the company almost as long, had suffered indignity, frustration and exile. Bugas, though a newcomer, had had his share of bitter experiences. Now they had a leader, and their leader had chosen them. Men unused to expressing their emotions, they sat in silence. Then suddenly Bricker slapped Bugas on the back. "You son of a bitch, I thought you distrusted me!" he cried. The emotion building up in the men exploded. They laughed and chattered. And then they got down to work on how Henry could become their leader in fact. They agreed that he should act immediately.

The next day, September 21, 1945, the board of directors of the Ford Motor Company met in the office of B. J. Craig, the treasurer and a member of the board. Present were Henry II, his mother, Bricker, Bennett, and Henry Ford, so frail that he had to be helped to his seat. Craig began to read his letter of resignation. After the first sentence Bennett angrily arose from his seat and started for the door. "Congratulations!" he snarled at Henry. He was persuaded to remain. After the resignation was read, the board formally elected Henry II president. The others left the room, leaving Henry alone with the furious, frustrated little fighter. Henry gave him the bad news, and Bennett ran from the room.

It was Bugas who caught the full blast of Bennett's rage. With a short-barreled .38 in his belt, he followed Bennett to his office. He knew that Bennett kept a .45 automatic in his top drawer. Bennett, his anger augmented by an apparent hang-over, sat at his desk.

Suddenly he exploded. *"You son of a bitch!"* he screamed. "You did this to me." As the words spilled out, he reached into his top drawer and pulled out the .45 automatic. Bugas was ready. He was confident that he could step quickly to the side, pull his gun, and fire before Bennett could shoot him. He felt a strange premature regret at the thought of killing Bennett. Not for Bennett, but for Henry and the company. The headlines that would follow the shooting, especially on company property, would be unfortunate.

The cold steel of his own gun must have brought Bennett to his senses. He calmed down. He even asked Bugas to go to lunch with him. Bugas said he had something else to attend to and wound up the visit. Then he turned and began the long walk to the door. Beside it was the target Bennett liked to shoot at. His back, Bugas knew, was a broader one. He reached the door, opened it, and left.

Davis had watched the confrontation of Henry and Bennett from his office, which was separated from Craig's office, where the board meeting had taken place, by a glass partition. He had not heard the conversation. He had seen Bennett turn and go quickly to the door and down the hall. Then Henry had left and, after a moment, Davis had followed him to his office.

"He's gone," Henry said.

"Good," Davis said. "Now can I fire somebody?"

"Who?"

"Harry Mack," Davis said. "I want to call him in Dallas and tell him he's through."

"Sure," Henry said. "Go ahead."

Davis got Mack on the phone. "Harry," he said, "you're fired and this time you can't get back because your boyfriend Bennett is gone too."

The only answer was a click on the other end of the line.

Bennett spent the rest of the afternoon at the incinerator in the back of the building, burning his papers. Then he left the factory, never to return. He received no balm from the man he had served in his own way for thirty years. When Henry Ford was informed by his grandson that Bennett was gone, his only comment was, "Well, Harry is back where he started from."

Bennett and his wife settled in the desert near Las Vegas. People who saw him over the years say that he mellowed. "They have a nice house," Jack Davis, who has also mellowed, told me, "with a lot of cats. I think the cats are supposed to keep the rattlesnakes away. My wife and I visited them a couple of times. He's not bitter at me anymore, or at Henry either. Just John Bugas."

On one of his visits, Davis recalled, the women went to bed and he and Bennett stayed up, talking over old times and drinking. Possibly due to the liquor, the conversation grew heated. Both men were in their seventies, and Davis had had three coronaries, but they staggered outside to settle the argument. Davis happened to get his right foot braced against a large rock and landed a lucky punch. Bennett staggered back, fell over a small rock wall, and landed in a cactus patch, out like a light. Davis saw that he seemed comfortable, and went back into the house and to bed. Next morning the two women and Davis were up and getting ready for breakfast when Bennett appeared in the doorway.

"What the hell did I fall over?" he asked, and they all sat down to breakfast.

While Bennett was burning papers in the incinerator Henry was calmly driving out into the country with Allen Merrell. It was only a temporary diversion because he was back on the job that night. Earl Newsom, reminiscing about that exciting period, told me that Henry had already asked him to help in the vital area of public relations—to restore the name Ford to its once high place in public opinion. Newsom had discussed the company with other motor magnates.

"They told me to stay away," Newsom told me. "They said that nobody could resurrect that pile of junk, least of all that poker-playing socialite. I found contempt for both the company and young Henry. After looking the company over, I could agree with them on that, but I was drawn to Henry Ford. He was courteous and thoughtful, with a grace and charm that comes from wealth and breeding. Like John F. Kennedy, he had a certain style. He was friendly and relaxed. But my view of the company remained the same, and I had pressing matters to attend to for other clients. I told him I was sorry.

"Then one evening, at eight o'clock, I received a call from Detroit. 'I've been named president of the company,' Henry said. 'The first thing I did was fire Harry Bennett. The second is to call you. Do I go there or do you want to come here?' 'I'll come there,' I said."

Even then Newsom had reservations about becoming involved with the Ford Motor Company. He knew that the motor industry community was prejudiced against public relations consultants, particularly the Madison Avenue variety. He strongly considered the possibility that these prejudices would affect his own effectiveness.

"But my personal feelings for Henry outweighed everything else. He was the most honest industrialist I have ever met, fearlessly so. I'd already sized him up as possessing tremendous courage and complete dedication to the task of rebuilding the company, and his actions proved my own estimation. I agreed to help him."

This was a period of great pressure and decisions, large and small. What about the guided tours around the Rouge? Should they establish a company paper? Newsom frequently dined with the Fords, and he liked Henry's wife Anne and thought the two little girls charming. (Young Edsel was not yet born.) Henry grew in his estimation every day. "He was incapable of an underhanded deal, he had more guts than any young man I ever saw. And the rest of Detroit was beginning to realize that he was developing into a leader."

It's difficult just to enumerate the problems Henry Ford II faced as the 28-year-old president of the Ford Motor Company; he had to solve them. The company was losing $10 million a month. The name Ford was losing what little prestige remained. The company had to make the transition from war production to automobile production. Dealers had to be reassured (they were, with the first 1946 model in the industry).

Bennett henchmen still occupied high positions throughout the company; Bugas volunteered to clean them out but Henry insisted on doing his own dirty work. Some of his dismissals were dramatic. A highly placed production manager had been throwing wild parties in a secret hideaway in the Rouge. Henry went there, found the door locked, grabbed a crowbar and smashed it open to the delight of the onlookers. The whole plant exulted. Young Henry was taking over.

With the end of the war, management and labor could no longer run to the War Production Board with their respective troubles, and chaos resulted. It was hard for the supervisory personnel to develop instant empathy with the people they'd been kicking around for years. But now the men had a union, and any time they had an excuse, real or imaginary, they got even by laying down their tools and walking off the job. Wildcat strikes occurred somewhere in the industry practically every day. These stoppages, combined with strikes at supplier plants, reduced the projected number of postwar cars, 80,000 before Christmas, to less than 35,000. Wages had been frozen, and now the men wanted a raise. Negotiations for a new contract would begin in November.

This was an ugly period in American labor-management

relations. The whole country was off on an anti-union kick. Union-busting, by both management action and legislation, was In. With Fordian foresight, Henry II saw that the incipient talks with the union would have broad national aspects, and discussed them in advance with Earl Newsom. They agreed that if labor and capital did not cease their bitter internecine bickering, the gates would open for the government to step in.

The union presented automobile manufacturers with a list of demands that covered several pages. Other companies publicly denounced the union; a top GM official publicly called Reuther a son of a bitch. Ford sought a better way. An experienced negotiator named Mel B. Lindquist was hired to work with John Bugas, now in charge of industrial relations. Countless suggestions were made and memos passed around, and meetings stretched out over weekends.

One Sunday night, Bugas and Newsom had supper together, then talked until early Monday morning. Newsom clearly recalls that in that conversation, in 1945, the guaranteed annual wage was brought up and seriously discussed. Out of that bull session evolved the idea of combining an amenable tone with hard facts: they would treat the union as an organization that had won the right to be respected, but they would remind its leaders that with respect came responsibilities; they would consider the demands of the union for greater security for its members but would expound forcefully the company's own need for security against wildcat strikes. After leaving Bugas, Newsom went back to his hotel and poked out the ideas on his portable typewriter. Early the next morning he met Bugas at the office and by 8:00 A.M. they had completed the letter to the union. Ford reviewed and amended it, and it went to the union over Lindquist's signature.

"That letter," Newsom recalled, "threw Henry onto page one."

For a company the size of Ford to accept a union as a

working partner with rights and responsibilities was a revolutionary approach to a problem beginning to be recognized in its full perspective. Hundreds of letters of approval poured in from average citizens as well as from representatives of government, universities, and institutions. Several institutions invited Ford to speak and a score or more universities offered him honorary degrees as a further inducement.

Not every PR consultant gets his client a choice of honorary degrees on the strength of one letter written in the gray Detroit dawn, and Newsom with understandable pride told Jack Davis about it. Davis grabbed the ball and took off with it. He studied the list of universities, compared them with the areas in which the name Ford needed shoring up, and selected a university in the midwest from which Ford would receive his degree.

When Newsom enthusiastically informed Henry of the arrangements being made, he was silent for a moment, then said, thoughtfully, "You know, Earl, I've always had a great respect for those letters after a person's name—Ph.D, LLD, you know. I always thought they represented a great deal—intellectual capability, hard work, accomplishment. I don't think I belong in that league. The only degree I wanted is a degree I can never have, an A.B. from Yale. I'm never going to accept an honorary degree from any university, ever."

(But, some years later, Ford changed his mind, and accepted an honorary degree from the University of Detroit.)

Newsom knew better than to argue the point. "All right," he said, "but you still can't hide. What you say and what you do is going to establish your image and that of the Ford Motor Company. I can't establish an image for you. I don't believe in image making. Even to attempt it would be an impossible and probably dangerous thing. A man creates his own image through his own words and his own actions."

Ford saw this. He has never liked press agentry. Newsom

recommended that he accept an invitation of the Society of Automotive Engineers to address their annual meeting in Detroit. "This is your home, these are your friends," Newsom said.

"But what will I say? I've never made a speech in my life."

"One thing you have," Newsom said, "is that you can afford to draw on experts, listen to them and take their advice. You won't be alone."

Ford agreed. His grandfather had only once, and then without advance warning, been called upon to address a group. He had muttered a few incomprehensible words, then fled. His grandson lived in a different world. He had to throw himself before the public if he was to establish his image.

But he still retained a strong trace of the Ford aversion to self-exposure. The National Broadcasting Company heard of the impending speech and asked to carry it nationally. "I'd rather not," Henry told Newsom. "It's hard enough just to stand up before all those people without knowing there are other people listening in." It was also hard for Newsom to convince NBC that Ford meant it; to NBC the refusal of free time just didn't make sense.

The Ford pattern of speech-writing was developed for his first address, and has changed little since. I was amazed at the elaborateness of what is to Henry Ford II standard procedure. I've written a lot of speeches myself, have talked with other speech writers, and what we all usually do is discuss the subject briefly with the man who is going to read aloud what we write, then bang it out and talk him into accepting it with as few changes as possible.

Before the first draft of the speech was written, Newsom arranged for experts in the broad field of communications to visit Ford in Dearborn and help him establish a viewpoint. Once the message and the tone were set, Newsom assigned four of his best men to write the speech, and contributed a great deal himself. Bugas and Davis were involved in depth, and technical information was, of course, obtained from experts within the plant. A total of 18 drafts was prepared before Ford was satisfied. When the various drafts were presented to Ford, he read them carefully, made suggestions for improvement and raised objections. "I don't *talk* like this," he'd say.

The day before the speech was delivered, Newsom was walking down Madison Avenue to Grand Central to catch the Detroiter when he bumped into Henry's wife, Anne. At the time the Fords spent most of their weekends in their apartment in New York or their house on Long Island. Newsom asked Anne if she was going out to Detroit to hear the speech. "Oh, no," she said. "He kept me up nearly all night reading it aloud. He practically knows it by heart and so do I."

Newsom was even more familiar with the speech, but nothing could have kept him away. He had promised Henry he would be there. "I felt for that young man standing up there all alone—I'd been 28 myself once."

The theme and title of that January, 1946, speech was The Challenge of Human Engineering. Sociologically, it represented the adjustment of one Henry Ford to the original ideas of the other. Henry II set forth mass production as a tool which free people use to make *more and better* products at less and less cost, a tool for *raising the standard of living*. [The italics are Ford's.] He hit on the universal advantages of *lower costs* —of more and better products brought within the budget of more and more people. Then he pointed out that while we have been developing our mechanical operations we have not successfully written into our equations whatever complex factor represents Man, the human element. Management must seek to solve the problem of human relations in industrial production, but management must continue to manage. He talked of the staggering amount of man days lost because of strikes— Ford productivity declined 34 per cent during the war period —and showed how much lower the cost of manufactured items would be if production had not had to absorb the expense of work stoppages.

The solution must be found, he said, for a closer understanding between management and labor. When free men give up the task of trying to get along with each other, and pass the buck to government, they surrender a substantial measure of their freedom. Failure in human engineering creates waste and inefficiency which handicaps the purpose of mass production—lower cost. He stated bluntly the intention of Ford to strengthen union leadership by urging and helping its representatives to assume the responsibilities they must assume if the public interest is to be served. What was needed was industrial statesmanship—from both labor and management. We must act on a more human and professional plane. A union contract should be written and agreed upon with the same efficiency and good temper as a commercial contract. Management has responsibilities toward its employees. Great masses of men work constantly at points below their top capacities: ways and means should be provided to help them rise to these opportunities. Information about company objectives and accomplishments should be made available to all. *Informed* employees are more productive, certainly, than *uninformed* employees.

After offering a sound program for continuing efforts toward better human engineering and mass production, he recommended giving the same hardheaded attention to human practice that we have given so successfully in the past to mechanical practice. The only approach we can take, he said, is to live up to the best industrial statesmanship of which we are capable. If we give the best we have, we can hope to get the best in return.

The response was immediate. Newsom went back to his hotel and was sound asleep when the phone rang. "Earl, what have you done to me?" Henry cried. He had been listening to radio reports of the speech. In the hastily prepared newscasts, thoughts and phrases taken out of context sounded more ac-

194

commodating to labor than the speech itself. Newsom assured him that later reports, based on a more careful study of the speech, would be balanced. They were. *Fortune*, for example, gave its approval. Ford was hailed as the leader of the new breed of industrial statesmen. The U. S. Jaycees named him Outstanding Young Man. His speech was received favorably by a broad segment of the political spectrum. Over at Bendix, Ernest Breech, a responsible conservative, read it with approval. So, at UAW headquarters, did Walter Reuther, a responsible liberal. Some 22 years later I asked Reuther if he remembered it.

"I certainly do," he said. "I read it with a great sense of encouragement. Nothing makes me happier than to see a young individual in business, or labor too, for that matter, give an indication that he is going to spend his future years being helpful and constructive. Not just business or labor, but the entire nation and the world stand to benefit from enlightened thinking and the courage and determination to stand up and say it publicly."

As for the negotiations that had triggered this entire episode, Malcolm L. Denise, vice president for labor relations of the company, who has been involved in all Ford dealings with labor since 1942, recalls that they represented a substantial departure from the preexisting pattern. Though company and union were far apart at the beginning, the negotiations proceeded with a lack of bitterness unusual in Detroit, and after the Human Engineering speech, union leaders realized that Henry Ford II really meant what his negotiators had been saying.

The company gave an 18½ cent raise, which at that time it couldn't afford; the union took definite steps to control its membership, agreeing that its own members could be fired for instigating or taking part in work stoppages.

Over the years, company and union have dealt with each other with less animosity, but Henry Ford's request that labor-union contracts be negotiated with the same efficiency and good temper as a commercial contract has never been fully realized. Bargaining time is still frequently marked by bellicose stands on both sides, positions from which each knows it is going to retreat according to the general principles of bargaining. Still, even after the catastrophic strike of 1967, John Bugas shrugged off any acrimony toward the union with the casual remark, "They've got to live, too." And not long after Henry Ford II reported to his stockholders that because of the strike 1967 was the company's worst year since its rebirth, he was asked by union representatives to serve on the committee for a dinner honoring Walter Reuther, with proceeds going to the Chaim Weitzmann University in Israel. He hesitated for a moment, then said, "Sure, it's for a good cause."

In the late Forties, Ford and Bugas, fully cognizant that many Ford employees had aged rapidly during their years with the company, presented a pension plan for which the company and employee would share the cost. The union, opposed to contributory plans, rejected it. Later a noncontributory plan was approved. This plan led to an effect on the American economy far greater than the hundreds of millions of dollars it directly administers. Its investment has influenced the stabilization of the stock market. One of Henry Ford II's more intellectual executives, Theodore O. Yntema, an economics professor before and after his association with the company as a vice president, insisted upon investing the funds of the pension plan in common stocks over the protests of the banker advisers. At that time, in 1949, it was customary to invest pension plan funds in government bonds.

"They said this was the only safe investment," Yntema, who is not shy about enunciating his economic observations, recalled. "Hell, anybody willing to be a little unconventional could see at that time that the stock market would rise and continue to rise. Henry Ford backed me up and that's where the money went. Albert Bradley of General Motors heard about

196

it, made an appointment, and I sold him, too. By 1968, other companies and institutions had joined with us to run the total investment up to over five billion dollars. This has had a profound effect on the stock market. You can be sure that the market will never go down appreciably because of it."

Though John Bugas brought up the guaranteed annual wage in 1945, ten years elapsed before union and company agreed on it under the face-saving change in nomenclature of *supplemental unemployment benefits*. Reuther told me that the union had to fight bitterly for SUB, but that after it was called to Ford's attention, the company became interested, hired technical experts to study it, and agreed to it. All of Reuther's ebullient dedication to the cause of the working man comes bursting out of him as he describes the long range benefits of SUB to both the worker and the nation as a whole.

Henry's daughter, Anne Uzielli, told me that she saw her father and Reuther with their arms over each other's shoulders, talking like old buddies, at one of the World Series games in Detroit in 1968. Reuther smiled at this accusation of consorting with the enemy, and said they weren't quite that chummy. He admitted liking Ford personally, however. And in answer to my direct question: Is Henry Ford II a leader in progressive labor relations? he said, "Yes, definitely, but I think you've got to give the union a little credit too."

The union prefers working with Ford to working with the other two automobile companies. "GM is mean, but they're smart," Reuther said. "They've got that tremendous depth. If one guy goes, they've got three more just as good ready to step in his place. As for Chrysler, they went through a period of mismanagement in the early Sixties that resulted in incredible incompetence from the very top to the very bottom. It's hard to believe that a company could get itself in a situation where it seemed you couldn't find anybody with any sense at all. But around '66, '67, they started coming back mighty fast. Ford isn't as smart as GM, because they haven't got the depth, but they're a lot smarter than Chrysler and they're more progressive than both."

Why, then, did the union lower the boom on Ford in the big strike of 1967? Reuther grinned. "Well, someday when you write a book about me I'll tell you that. In the meantime I'm afraid I just have to refuse to answer. I've been completely honest with you and I want to continue to be. How we make our tactical decisions here is a little secret that we have and one that we intend to keep. Several factors are involved in such decisions, most arrived at scientifically after a great deal of study and research, but there's a little bit of hunch involved, too. Anyway, don't get the impression that we want or should have complete unanimity with industry. When this happens a most sterile and unproductive situation results. Our differences with Ford make up a stimulating and challenging relationship. The free enterprise system, free society, is based upon diversity of opinion."

In the 1967 strike, the major issue involved the variation in the pay scales of the skilled and unskilled worker. The craftsmen of the union were making less money working for automobile companies than their counterparts on the outside. They wanted a big increase. Automotive workers, on the other hand, knew very well that the more the craftsmen received the less would be left for them. In effect, the automotive industry faced an internal union problem.

For months before the strike, all Detroit knew there was going to be one, but no one knew where. Before the expiration of the contract, numerous meetings were held, with and without Henry Ford II, to determine what the company's response would be if the lightning struck Ford. The other companies were having similar sessions. They all faced the fact that whatever company was hit, it would be a long wait before the contending factions within the union could get together. The

Ford people determined in advance approximately what the company would agree to.

Finally, then, the ax fell, Reuther knows why, on Ford, Company and union were far apart, and in September the plant closed down. Ford had resolved to wait until the workers cooled off before progress could be made. But it was an agonizing wait. Here was this magnificent production mill standing idle, and idleness is something a Ford can not abide. Weeks went by. Finally resistance began to thaw.

The press sensed the possibility of impending settlement. Automotive strikes are big news as the industry affects us all indirectly; in Detroit the effect is direct. Reporters from local papers and distant ones, newsmen from radio stations, television crews, all kept a constant vigil. If a secretary came out of one of the many meeting rooms to go to the pink-doored ladies' room, newsmen pounced on her with questions. This type of coverage produced some wild rumors, and both sides agreed on a 24-hour complete blackout of news: no one from either Ford or union would give any information whatsoever to the press. The original 24 hours stretched out into twelve days, twelve days of an army of newsmen reporting nothing.

Late one night a reporter with nothing better to do was leafing through the company telephone directory in the press room. He noted Ford's number. Everyone had observed that the lights were on in Ford's office on the twelfth floor. On the spur of the moment, the reporter dialed his number. Who should answer on the first ring but Ford himself. The reporter, somewhat startled, asked the first question that popped into his mind, which was, naturally, Is there any hope for settlement?

"Oh," Ford said, "we can settle it if we give Walter $5 an hour." In seconds the remark spread through the press corps. When it reached Walter Reuther he turned white and his jaw set.

"Get me Malcolm Denise," he snapped. He angrily in-

199

formed Ford's head of labor relations that the remark was a violation of the news blackout, that it was not true, and concluded: "You either retract that statement or I'm calling a news conference."

Within an hour a retraction was passed out; it was only a joking remark and had been misinterpreted. Then the speculation began. How many high-priced PR men had frenziedly gotten together to prepare that statement?

The penultimate bargaining session lasted 48 hours. Three of the negotiators keeled over, and a doctor warned that it would be dangerous to continue. The final session began at 10:00 A.M. on a Saturday and the agreement was reached Sunday, October 22. The original Ford offer was 13 cents across the board. The final offer was 20 cents increase to the unskilled workers, 50 cents to the skilled workers. Everyone was satisfied. Denise, reviewing the entire period of negotiations with me later, maintained that even with hindsight, there was no other way the agreement could have been reached. "If we'd made that offer at the beginning," he said, "before they had to tighten their belts a little, it would have been turned down flat."

The strike provided a deeper insight into Henry Ford II. An impulsive man, a man of great personal industry and a hatred of idleness, he was nevertheless able to give at least the outward appearance of patience as he rode it out. He had resolved not to shoot from the hip, and he didn't.

Chrysler and GM had kept right on grinding out cars, and no doubt selling a few to potential Ford customers. After the Ford settlement, the two other companies signed with the union on terms generally similar.

Talking with Henry Ford II and Malcolm Denise about the strike after it was all over, I was impressed with the combination of sadness and equanimity with which they accepted their huge losses in production and profit. They took it as unfortunate but just one of those things. Yet, the seven-week strike had taken a tremendous toll in loss of pay to union members, loss of income to the company. Total sales of Ford cars and trucks in North America dropped from 3,240,000 in 1966 to 2,434,000 in 1967. The worldwide drop in cars, trucks, and tractors was a million units. Total sales figures dropped from twelve and a quarter billion dollars to ten and a half.

Most drastic of all was the decline of net income—$621 million down to $84 million. In 1966, Henry Ford II and president Arjay Miller both received bonuses of $415,000; total bonuses paid amounted to $48 million. In 1967, none of the major officers received a bonus, and the total paid was less than $6 million, taken out of the reserve. It was a pretty dreary spring in Detroit suburbia in 1968.

9

THE SPRING OF 1946 would have been a dreary time too had it not been for the new spirit that infused the company and replaced the fatigue of strain and war production. One chubby 28-year-old with a magic name and glowing personality had uplifted sagging morale and caused the euphoria throughout the factory.

"He breathed the spirit of life into this place," Jack Davis said. The irrepressible sales manager, in the glory of the moment, had huge signs erected over the plant saying BEAT CHEVROLET, surely the most absurd aspiration since Spartacus. Despite the intoxicating atmosphere, under existing conditions Ford would have had a hard time beating anybody. Manufacturing automobiles requires more than a nice young man, even if he is an outstanding one.

The company's momentum had diminished substantially

since the Model T. Leadership and management expertise had been squelched, not encouraged. Without war contracts and money stashed away in banks (at zero interest), the demise might have come long before. Now the momentum was gone, war production was gone, cash reserves were going, and one man's charisma was no substitute for them. Yet at first that was all Henry Ford II had. He didn't even know enough to know how little he knew. Only through studies necessitated by the Office of Price Administration did he learn that the company would lose $300 on every car Davis was planning to beat Chevrolet with. The total losses of the first quarter of 1946 would amount to $22,000,000. Ford knew next to nothing about management— where would he have learned it?—and nothing at all about cost analysis.

He started by setting up management meetings. The three top lieutenants, Davis, Bricker, and Bugas, headed sales and advertising, manufacturing, and industrial relations, respectively. Other departments were not as strong. Herman L. Moekle, for example, who headed finance, was primarily a lawyer with some accounting experience.

The makeshift organization did manage to bring out a postwar car, basically the same as the 1942 model. But the deeper Ford got into management, the more he realized his limitations. This in itself was growth. Davis, looking back on Henry's development, recalled him first as a pleasant young man whom he would have been happy to have in his department as a trainee.

"When he was released from the Navy he must have looked around and seen the sorry shape the company was in, and realized that it was completely up to him. I think Henry felt keenly his responsibility. I think he realized he just had to assume leadership. His brother Benson didn't seem to want to and Billy was far too young, so Henry knew it was up to him. He was the top Ford man. And I think he was impressed with this role every day. It provided a self-generating power.

"From then on he had determination, a lot of courage, and confidence in himself. He was willing to learn. He seemed to appreciate that it was a gigantic task he was undertaking. He became really wedded to the Ford Motor Company. He blossomed quickly. He studied a lot, studied his men, and made intelligent inquiries about company activity. He didn't just step in and take over, it was more of an evolution."

One day, out of a clear blue sky, Ford told Earl Newsom, "Earl, I just don't know enough about manufacturing to run this damn place."

Newsom, commenting on the remark to me later, said, "But he did know enough to go out after Ernie Breech."

Even Breech apparently did not at first realize the full extent of the reorganization necessary. Driving to his office one morning in August about a month after he had officially signed on, he stopped his car and sat motionless. As he told his biographer, "For the first time in my life I was overwhelmed. Not afraid, but very disturbed. Our problem seemed almost insuperable. Things were in a mess. It would take years to get them under control."

Chrysler, General Motors, and even Studebaker were going into postwar production. Despite the fact that it was first to market with a 1946 model, Ford was in poor shape. Manufacturing plants were obsolete. The company had few dependable sources of supply. It would take years to install proper accounting methods to obtain any semblance of financial analysis and controls.

One of Breech's first steps, taken with the full support of Henry Ford II, was to set up a modern organization featuring a program of decentralization. Breech had no hesitancy about bringing the General Motors system to Ford, since Peter Drucker's book, *The Concept of the Corporation*, describing the GM system in detail, had just been published. Breech passed the book out among the Ford executives. "I made everybody from Henry on down read it," he said, and from the tone of his voice I could see he didn't get much feedback. ("Sure I read it," Ford told me. "I didn't have any choice.")

I think the best way for me to explain the system is, surprisingly enough, through the words of a regular Army officer, Colonel Harold G. Moore. Colonel Moore, back from Vietnam, was one of the 1967–68 Fellows of Harvard University's Center for International Affairs. The purpose of the Center is to broaden the individual's knowledge of the field and it is attended by a score of high-ranking officials of several countries each year. The Ford Motor Company annually brings the group out to Dearborn for a comprehensive program in the workings of a major corporation. I spent a couple of days with the Fellows and improved my own insight into the Ford company through their impressions. They commented often on the intellectual force of the executives they met. They had expected to find men of corporate capability, but were surprised by the enlightened and stimulating ideas bouncing around.

When I asked Colonel Moore his impressions of the company, he said, "The thing that strikes me more than anything else is the similarity to the military. This company is organized along military lines. It's a well-disciplined organization, with a clearly drawn chain of command. They even use the same terms—*line* and *staff*. I was interested in their analysis of their mission and after only a couple of sessions I found the message coming across loud and clear. *Their mission is to make money for Ford.* They are all tremendously professional and it's obvious that anybody who's a phony wouldn't be here."

Line and staff are the key words. Under the one-man rule of Henry I, there was no delineation between these two functions, if indeed there was any delineation between anything. In the decentralized, profit-center system, just as in the military, duties are clearly divided between the staff, which plans and advises, and the line, which executes. The line and staff breaks

206

down the competitive instinct of mankind into two separate manifestations, individual and group. The staff furnishes advice and guidance, then turns the line loose to accomplish those goals. After the battle, or the financial report, it dishes out rewards—promotion, medals, money, privileges; they are all the same.

When the system is working perfectly, each squad leader tries to gain his objective faster than the squad next to him. The platoon leader is pushing them on in an effort to outdo his rival in the next platoon, and the company commander is right in there pitching, too, in competition with the companies on his flank.

I don't want to carry this industrial-military analogy too far, but you can nevertheless see what happens when the general principle is applied to industry. With individual units of General Motors—Chevrolet, Buick, Cadillac, et al.—each trying to outdo the others with enlightened guidance from central headquarters, GM was making billions while Ford was breaking even.

It was a proven system, and Breech set out to move it over to Ford. It was about as easy as turning a coal mine into an international bank. Many processes had to be changed; the most complex was establishing profit centers. The people at Ford really had no idea how much it cost to manufacture a piece of steel, an axle, an engine, or an automobile. Nor had the majority of personnel, brought up under an eccentric with a phobia about bookkeepers, either the interest or the inclination to learn.

To help him with the job Breech brought in scores of men from General Motors. Men at the top, like Lewis D. Crusoe, once Breech's right-hand man at Bendix, had to be wooed; lower echelon personnel came with alacrity. GM had long maintained a wealth of personnel and had brought them along slowly. Now there was a challenge, many vacancies, and the chance to be with Breech, an unparalleled leader and teacher. Few were disappointed. Ford Finfgeld, one of almost a hundred minor executives who exited from the Fisher Body Company, told me that he had more downright fun and progressed further in his first six months with Ford than he had in 16 years with Fisher.

By 1948, two years after Breech began reorganizing the company, 98 of the top 100 men in finance were his boys. Their task was doubly complex, for they had not only to eliminate the old order, but establish the new.

One of Breech's financial tigers, Gerald J. Lynch, who went on to become chairman of the board of Menasco, was one of a task force of more than a thousand assigned to review war contracts. For a period of several months this battalion of accountants wasn't sure whether the company should refund more than $20 million or seek renegotiation.

"When the history of the Ford Motor Company is finally written," Lynch said, "it should be noted in bold type that Ford was saved from imminent oblivion or at least a complete change in ownership by Mr. Ernest R. Breech. . . . In my opinion this rescue operation under forced draft while in competition with the most successful company in the world, ranks with Alfred E. Sloan's structuring General Motors as the outstanding corporate achievement of the twentieth century."

According to Breech himself, the company lost $8.5 million during the depression period from 1931–40, but made $5.5 billion during his regime, 1946–60.

Breech said: "What we went after was precisely what it will take for any firm to be competitive in the rich but hard-fought market of today and tomorrow. And what it takes, above all, is competent management, flexible and big enough to respond swiftly to changing market conditions; research and engineering adequate to meet the enormous strains of modern product competition; plants and machinery efficient enough to compete with the best in industry; and a financial control system which provides some forecasting, that keeps operations efficient, and is geared to produce peak profits."

One of Breech's first steps was to set up the profit centers, each held accountable for its profit performance. The monolithic company was composed of many huge plants and operations, producing everything from steel to finished automobiles. In order to be able to judge the performance of an individual operation, a measurement, price, had to be established for its product. But as that product was created out of Ford raw materials in a Ford plant by Ford workmen for Ford use, determining its worth in cash seemed an insuperable accounting problem. There was, after all, no other market for a Ford engine: Chevrolet didn't need one. Even when the accountants finally arrived at a figure for each item they referred to it as the shadow price, for it was an artifice.

By assigning an intracompany price to each product, including those composed of other products, a profit percentage could be established. This, then, became the yardstick by which the operation, and its manager, is judged. With strategic advice available to him from the staff, each manager must make such decisions as whether to replace existing equipment, old or new, to better his performance. If he spends millions on a new plant or process and shows a 15 per cent profit, he gets his decoration in the form of a bonus and a boost toward the next rung on the ladder. If the new plant proves to be only a monument, with it comes a ticket for early retirement.

After putting this system into effect, Breech had to convince his personnel, from managers to foremen, of its value to the individual. Motivation had to be restructured on every level. One day, walking through the plant, Breech brushed against a worker who accidentally got in his way. Before Breech could raise a finger, the foreman threw the innocent offender against the wall. Breech was horrified. A friendly fellow as well as an efficient administrator, he believed that the key to the improvement of individual performance lay in incentive and pride, not in fear and physical violence.

209

In 1948, Breech called a meeting of several hundred of the top management men and presented his program in detail. He showed how increased individual performance produced extra individual compensation. And finally his managers bought the program: positive rewards for positive performance measured efficiently by the yardstick of profit.

Should the yardstick show loss, of course, the rewards were commensurately negative. Earl Newsom told me of an occasion when he and Breech planned to have lunch together after a meeting. Breech excused himself for a couple of minutes, and took one of the managers aside. When he rejoined Newsom he apologized for the delay with the explanation that the manager was not producing, and that he had been given six weeks to get his operation in order. A couple of months later Newsom asked Breech about the outcome. The manager had not delivered, and he was no longer with the company. But he had not been dismissed before he had been given a fair and candid appraisal of the situation, a few words of advice on what he should already know, and a reasonable length of time to rectify mistakes and indicate positive progress. Nobody removed his desk in the middle of the night or threw him off a running board.

An operation that needed immediate attention was the engineering and product-planning department. Breech changed its velocity, direction, and size. Henry the One could close down a plant and then bring out a new model in little more than a year; the postwar industry had to look at least three years ahead on new models, and determine its annual output over those years. If an automobile company overestimates its volume in its financial plans, the overcapacity will result in reduced profits. But an underestimate of projected output will mean overtime, and hasty, inefficient remedial efforts.

Though the period in which Henry Ford II and his executive vice president first started working together is referred to in company histories as one of rebuilding and reorganization, what it really amounted to was the creation of a viable, modern corporate entity from scratch, or, better, from *minus* scratch, for the old adhesions had to be broken down before the new growth could begin. Who can calculate the man hours devoted to drawing and redrawing organization charts and dictating memos? The stock of the paper company supplying Ford must have jumped a point or two, for example, when the corporate planners proposed the creation of a Ford Division within the Ford Motor Company. After all, what was the Ford Motor Company but the Ford Division?

It was in relation to the creation of the Ford Division that Breech told me of the excellent learning capacity of Henry Ford II. "Our doors were open to each other at all times," he said. "We had an excellent team. Henry would bring people into my office and I would take people into his. Frequently he would come into my office with some fresh idea. He'd ask, why not do it, and more often than not, after thinking about it, I'd agree with him. Then the first thing I knew, he was going ahead and putting it into effect. We had a great deal of complaints, criticism, and reluctance on the part of some of the other executives when we set up the Ford Division. I remember Jack Davis saying, 'What am I going to do?' Meaning, what would his job be. But in spite of Davis's complaints, Henry said, 'We're going to do it this way. Not only will we do it,' he said, 'but we're going to do it now.' It almost meant a revolution within the company but he did it, did it *now,* put it into effect and made it work."

Though Breech never told me so, he himself could take a great deal of credit for enabling the young president to develop his blunt forcefulness. Talking with the current executives of the company, more than 20 years after Breech came in, I was repeatedly told that Breech and the seasoned executives he brought in with him provided the umbrella under which today's top leaders of the company could learn corporate expertise without

getting sunstroke. They learned it so well that they took up where
Breech and the GM system left off, and have developed a new
concept of corporate organization, the *Ford* system. Today, for
example, after all the furor in setting up the Ford Division, it is
only a marketing agency.

Ford himself mentioned several times the importance of the
three P's—people, profit, products. "Of the three," he said,
"people really come first. Profit is the ultimate objective. But
profits come only through bringing out a superior product, and
that brings us right back to people."

The founder of the company had almost a fetish for bringing people up through the ranks. His grandson, aware of the increasing amount of college recruiting by industry, came into the
company with the inclination to pour college graduates into his
personnel pipelines to the future. Before joining the Navy he
had wangled a job for a member of the Yale crew in the personnel department. His grandfather, having his fun, needled Harry
Bennett about the interloper in his own personal domain. Bennett dispatched two hand-picked tough guys to teach the trespas-
ser a lesson. Envisioning a big oarsman with tremendous
shoulders, Bennett saw to it that his musclemen were also giants.
But when they found their victim they didn't know what to do
with him. He was a former crew member all right, but he'd been
the coxswain. He wasn't much more than five feet tall. Bennett,
who had a sense of humor, got a laugh out of the incident and
let young Ford's college friend stay on. He was one of the first of
many thousands from hundreds of schools.

The predisposition on the part of Henry Ford II toward
college-trained men was a factor in a personnel package deal
unique in industrial history. I'm referring, of course, to the
famous Whiz Kids, a ten-man group from which have come two
presidents of the Ford Motor Company, a Secretary of Defense
who made his mark on the entire military establishment, the
chairman of the board of one of the world's largest conglome-

rates, and others prominent both at Ford and at other major corporations.

The leader of the group was Charles B. "Tex" Thornton, a brilliant young officer who had become a full colonel in the Air Force—in a desk job—in his twenties. As head of the Office of Statistical Control, he had supervised the accumulation and proper use of data of utmost importance to the prosecution of the war. When the war ended, Thornton, with fellow officers Francis C. Reith, George Moore, and Ben D. Mills, thought of forming a company of their own. They didn't know exactly what the company would do, except that it would perform a service rather than manufacture a product.

"We were thinking along the lines of A. C. Nielsen Company, which then rated radio shows," Mills told me. "We decided to expand our number, and I made up a list of 25 officers selected from different sections of the Air Force. They all had good backgrounds. I listed characteristics which I thought would be valuable and rated each one of the officers according to these headings. As I recall, I had a sheet of paper about 36 inches wide. Then we narrowed this group down and eventually came up with ten. Thornton made the final selection, and it's interesting to note that he was the only one of us who knew all the other nine."

All were college men, some with advanced degrees, and most had studied statistical control at the Harvard Business School. Robert S. McNamara had been a faculty member at Harvard, Arjay Miller a teaching fellow at the University of California, and J. Edward Lundy on the economics faculty at Princeton. Their expertise had been intensified in military service.

Robert S. Young of Allegheny Corporation, a catch-all, first-generation conglomerate that included among its holdings the ever-prosperous Chesapeake & Ohio Railway, invited the group to join him. Not all the members were in favor of

213

Allegheny, however. About that time Arjay Miller read an article in *Life*—"I still remember the date; it was October 5, 1945"—about Henry Ford II and the challenge he faced as the new president of the Ford Motor Company. He proposed that the group offer their talents to Ford, and he was so persuasive that the other nine went along.

Curious as to what had made such an impression on him, I looked up the article in, as it turned out, the October 1 issue of *Life*.

Written by Gilbert Burck, it was a warm and perceptive profile of an earnest young man and a rundown old company. It told of the influence of his sociology studies on the young president, which appealed to the university-trained officers, and commented on Ford's "blunt frankness and intolerance of pretense," which appealed to the positive young statisticians. Referring to his naval service, Ford was quoted as saying, "I learned to do what I was told when I was told to do it," which struck a note of sympathy.

With uncanny prescience, Burck conceded that it was possible "to imagine his becoming as arbitrary as his grandfather when he got as experienced and confident," but that it was easier "to imagine his combining his frankness with knowledge and experience in a way that will make him an unusually able practitioner of human relations . . . it is hard to imagine his going off half-cocked so long as he retains his personal ability to value other people's knowledge more highly than his own." The article attributed to Henry II a reasonableness in regard to labor and mentioned his interest in a guaranteed annual wage. It described his ambition to make Ford first again.

Burck made such a convincing case that Thornton sent a telegram to Henry Ford II himself. It was a forthright and aggressive message, which, one of the group said later, "bordered on impudence," but it appealed to Ford. He likes blunt, aggressive confidence, and his response was immediate. He once told me, talking about another episode, that he "did it the way I do every-thing—go right at it."

The next day Thornton got a telephone call inviting the group to Detroit. All were excited about the prospect except one—McNamara. He had been invited to return to Harvard as full professor, and said he wasn't interested.

"Well, you'd better get interested," Thornton snapped. He knew that McNamara's wife had been hospitalized for months with polio, and that he owed more money than he could repay on a professor's salary. "Didn't you tell me you were broke? Come with us. You owe it to your wife."

The officers made the trip, met Ford, whom they liked, and were grilled extensively by John Bugas. Ford in the meantime had been checking on them on his own and he bought the package. Their official employment began February 1, 1946. Thornton suggested the salary to be paid each member of the group—their ages ranged from 26 to 34—and Ford agreed with-out quibbling. One of the group postulated that Ford wanted them not only for what they could contribute but in order to have some men his age around him. And Ford himself said later, referring both to the Breech veterans and the Thornton economic intellectuals, "You couldn't help but learn from such a group. Every day of the week I learned something—even by osmosis."

McNamara, when Secretary of Defense, reminisced to Bob Considine that "what kept us going was the example set by Henry. He had to face a lot of his problems alone. He could have done what a lot of other rich men's sons have done—turned his back on all the difficulties and become a playboy. But Henry had great guts when needed. That's the only way I can describe it."

The ten young ex-officers had strong ideas about how to run the company. "We'd been working under the line and staff concept," Thornton told me. "I was just as positive about decen-tralization and accountability as Breech and the GM group." But the background was different and the emigrés from the Air

Force had to learn what was going on at the factory. In a thorough indoctrination program, they went around asking questions of both top executives and lower echelon supervisory personnel.

A popular radio quiz show at the time featured some very bright children known as the Quiz Kids, and the application of the name to the inquisitive young men of the Thornton group was a natural development. The appellation later became Whiz Kids, and though few of them liked it, the name stuck. Years later, after McNamara had risen to the presidency of Ford Motor Company and given an impresario performance as Secretary of Defense, he was still being referred to as one of the Whiz Kids—as well as being blamed for the Edsel.

Though appalled by the horrendous inefficiency of the company, particularly in finance, they kept their sense of humor. One time they asked someone in the controller's office about the financial projections for six months hence and received the perfectly serious answer, "What do you want them to be?" Miller made a personal study of the records, and when the others asked him his opinion, he replied, "What do you want them to be?"

The Whiz Kids soon knew more about the company than any of the older employees. But they still had something to learn about judgment. In May, Thornton drew up a letter for Ford to sign which would give him broad authority. Ernie Breech had in the meantime agreed to become executive vice president and Ford showed the letter to him. "If you sign this letter," Breech said, "there's no need for me to join the company."

Many years later Thornton told me, "At the age of 32 I could be more adamant than patient." Assigned to Lewis Crusoe, Breech's executive assistant, he found it difficult to live with his differences of opinion on company policy.

"One of our disagreements grew out of Crusoe's desire to pattern Ford after GM," he said. "My point was that if we were going to be exactly like GM then we couldn't be better—and I wanted us to be the best. My wife and I talked it over and then I told Crusoe I wanted a change, either in or out of the company.

He got angry about it, which surprised me, because I thought we got along well personally. Anyway, I left."

He did all right. By the time I interviewed him, he was chairman of the board of the huge conglomerate, Litton Industries.

The Thornton group had originally intended to stay together in the company, but Ford and Breech decided they could be more effective if assigned to individual jobs. Arjay Miller, for example, on the death of the elder Henry Ford, worked personally with Henry II to settle the estate, then went into the finance department. In 1949, Ted Yntema, an economics professor serving as consultant to the company, came in full-time as vice president in charge of finance. When, long after his retirement, I asked Yntema if making the transition had been difficult, he looked at me and asked, "With Miller as my assistant?"

Miller was president from 1963 until 1968, when with Bunkie Knudsen's arrival, he was named vice chairman. The next year he became dean of the Stanford University Graduate School of Business.

McNamara, who awed his confreres with his brilliance, became head of the Ford Division and then, on November 9, 1960, president of the company. (Henry Ford II had become chairman on the resignation of Breech four months before, and retained the presidency during that period.) He held the position less than two months. John F. Kennedy had just been elected President of the United States. Ford received a call one Sunday night a little later with the tip that McNamara was going to be offered the post of Secretary of the Treasury in the new administration. Next morning McNamara agreed that he had been sounded out about a cabinet post.

"But if it's Secretary of the Treasury," he said, "I'm not going to take it." Next thing Ford knew McNamara had agreed to be Secretary of Defense. "I think he's done a great, great job," Ford said after McNamara had left the cabinet in 1968 to become president of the International Bank.

217

J. Edward Lundy also went into finance, and became executive vice president and member of the board. Though his rise in the company was not as swift as McNamara's or Miller's, his individual interest in personnel has perhaps been of greater value over the long haul.

Jack Reith, after a magnificent performance helping Ford and Breech restore order to the chaotic overseas operations, prepared a master reorganization plan of which the introduction of a new middle-priced car later named the Edsel was a too-well-remembered part. He left the company shortly afterward.

Ben Mills eventually became vice president in charge of purchasing, charged with establishing purchasing policy in a staff capacity. By the time of the departure of Miller in 1969, only he and Lundy were still with the company.

Wilbur R. Andreson stayed only a few months; he and his wife, both from California, didn't like Detroit in winter. George Moore became a dealer. James O. Wright reached the level of group vice president but left to take the presidency of another company. Charles E. Bosworth also attained the upper executive echelon and retired in 1967.

"Looking back on those days," Tex Thornton told me, "I'm even more impressed with Henry Ford. He was young, inexperienced, in a company with a general flavor of losing. You'd presume that he would be inactive and ineffective. What he had was the courage to bring in new men, and a new approach to permit the environment for new life. What made the difference between the company as it is today and what might have been was the courage that young man had. He brought in experienced talent—Breech and his group—and he brought in young talent in us. Call it luck, call it intelligence, he had it. Ernest R. Breech gave effective operational and inspirational leadership to phase those two groups together with the old Ford group that stayed on, so that three teams worked as one team. But it was Henry who brought us together in the first place."

10

WHILE THE gnarled old trunk of a company was putting forth new shoots in the form of personnel, organization, plants, and equipment, it still had to produce hardware. All automotive companies, in the immediate postwar years, had brought out up- dated versions of the 1942 models. Ford planned a smashing new model for 1948. Breech decided that the model on the drawing board would be too big, heavy, and expensive to com- pete in the low-priced field, and it was brought out instead as a Mercury. But that left Ford with the tired old 1942 model.

On the morning of September 4, 1947, while driving to the office, Breech received the inspiration to start afresh. He recom- mended to the policy committee that morning that they waste no more time or money phonying up the old Ford, but begin a crash program, immediately, from scratch. Not completely satisfied with the design of Eugene Gregorie, the Ford stylist, he took Henry, Jack Davis, and Harold Youngren of engineering over to visit George W. Walker, a free-lance designer. As the four men discussed their ideas for the new car, Walker started sketching it. His design was accepted, and Gregorie quit in a huff.

With a spirit of teamwork that would have made Edsel Ford glow, the factory brought the new car out in record time. During the period from drawing board to metal reality, young Henry must have been overwhelmed by the high-powered executives Breech had brought in. Even the second and third echelon people who had left GM for a future with Ford were older and more experienced than the young president. But when the car came out, Henry Ford was in his element. Jack Davis, who was entrusted with introducing the car, was delighted with Henry's creative pictorial sense. He was particularly good at suggesting and selecting photographic angles to bring out the best features of the new car.

Though the 1949 Ford was a tribute to the production and organizational genius of Breech and his top-flight associates, the presentation of the automobile demonstrated the direction Henry Ford II was bringing to the product. The car was introduced in the gold-and-white ballroom of the Waldorf-Astoria. Champagne flowed. Orchestras played. Hundreds of thousands of people inspected the first truly postwar beauty.

Davis had to fight off would-be dealers; there were 25 applicants for every opening. Though Davis later said the car had 8000 bugs in it, a hyperbolic comment taken mistakenly as serious criticism, he knew he could sell that car. It was sleek with elegant simplicity and a minimum of gingerbread and chrome. It was long and low for its time, and no running boards marred its lines.

Promotional and advertising photographs showed the new Ford at a country club or in the driveway of a stately mansion. Henry I had brought out a car for the masses; the 1949 Ford established Henry II as the producer of the classless car. Anybody could drive it; you could even be rich.

In 1949, the company's total sales, including the new Lincoln and Mercury models, passed the million mark. Plymouth was definitely put back into third place, and though Chevrolet felt no hot breath on its rear windows, it heard footsteps. Despite the heavily augmented payrolls and vast capital improvements in the works, Ford Motor Company showed a profit of $177 million.

During the Korean War, for which the factory furnished large amounts of materiel, Ford continued to grow. Organization had brought order; every man on the organization chart knew what he was supposed to do and who would see to it that he did it. Breech was particularly proud of the engineering department, whose personnel quadrupled and whose budget was increased by a factor of nine. Del Harder, who had coined the word automation, automated manufacturing. Defining it as the use of machines to run machines, Peter Drucker compared the automation installed under Henry Ford II to the assembly line developed by his grandfather. The 1952 model Ford, second generation of the '49 with the 8000 bugs removed, gained on Chevrolet, and the 1954 model either outsold it or came mighty close, depending on whose figures you believe.

The Gold Dust Twins, Ernie and Henry, were elated with their progress. But there was still some sludge in their engine. After 15 years, Mercury was selling only about one out of every 150 cars manufactured in the country. As a car owner's income increased to, say, $5000 in the mid Fifties, he began dreaming of trading up to a more expensive car. That car was more often than not a BOP—Buick, Oldsmobile, Pontiac. "We're growing customers for General Motors," Lewis Crusoe, head of the new Ford Division, said.

In January of 1952, Henry Ford II appointed Jack Davis head of a committee composed of several top executives to make a full study on how to get more of the middle-priced market. The directive setting up the committee hinted strongly at a new car with a new name and a new dealer organization. The Davis committee produced a six-volume report, known as the Davis book, which clearly reflected Davis's personal experiences along this line, as with the Zephyr, Edsel Ford's attempt to break into the medium-priced market, and his observation of General Motors flops like the Marquette, Viking, and La Salle.

His recommendation was modest indeed in the light of what was later adopted. He recommended a new car that would be a little bigger than Ford to compete with Pontiac, and another version of the same name which would be a little smaller than Lincoln to compete with Buick.

The company at the time had only two body shells, that for Ford and Mercury which covered more than 97 per cent of all models, and the Lincoln which took care of the rest. Davis would continue using these shells for the new car, with interchangeability of parts, and would peddle it primarily through existing dealers, though a few would be set up in large communities to handle the new car exclusively. Purely for convenience in referring to it, he called it the E car, in which E stood for experimental.

But the top echelon did not buy the Davis book. Henry and Ernie were big and they wanted to get bigger. One indication was the creation of a more prestigious title for Breech; in 1955 he became chairman of the board. H. F. II remained president and chief executive officer. It took two men to fill Breech's shoes as executive vice president: Harder for manufacturing and Crusoe for cars and trucks. Both rode clouds to work.

Crusoe, as head of the Ford Division, had not only pushed Ford automobiles to their highest penetration point, but had, as a kind of sideline, brought out a surprisingly successful new car. Designed merely as a competitor to the Chevrolet Corvette, the two-seater Thunderbird suddenly became the In car of 1954. It had pizazz with a capital P.

With the stubbornness of a drunk looking for trouble until he finds it, Henry and Ernie set up the Product Planning Committee on top of the Davis committee and named Crusoe chairman. About this time, early in 1955, Jack Reith returned from so excellent a performance in France that Crusoe gave him the ball. Reith ran with it. He drew up a far more ambitious plan and presented it in a masterpiece of exposition.

Reith pointed out that in the price range between Mercury and Lincoln, Ford had nothing. In that Ford vacuum GM offered two cars, the big Oldsmobile and Buick, and Chrysler the De-Soto and small Chrysler. In effect he proposed an increase to three body shells with a total of seven products. From the top down, there would be the Lincoln, a big new Mercury, an almost as big new E car, the standard Mercury, a smaller edition of the E car, the new Ford Fairlane, and the standard Ford.

Incidentally, in fairness to the planners of both committees and in answer to those who criticize Ford for not bringing out a compact car at that time, I should point out that the company had been making exhaustive studies of the potential of a light car all along and had even designed one. But from the pragmatic standpoint at that point in time—that's the way they talk at Ford's—the American people just didn't want an economical small car. Remember the Henry J, the Willys, the Hudson Jet, the small Nash? Only the Nash ever got anywhere, under the name of Rambler American. Dealers couldn't give the economical Ford Mainline away, and it was discontinued. As for the small foreign cars, in the early and mid-Fifties they were curiosities.

Reith's program called for an entire new dealer organization to sell the E car, but the car itself was to be only part of a comprehensive package involving a major reorganization of the company. Reith did not spring his program on the board of directors without warning that April 15, 1955. Nobody with any sense would have thrown a program of this magnitude before a board without softening up its members first, and Reith had plenty of sense. He planned his pitch, discussed it, and organized his forces long before the meeting. He was tireless, enthusiastic, and almost hypnotic and he had Crusoe behind him.

When the proposal was brought before the board, it was adopted unanimously. Henry Ford II was present, and he voted for it. McNamara was also present.

As for Ernie Breech, the chairman, he has since maintained that he was the only person in the room opposed to the car, but that he yielded to the majority. Several executives with whom I've discussed the ensuing fiasco maintained that Breech could have prevented it if he had strongly disapproved it, but they said so off the record. Not Jack Davis, who doesn't know how to speak anonymously.

"You may think that the Edsel is a dead issue," he told me, chuckling, "but it's no dead issue as far as a fellow like Ernie is concerned. He's got to prove to the world that he can't be blamed for the Edsel. The truth is that he was the one man who could have stopped it. The Edsel was Reith's baby. He worked it up and made a presentation for it—for Crusoe, he was working for Crusoe—at the board meeting. I wasn't there, I had just had a coronary. But I'd headed the committee to consider and make a separate recommendation on the Edsel, and the Davis committee recommended against it. Further, I'd shown Breech a copy of my report before the meeting and he had agreed with me. I asked Ernie later, 'Why did you go along, Ernie? You had my report, you said you were against it.' And Ernie just shrugged and said something about not rocking the boat. He was chairman of the board. He could have stopped it. He could have put sand on the track. He may be kidding himself, but he's not kidding me. Further, I believe if Breech had opposed it, Henry would probably have gone along with him. Breech was chairman of the administrative committee and Henry listened to him."

The decision was made. The Special Products Division was set up to produce the new car. Several top executives were shuffled around in the reorganization. The wheels started to turn. The E car was underway, with the full force of the Ford Motor Company behind it. Thousands of details had to be determined, including such major criteria as who would buy it, what it should look like and what special features it should have before it could be designed, engineered, produced, advertised, and sold. Exhaustive research studies were made.

Just one, but one of the most interesting, concerned the name. At the beginning, as a matter of routine deference, the three Ford brothers were asked if they wanted the car to be named Edsel. Henry and Bill demurred politely, Benson forcefully. "Over my dead body!" he said. Benson knew that Edsel Ford had never particularly liked his own name. After naming his first son Henry, he and his wife named their second Edsel, Jr., but three months later they changed it. The name Benson was probably chosen with a sense of desperation; its bearer isn't quite sure where it came from.

But if not Edsel, then what would the new car's name be? Someone got the brilliant idea that for a poetic name one should go to a poet, and Marianne Moore was asked to make a few suggestions. She entered into the spirit of the thing with zest, and came up with several beauties. The one I like best was Andante con Moto. Get it?

But this was too serious a matter to be entrusted to one female poet. Other nomenclature nominees prepared lists totaling some 18,000 names. Special research teams went out to test them on the public. If you were one of the lucky thousands to be consulted, you were asked not only how each name struck you, but also what it reminded you of. In addition, you were asked for a word meaning the opposite.

Another way of testing names was to get a group of people together in a darkened room and flash selections on a screen. Gayle Warnock, in charge of publicizing the new car, remembers participating in such a screening.

"It was deathly serious," he said. "We sat there motionless and soundless in the dark, staring at the screen. We were all so intense that when the name Buick was flashed there wasn't a murmur in the whole group."

The advertising agency selected to handle the new car, Foote, Cone and Belding, which had compiled the original list of names, eliminated twelve thousand of them. Now it became a question of time, for although the car was still two years away, the dies that would stamp out the parts for it would have to bear the name. The agency assigned its New York and Chicago offices, working independently, to a crash weekend program to eliminate 5990 more. Each office was to come up with a list of ten names. As an added inducement, the employee who chose the winner would be given a new car. Names of members of the Ford family were specifically excluded. Of the two lists submitted by each office four names were the same: Pacer, Ranger, Corsair, and Citation. Warnock says that Citation had the inside track.

The names were proudly presented to the executive committee in early 1956. It so happened that the three Ford brothers were all out of town—Henry was vacationing in Nassau. Breech looked at the four names and said he didn't like any of them. He skimmed over some of the rejected suggestions, saw the name Edsel, and said, "Let's call it that." He called Henry in Nassau to tell him the committee's decision. Henry, though somewhat taken aback, agreed to go along with the choice of the committee, and undertook the job of talking Benson and Bill into accepting it. The four rejected names became the designations for the four models produced.

As to whether the Edsel was really a good car or not, you can get any answer you want. It contained such newfangled gadgets as push buttons mounted on the steering wheel for shifting gears, and the two big models contained the most powerful engine on the road—345 hp. To most people today the Edsel's most distinctive feature was the nose grille, which has been described variously as a toilet seat, a man sucking a lemon, or a sex symbol. George Walker, then vice president of styling, said it should have been named Ethel instead of Edsel. It must not have been too bad from the automobile stylist's viewpoint, however, for at least one repeated a modification of it ten years later. From a distance I have trouble telling the '57 Edsel and '68–'69 Pontiac apart.

The projected sales figure for the Edsel was a minimum of 200,000 the first year. Two years and some two months later, a little more than half that number had been sold. It was a period of recession; all auto sales were off. Estimates of how much the Edsel cost the Ford Motor Company range from $200 million on up to a third of a billion. In 1958, dividends were reduced from $2.40 per share to $2.00 and the stock fell 20 points. Still, nobody got fired. Henry Ford II could hardly fire himself, and Breech was on record as qualifying his vote, however mildly. Warnock did leave the company, but returned. Later Ted Mecke assigned him to beat the drums for the Cougar, a sure thing. "This way you can bat .500," Mecke told him.

Though the Edsel has almost entered the language as a symbol for corporate failure, it does not hold the record. General Dynamics lost $425 million on one airplane. Anyway, it was far from a crushing blow. Ford came back.

So, for that matter, did the Edsel. It's now a collector's item worth more than its original cost. Some collectors have several, and others keep a spare to cannibalize for otherwise unobtainable parts. There are Edsel clubs. Ten years after its discontinuance in November, 1959, there were more than 43,000 Edsels still registered in the United States.

11

I MENTIONED REITH'S *succès d'estime* in France as one of the many factors involved in the Edsel episode. Henry Ford II seems to have a weak spot for the international operations of the company, especially in the United Kingdom and Europe. He would have liked to have devoted more attention to revitalizing the company's operations abroad during his first hectic years as president. His first visit to Europe after the war was in early 1948 when he inspected the operations in Britain, Germany, and France.

The company was in sorry shape, but then so was everything in those postwar years. John S. Andrews, who retired in 1969 as chairman of the board and president of Ford of Europe, was with Henry on some of his early European visitations. Andrews, a tall, slender, soft-voiced and thoughtful man, stopped by my table at the Dearborn Inn one night to say a few words, and got carried away talking about Mister Ford's interest in Europe. Ford saw the poverty and hunger of war-torn Europe and revealed his sorrow and sympathy to Andrews. Improving the welfare of the people was a strong factor in Henry Ford's desire to get the company's European activities in full operation again.

"No other American industrialist places such emphasis on activities abroad as Mister Ford," Andrews said earnestly. "He sees not only the business potential in the emerging nations, but the need to furnish opportunity for their people."

Ford is comfortable in Europe. Like his grandfather, he appreciates the industriousness of the German people, but he also likes the ambience of France, particularly in Provence. He has a high respect for European scientific and technological advances, as evidenced by his importation of the Austrian method of steel production and the English Pilkington glass process. He has commented favorably on the revolutionary new Wankle engine, and told me of his admiration for European-built automobiles.

One of his happier periods was his term as alternate delegate to the United Nations in 1953. "I watched him become an internationalist," Forrest D. Murden, Jr., a career member of the delegation, said. "When he first came in I was predisposed to consider him just another prominent capitalist who might prove onerous. Anyway, I was busy. After he had been there for four days he came in like an ingratiating puppy asking if there was anything he could do and I told him to go away. 'I'll get around to you later,' was actually what I said. But as time went on he became knowledgeable about the operation and made an excellent delegate. All the guards called him Henry, so did the switchboard operator, and most of the secretaries. I think he liked it, being accepted as a person, not a Ford. He became aware of the problems of the world, and the American role in helping to solve them, particularly the role of American capitalists, entrepreneurs, industrialists.

"I'd intended to return to the faculty at Columbia University but Henry asked me to serve as liaison between the company and its *pro bono publico* operations. In Detroit he was a different man. The shield was up, all those layers of insulation. I could understand the necessity, but I regretted them. Of all the people I've worked with, I've never had the personal rapport with anyone that I've had with Henry. I have found him to be warmer than anyone I know. I've never known him to do a mean, thoughtless thing. But he so rarely has a chance to be himself. The UN was a different world to him, one he could relax in. Everyone was used to celebrities—we bumped against them in the hall every day—and dedicated to a higher ideal. Nobody wanted a thing from Henry Ford. He could let people call him Henry and enjoy it. When I was with him at the company, traveling abroad was the same thing. In Dearborn he had to be the unapproachable Mister Ford. In Europe he could be Henry."

In his first trip to his dominions in 1948, Henry could do little more than dream of Ford's future overseas. The Marshall Plan which helped put Europe back on its feet was still being debated in Congress. His first stop was England. The Ford plants had continued operations during the war, chiefly manufacturing tractors, but organization was in a frightful state. He brought Ernie Breech back with him later that year to help straighten things out.

In Germany the Cologne plant was in fair shape but the morale of the people was pitiful. Even in the rubble, however, he demonstrated his confidence in the future: he tried to buy Volkswagen. Ferdinand Porsche, who founded Volkswagen, had visited the Ford plant years before to study American mass production of automobiles and had installed American methods in the Volkswagen plant. Porsche was still being held by the French when Ford made his first postwar trip to Germany, and Heinz Nordhoff had just taken over the battered buildings. There was little reason at the time for anyone to believe that Volkswagen could become successful in Germany, much less in the world. Yet Henry Ford II had the foresight to set up a meeting with Nordhoff at the Frankfort Airport. Nordhoff had no authority; he was virtually an employee of the British government, which occupied the sector of Germany in which the plant was located. Ford visited the British general in charge of the occupied zone, but there was no way to pry Volkswagen loose from British control. He offered Nordhoff a job with Ford, but Nordhoff had dreams of his own and they paid off. All Ford could do in Germany was to get plans underway for the future.

France was the biggest mess of all. The plant, at Poissy, had suffered little war damage, but it reflected the condition of the country as a whole. The bitterness between the collaborationists and the resistance movement still persisted. The company was up to its *oreilles* in debt. It still owed money borrowed before the war, and immediately after the war it had sold debentures in order to buy new equipment. All Henry could do on his first trip was to throw in some more good money after bad, but that wasn't enough; the company borrowed $9 million more from banks. The next year its only real asset, its president, resigned, and François Lehideux, the bankers' choice, replaced him. Lehideux's experience was in running a department store; his only connection with the automobile industry was his wife, née Renault. Breech and Ford met with the bankers in a long session with a Ford executive interpreting. The bankers, thinking themselves secure behind the linguistic screen, made some pretty snide comments about both the company and Ford himself. Midway through the conference, according to Breech, Ford suddenly dispensed with the interpreter and took over in French, enjoying the pleasure of seeing some red faces across the table.

The bankers agreed to the Ford solution: Lehideux would

continue with an impressive office and salary to save face, but an American management expert would be brought over to run the show. Breech put in a call to Crusoe in Dearborn, and Crusoe recommended Jack Reith. Breech told him to put Reith on a plane and get him to Paris by Saturday or Sunday. "It's only Wednesday today."

Reith found that in addition to all his other problems, he had Lehideux to contend with. Apparently the face-saving program had not placated the Frenchman, because he put mysterious obstacles in the way of a work permit for Reith. His timing was poor, for Ford and Breech were no longer interested in playing games. They threatened to call a special meeting of their shareholders, throw Lehideux out on his *derrière,* and elect Reith chairman of the board immediately. The work permit came through, but it was too late for Lehideux to sew up the cut he had made in his own throat. Reith maneuvered him out, and himself in.

With Ford technical experts flying back and forth across the Atlantic to assist him, the new chairman immediately started improving the company. The French Ford, called the Vedette, though larger than its largest competitors, Renault and Simca, was a good car. The new expertise in production and cost controls started Ford of France back toward recovery. In 1953 the company enjoyed a swing from the loss of $3 million the year before to a profit of $1 million.

That set the stage for the second act. Ford production in Britain and Germany was now coming along strong, and so Henry Ford saw that if he could get his name back from the French company, he could import cars built in England and Germany into France cheaper than he could make them there. Reith set up an appointment with the executives of Simca (Société Industrielle de Mécanique et Carrosserie) and demonstrated the pilot of a new model Vedette. It would obviously be an excellent addition to the Simca line. As a clincher, Reith produced a clay model purporting to represent an equally attractive but smaller car which would compete directly with the existing Simca. A merger was soon consummated. For 15 per cent of its stock, Simca took over Ford of France's plants and both Vedettes, real and dummy. Henry Ford II got his name back, and set up a new wholly owned company to market Ford products in France. He later sold his 15 per cent interest in Simca to Chrysler.

Reith's job was done and he was ordered back to the States. The French gave him the Legion of Honor and pleaded with Ford to permit him to remain in France to perform more miracles with Simca. Instead, however, he walked across the ocean to sell the Edsel.

In England an equally complex situation existed. Ford Motor Company, Limited, the English concern, had grown out of the long friendship of Henry the Elder with Percival Lea Dewhurst Perry, First Baron Perry, who in 1904 had paid 50 pounds for a five-year franchise to sell Ford cars in all of Europe. For reasons which had seemed good at the time, the English company, in which the parent company owned 60 per cent, in turn owned a controlling interest in the Ford companies of Italy, Egypt, Spain, Holland, and Denmark. Ford of Denmark owned 60 per cent of Ford of Sweden, which in turn owned 48 per cent of the Finnish company. The English company had also sold rights and patents all over Europe.

The organization was bad but the production was good. Ford held undisputed first place in England. The British government in the postwar years desperately needed exports in order to get outside money, and enabled the Ford plants to obtain equipment and raw materials. In addition to developing a highly successful diesel-powered tractor, the English factories produced the Anglia and Prefect and the ridiculously small but ridiculously cheap Popular, and later added the new Consul and Zephyr. (Years later, the leading model was the Cortina.)

Operating within so diffuse a system would be difficult at

best; under the firm new Breech method, it was hopeless. There could be no coordination between all of these companies and Dearborn; the developing managerial direction, so badly needed in Europe, was practically unavailable. The British would have been happy to exchange their ownership in these floundering operations for Dearborn expertise, but under the rigid postwar governmental regulations the swap seemed impossible to accomplish. God knows how many man-years and transatlantic passenger-miles it took to work it out, but eventually the exchange was made. Ford of England had built up a large surplus, but had been unable to pay it out in dividends because of governmental restrictions. In a procedure the British called a scheme of arrangement, the English company declared a large dividend of some 7 million pounds. The American company, which couldn't take the money out of the country anyway, simply gave it back to Ford of England in exchange for all the ancillary Ford companies. The other stockholders, who couldn't receive the money in cash either, were paid off in preferred shares. Now Ford in America could make some sense out of Ford in Europe.

Ford of Italy was reduced to a distribution operation, since governmental restrictions made it impossible to compete with Fiat in manufacturing. In Spain, *El Caudillo* said manufacturing *sí,* assembly *no,* and he was left with neither.

The result of the reshuffling was an eminently workable system of communication and control with all the English and European companies. Even the merger of two of the largest British companies, Austin and Morris, into the British Motors Corporation failed to impede the increasing prosperity of Ford in England. One reason was that the company returned a high percentage of its earnings to capital investment. Another was the insistence on quality. Although Ford products, with the exception of the Popular, made no effort to compete with other brands in price, they offered solid value which both the British, and their customers all over the world, appreciated.

Henry Ford II himself, incidentally, though fond of the English people, is pretty critical of their products—non-Ford products, that is. We were talking about his personal preference for European cars and, because I happen to have one myself, I asked him what he thought of English cars in general.

"Well," he said, "the English sometimes turn out a substandard product. They just don't seem to give a damn. I don't know whether it's because of the government's attitude—the emphasis on socialism—or whether it's the attitude of the people themselves, but anyway the workmen turn out these shoddy little cars that won't stand up."

"I've got an MG 1100," I said mildly. "You know, that's the little sedan. . . ."

"It's got a top on it like a box," he said. "Americans want a more graceful, more flowing line. Sure, it's practical and functional, but you'd go broke trying to sell it in this country. They had an engineering genius in there who was only interested in getting his ideas across. He couldn't care less about following them through."

"Well," I said, trying to defend my baby, "it's got that crosswise engine in it and front wheel drive which seems to me pretty efficient. There's a lot more room in the back seat of this little car than there is in my American car."

"The American people who buy the cars I manufacture don't want things like that," he said. "They want beauty and style and power, and they pay for it."

The truth of the matter is that he was right about my car in some particulars, although I'd be damned if I'd tell him so.

Ford let himself in for some intense criticism in 1961 when, after Breech had departed, he bought the entire English company, lock, stock, and the 45 per cent minority interest. President Eisenhower, during whose administration negotiations began and whom Ford had supported, was pleading for restraint in spending abroad because of the gold shortage in the United

States, but Ford went ahead anyway. Representatives of both American and British government and press crawled all over him. He didn't have to explain his actions, for it's pretty obvious to everyone that Henry Ford II wants to control everything that has his name on it, but he did admit that it was inopportune timing.

Contrary to some reports, the government never requested him to cancel the deal. "Secretary of the Treasury Anderson was a gem about the whole thing," he said. "He just wanted to know what we were doing, and we kept him fully informed." As for the gold flow, he could well justify the expenditure of some $368 million abroad by pointing out that his expenditures abroad came out of earnings abroad, and that in the decade before the time of purchase the company's gold flow had brought almost $2 billion more into the United States than it had sent out.

The deal paid off in both the United States and Britain. Ford became the leading American automotive firm in retail sales overseas and for years English-made Ford products brought in the largest supply of revenues to Britain.

The fortunes of the German operations have not been so heady, but at least the situation there bore out the astute foresight of the 30-year-old who tried to get Volkswagen when the rest of the world was laughing at it; Volkswagen, until its decline in the late Sixties, was hard to beat on its home field. The Ford-made Taunus, a bigger and more expensive German car, nevertheless sold well and made money. Two new models, the Escort and the Mustanglike Capri, manufactured in both Germany and England, were introduced in 1968 and 1969 respectively. A new car, the tiny Corcel, was also introduced in Brazil.

When the chips are down Henry Ford II doesn't bluff; he calls. In early 1966, the Palestine Automobile Corporation, Ltd., and the Ford Motor Company began negotiations that would lead to the assembly of trucks and tractors in Israel. The corporation had been distributing Ford products in Israel for 30 years. It had headquarters in Tel Aviv and some of its dozen branches and dealers are located in familiar sounding towns—Jerusalem, Beersheba, Nazareth. The corporation had doubled its sales in the last few years, was now selling 25,000 vehicles annually, and the demand was rising. Assembling vehicles locally, from parts manufactured in the U. S., Germany, and England, had proved to be good business in similar operations in Morocco, Pakistan, Turkey, Thailand, and the Philippines.

Helping ambitious people of all nations expand and prosper has long been the policy of the Ford Motor Company, and the Israelis were not excluded. Ford sent off a letter of intent to enable the Palestine Automobile Corporation people to proceed with their plans.

News of the forthcoming operation was not so happily received by the Arab League. Although there were prosperous dealers selling Ford products in Lebanon, Syria, Jordan, Iraq, Yemen, Saudi Arabia, and the United Arab Republic, and enjoying full cooperation with the parent company, the Arab League threatened to boycott all Ford products if the company went through with the Israeli deal. Henry Ford told his close personal friend Max Fisher, "Nobody's gonna tell me what to do." The arrangement with the Palestine corporation stood.

The Arabs did not back down either, and the boycott went into effect. I've been told that this was smart public relations on the part of the company, a dramatic gesture in its continuing effort to counteract the anti-Semitism that perished with its founder. But Mister Ford relegated his personal feeling to a minor part of the decision.

"It was just pragmatic business procedure," he told me. "I don't mind saying I was influenced in part by the fact that the company still suffers from a resentment against the anti-Semitism of the distant past. We want to overcome that. But the main thing is that here we had a dealer who wanted to open up an agency to sell our products—hell, let him do it."

When Henry Ford II took over the company he inherited a peculiar situation with Ford of Canada. The parent company owned only about 40 per cent of the voting stock. The traditional peaceful coexistence of the United States and Canada was also found in their two Ford Motor Companies. The sixth Ford car ever built was sold in Toronto, and Ford of Canada was established less than a year after the parent company. One of Canada's first cars was sent to India, and it was through Ford of Canada that the car penetrated into the furthermost reaches of the British Empire. Ford of Canada was actually the biggest automobile concern in the entire British Commonwealth, including the United Kingdom. In the Fifties, Ford of Canada went through the dichotomous process of becoming both more Canadian and more American. It moved its headquarters from Windsor, across the river from Detroit, to Oakville, near Toronto, thus taking on a more Canadian atmosphere. But it also increasingly adopted the management technique pioneered south of the border.

Ford of Canada was the total owner of subsidiaries in India, Australia, New Zealand, Malaysia, Rhodesia and South Africa. In the austere period in the British Commonwealth following the war, Ford of Canada and Ford of England were in competition with each other, for the shortage of dollars made it less difficult for a customer in the sterling area to buy an English-made Ford. But through the Fifties the Ford penetration in the areas served by Ford of Canada increased. One exception was India, where the new independent government, as in Spain, insisted that automobiles be manufactured there. In 1945, the company placed the Indian operation in voluntary liquidation, which is corporationese for saying the hell with it. The Rhodesian operation was sold sometime later.

The Australian subsidiary of Ford of Canada had better

than 15 per cent of the entire automobile market in the Fifties, then slumped. New Zealand had its own separate company, as did Singapore and South Africa. If, by the way, you bought a sharp new Ford Fairlane in South Africa in 1969, you bought a car that was made in Australia under direct organizational line from Toronto and designed and engineered in Dearborn. If you happened to buy a gleaming product of the brand new assembly plant in the Philippines, it too came down the organizational chart from Ford of Canada.

Mister Ford's internationalists in the company are so enthusiastically voluble I came away from conversations with them feeling like a sparrow caught in a badminton game. For a more objective explanation of what Henry Ford II and his operations mean to the world, I'll use the words of someone outside the company. Nathan Cummings, chairman of the big conglomerate Consolidated Foods and 21 years older than Ford, has no motive other than friendship.

"Henry's dedicated to his business," Cummings said. "He lives it, breathes it, sleeps it. He works like the devil. All this drive has a direct influence on the entire world. In some countries Ford is the major factor in the national economy. Through the high standard of living Henry sets for his own employees he improves living conditions in every country he does business in. He doesn't chisel. He's no crusader, just a clear thinker. By paying good salaries, supplying better transportation, he's elevating the standard of living all over the world. He's also increasing the customer potential for his own products—don't forget that. But he's creating new customers for *my* products, too, for everybody's products."

Having a completely self-sufficient operation across the border provided an irresistibly titillating opportunity for the Ford publicity people during 1968.

Concern over the increasing sales of small foreign cars in North America has been building up for years. A 1968 *Wash-*

ington Post headline over an automotive story described the situation neatly: SMALL CARS GIVE DETROIT BIG HEAD-ACHE. Volkswagen, of course, was leading the import parade, with GM's German-made Opel a poor second, but the two Japanese leaders, Toyota and Datsun, were suddenly beginning to appear like mosquitoes at twilight, especially on the West Coast.

The Japanese cars in particular bugged Henry Ford II, not because they were biting him so much as because he couldn't bite back. Ford has gone out on a limb publicly in favor of free trade and against restrictive tariffs even for the foreign cars that compete against him in this country. In his personal conversations with me he reflected the same attitude. Sure, he'd like to have as customers some of the almost half a million Americans who bought Volkswagens in 1968, but he wasn't bitter about it for a very good reason: he was doing okay in Germany with the Ford and Capri. They were bigger cars, with a higher profit potential. As a matter of fact, Ford almost built the German Ford right here in America, under another name. For several years, the factory spent a lot of money on its prototype—its working title was Cardinal—for home consumption.

"We just finally decided," Ford told me, "that we couldn't manufacture a subcompact car in this country. We considered all the problems of tooling and manufacturing it and the inter-changeability of parts and putting it on the highway, and I just didn't think the people would buy it."

"Do you still think you were right?" I asked.

He glared at me over his teacup and his half glasses and said, "You're damn right I still think I'm right. At first it was a lousy car. We brought a few hundred over here and had too many troubles with them. They worked out all the bugs over in Germany, and it's a good sturdy car and it's doing damn well. But we still don't intend to bring it over to this country. We do bring the Cortina over from England, and we sell quite a few of them, but that's another matter. There are a lot of reasons why we can bring the Cortina in."

"Well, what about the Japanese imports? Do they bother you?"

"They sure as hell do. They're turning out mighty good cars and I don't like the way they're cutting into the American market. I haven't got anything against open competition. If they can build a better car and sell it for less money, let 'em do it. But what burns me up is that I can't go into Japan. We can't build, we can't sell, we can't service, we can't do a damn thing over there. Ford Motor Company still owns land in Japan, and we still have a building there that was put up before the war. I understand it leaks like a sieve but it's still there, built with our money, and we can't use it. I'd be in there tomorrow if the Japanese would let me. I'd be manufacturing cars and I'd give the Japanese a run for their money. But they won't let me in and that's why the whole thing is unfair. I think this country ought to have the guts to stand up to unfair competition. The Australians had the guts to do something about it. Why can't we?"

Mister Ford has been just as vociferous in public in his declared war with the Japanese as he was with me in private. Before a whole roomful of reporters in the 1968 year-end press conference, he let go with another salvo, this one reported around the world. "One of the big problems we have in the automotive industry in the United States is a problem with the Japanese," he said. "I think the Japanese are playing it kind of stupid on a worldwide basis, because they are going to trigger protectionism in the United States if they keep acting the way they're acting."

I had the feeling that he was almost as angry about the Japanese giving American protectionists ammunition as he was about the direct competition of the Toyota and Datsun.

Henry Ford II projects his prejudice against tariffs beyond

242

the American coastline to the emerging nations. He believes that reducing artificial trade barriers is a means of expanding their growth. Some of his own people have advised him against expounding his views in public, but they might as well shout their protests to the earmuffed workers in the stamping plant. Although few people in public life, much less industrialists and automobile manufacturers, would have said it publicly even if they believed it, Ford delivered a speech on free trade. His only qualification was to give his speech writers a hard time in preparing it; if he was going to say it, he wanted to say it well. His message was that free trade is good for the whole world, but another, unsaid, message that I get loud and clear is that Mister Ford is a pretty self-confident individual. He doesn't want protection. He and his products can take care of themselves, thank you.

I came away from the visit in which we discussed small cars with the definite impression that he had no intention either of building a small car in the United States or importing another one from overseas. But in the fall and winter of 1968, rumors began coming out of Detroit to the effect that Ford was going to bring out a small car; the reporters on the automotive beat even gave it a name, Delta. I went back to Mister Ford to find out what gives. I was assured that what he had told me was absolutely correct, and to stop being a worry wart. At his annual year-end press conference in December, 1968, the chairman announced that the company would introduce, in the spring of 1969, a new car called Maverick to compete with the imports. It is not a subcompact, a replacement for the compact Falcon, and the first models were made not in the U.S., but in Canada. A true subcompact was scheduled for 1971.

As for all the printed rumors on the new product emanating from Detroit during the year, the Ford publicity boys had enjoyed them immensely. There's nothing like a good rumor to get car *aficionados* talking. I won't say that the rumors were exactly planted, but there sure was a conspicuous lack of desire to clear up the confusion. "We love curiosity," one of the PR men said. "The more confusion, the more questions people ask. Then newspaper editors feel they have to answer the questions whether they know the answers or not, which leads to more confusion, which leads to more talk."

Remembering all the fuss about the selection of names which were never used for the Edsel, I asked the question around the factory: Why Maverick? Apparently its choice involved far less of a production than the choice of the names Citation, Corsair, Pacer and Ranger, but much more of one than the arbitrary selection of the name Edsel. Maverick grew out of Mustang, and Mustang was the result of the desire for an epithet signifying raw, untamed horsepower and a fun car.

The name Mustang had been kicking around the factory before the first pencil line was on the drawing boards. (As a matter of fact, two experimental cars called Mustang I and Mustang II had been built and demonstrated.) Just in case some better name might be lurking in the dictionary, however, J. Walter Thompson, the advertising agency assigned to the new product, had a list of 6000 words selected. Later models, Bronco, Torino, Cougar, all took their names from the list. Lee Iacocca's favorite was Torino. At this writing, the prime choice of Henry Ford II has still not found a grille to call home. He wanted to call the Mustang T-Bird II.

After Mustang, Maverick was easy. What else has a 100 per cent American, western ring and begins with M? Once Detroit latches onto a good thing it hangs onto it. It was no coincidence that the Maverick was introduced on April 17, the same day of the year the Mustang came out.

I think it's a little interesting that the company would follow up a successful car named after a horse with another named after a cow, but other than that Maverick is a strikingly appropriate name for any Ford product, including the two named

Henry. To refresh your Texas history, an early settler named Samuel Augustus Maverick accepted a herd of four hundred cattle from another settler who owed him $1200. As anybody who has ever seen a cowboy movie knows, cows in those days roamed the open range and were identified at round-up time by the brand of the owner. Maverick, however, didn't like the idea of sticking red hot iron on calves, and refused to do it. Something like Henry the One, who used the back door for weeks to avoid disturbing mama robin's nest on the front door.

Anyway, any member of the bovine family without a brand on it became known as a maverick, and out of that came the connotation of a stubborn individualist, which sure fits both Henry Fords. Maverick, the man not the cow, had another trait in common with the grandfather. Although anybody with a rope and a hot branding iron could easily add another calf to his herd, Maverick really didn't seem to care. He wound up with no more cattle than he had started with, but he sold them for twice the amount he had paid for the original herd. In the meantime he was building up enormous personal wealth. When he died he owned huge chunks of Texas from San Antonio to the Mexican border, plus some islands in the Gulf. One of his descendants was a Congressman from Texas, Maury Maverick, who also added a word to the language. He called the jargon of the bureaucrats gobbledygook, and it stuck.

The metal Maverick of the 1970's is an odd hybrid, resembling the crossbreeding of the Falcon of the Fifties with the Mustang of the Sixties by Gene Bordinat's geneticists in the Ford design center.

A big difference between the car and the cow is that it has the brand, both corporate and personal, of Ford all over it. It has some of the rudimentary simplicities of the old man; you can replace a banged-up fender with a wrench instead of with an acetylene torch and put in a new set of spark plugs without taking a course in automotive mechanics. It has the short rear

245

deck of Edsel Ford's first classic Continental, and a slanting hood as European as Henry Ford II's sideburns and slash-pocket jacket. Gene Bordinat, however, says that it's strictly American. His word for it is sassy.

To continue this stooping to personalities, the Maverick reverts back to cost-conscious McNamara in size and economy (103-inch wheelbase and under $2000), but it also has a touch of Lee Iacocca, who likes to say that the American people want economy no matter how much it costs them. Though it was introduced with few accessories, and the idea was to push the basic, stripped model, it allowed for such extras as a larger engine, automatic transmission, and air-conditioning.

The car also indicated in a paradoxical way the inability on the part of all American manufacturers to leave things alone. The Falcon, after its smashing success pushed dividends and stock up, kept getting wider and longer and more powerful and more expensive. The Maverick just started the whole cycle all over again for, despite all the drumbeating, all it is in size is an updated Falcon. A Volkswagen it is not; it has an 8½-inch-longer wheelbase. Nor is it a Toyota. It is the North American answer to their challenge.

Mister Ford's personal preference is for raunchy cars. He has a good-humored contempt for small imports—he always refers to Pat Doyle's Volvo as "that Volkswagen." It's a little difficult for me to believe he has a gut feel for the Maverick or the even smaller car projected for the Seventies. Like the plain little '59 Falcon, they are marketing necessities. He seems to be aware of the paradoxical situation he's in, and has his own way of handling it firmly but gracefully. He takes part in styling discussions involving differences of less than an inch, no picayune matter in automobile design, and any time Mister Ford participates, he does so vociferously. Once he set forth his views forcefully and at some length on a comparatively minor matter of styling but when he finished his top executives were still adamantly opposed. The chairman of the board gave up and accepted their recommendation. Then he grinned.

"Well," he said, "I just wanted to tell you how I feel about it. I'm just one guy and I never even bought a car in my life."

One of the executives who was at the meeting, Will Scott, philosophized at some length on that comment. "Despite the fact that he does not live the life of a typical wage earner, fighting the mortgage, and trying to get the kids through school, Mister Ford has some kind of a quality, a feel and understanding of what makes people tick, and what kind of cars they like and why they like them. He has been in the forefront of sensing trends and changes in the car market. It's tough to make decisions in this business because they last a long time and they're costly. After a certain point they can't be turned around. So once you launch a major program in an automobile company, it's an awesome thing. Thousands of people get into the act and it's almost impossible to turn something around without causing a chaotic situation. Decisions have a lot riding on them and they should have, for the reward of making decisions is so great in this business. Your reward in the automobile business is simply survival. If you do things right, you don't go out of business. And that's not so bad when you stop to think about the thousands of companies that have gone down these tracks before and aren't around anymore.

"Mister Ford has a great problem in refraining from imposing his personal views on important decisions when he finds a pretty strong collection of executives who want to go the other way. He knows that by saying so, or snapping his fingers, he can make it happen the way he wants it to happen. But he endeavors to surround himself with people who have the guts to make decisions or recommendations to him. Many's the time I've seen him approve something, particularly in the styling area, that he didn't personally care for. He approved it because it was proposed to him by the people who have to sell it. More than once in this kind of situation, after expressing his own views and hearing the views of those at odds with him, he'd finally say, 'Okay, you've got to sell it. It's approved.' Then he'd turn and walk out of the room. He had it both ways. He'd refrained from imposing his own personal will on top-flight people, but he still wound up putting the monkey right back on their backs.

"I'll never forget one time we had a hell of an argument about what we call a wide wheel cut. He wanted a lot of wheel exposed, a sporty looking wheel opening, but the stylist was arguing for a narrow wheel cut. We had two meetings on that one issue. Mister Ford finally gave in. But he said, 'Well, after you get this car in production, why don't you make one just for me, with a big wheel cut in it.' That was his way of backing off, of telling his people to call the shots the way they saw them. He's a fascinating manager of people."

One of the battles that raged over the Maverick concerned the issue of a two-door model versus a four-door. The car was originally planned for a 103-inch wheelbase—eight inches less than the standard Falcon. Gene Bordinat, who as head of the design department must tiptoe along the razor edge between esthetic beauty and what will sell, and Lee Iacocca, who wants to sell cars but realizes that esthetic design has a great deal to do with the furtherance of that desire, wanted to bring the car out in a two-door model only. This design would be unique and sporty. But it would preclude the possibility of bringing out a four-door later on the same wheelbase. To keep the same lines, the same motif, a four-door, six-passenger model would have to be four inches longer. This would be tantamount to another car, which would entail another investment.

Mister Ford wanted both the two-door and the four-door built on the same wheelbase, which would of course result in a greater interchangeability of parts and a lower investment. The four-door, six-passenger model would be like the sporty two-door, only stretched out. The savings involved would run in the millions. However, they just couldn't get all this on the 103-inch wheelbase. Both cars would have to start at 107. But Bordinat and Iacocca staunchly defended the 103-inch wheelbase, which would mean a less expensive initial investment and a smaller, sportier-looking car. Finally Ford approved their concept.

But he didn't forget. At the next meeting he turned to Iacocca and said, "Lee, how long will it be before you come in and ask me for the four-door?"

Bordinat, who was telling me the story, laughed and then gave me his interpretation of that remark: "I'm used to your nickeling away at me."

"Everyone squirmed," Bordinat said, "but Lee's pretty fast on his feet, and he said, 'I can tell you when. We'll make this promise. If the two-door is not successful, it will take six months on the marketplace to determine it. And if it isn't, we will not bring in a four-door to save it. It will be beyond saving. A four-door can never save a two-door. But on the other hand, if the car is very successful, and we feel we can get further incremental volume by bringing in the four-door, we'll be back to ask you for it. But the two-door will have to be six months on the marketplace before we can determine that.'

" 'Okay,' Mister Ford said, 'I want you to make a big note of that in the record.'

"So we know exactly where we stand. We won, but there isn't going to be any hanky panky about it, no sitting back and thinking he's forgotten the deal five months from now."

Bordinat says that on the basis of his close proximity with Ford over a period of several years he knows everything the chairman likes. He can design a car that will knock Ford's eyes out—wide wheel openings because Ford likes to see wheels, for example, and the whole thing flaming red. But Ford knows he knows, and Bordinat knows that Ford knows. They kid each other about it. But they both also know that Bordinat has to design a car which will prove itself on the market.

"It's the job of design to support marketing," Bordinat has said. "That is the designer's whole reason for existence. Even if he reached unparalleled heights of beauty and created products rivaling the Mona Lisa every hour on the hour, it would serve no purpose unless his design helped to sell the product."

Elgar F. Laux, then vice president-sales, put it even more strongly. "Styling is always the number one reason for buying anything as far as automobiles are concerned. Styling is *number one*."

Henry Ford, then, invites the collective judgment of Bordinat and the men who must sell the cars—Knudsen, Iacocca, and the other top executives. "That's their responsibility," Bordinat said. "If he usurps that responsibility he can't in justice can them. That's the risk we run. We all have to stick our neck out. He has the powerful right of veto, he makes the decisions. I don't know if you've looked at the organization chart, but if you read what the functions of the chart are, all committees are recommending agents to the chairman. And that's all."

I remembered someone telling me that at another meeting Ford had cut off an objection with the flat remark, "I'm in the captain's chair." I mentioned it to Bordinat.

"You're damn right he's in the captain's chair," Bordinat agreed. "But when you posture yourself as a fellow making decisions, you join the group which makes the proposal if you agree with them on it."

"But when you're working for somebody who can make up his mind, you know where you stand."

"No question about it," Bordinat said. "And that's good. We get paid an awful lot this way. We sweat, but we get paid for it too."

Bordinat does all right. He has a showplace of a home overlooking a small lake, a seven-acre estate in Frenchmen's Cove in Jamaica, a partnership in a Polynesian restaurant across

Grand Boulevard from General Motors, two Continentals, and a wardrobe that fits his image.

Another man who has done all right fighting with Ford is Lee Iacocca, who typifies the new Ford Motor Company. J. Edward Lundy, one of the most perceptive developers of personnel in industry, paid Iacocca a supreme compliment when he said that few men since Jack Davis retired have shown such a grasp and knowledge of the company's operations. Though he has engineering degrees from Princeton and Lehigh, Iacocca came up the ladder through sales. He became head of the Ford Division in 1960. The time was as ripe for him as Gorgonzola in August, and he made the most of it. More than any other executive in the company, he represents the revolt against the sharpened pencil policies of Breech and McNamara, and the new era of high performance. It's significant, too, that he came in a couple of years after Henry Ford II had finished studying to become an executive, as Breech put it, and had become one.

Oddly enough, Iacocca was one of the few executives whom McNamara discovered in a comparatively lowly position and pushed upward. That was about all McNamara and Iacocca had in common. One had a slide-rule mind, the other a telepathic gut. McNamara hit his timing right with the Falcon, and Ford went along with him. But it was more of a logical development than the gut feel so vital to the automotive industry. People don't buy cars on a slide-rule basis. True, the Falcon, introduced in 1959, sold a record number of cars in its first year. But does this represent a positive desire on the part of the American people for unadorned economical transportation, or was it a reaction to the grotesque fins and chrome arabesques of the ponderous cars of the Fifties?

Iacocca *likes* cars. He likes to go to the races. He likes to drive cars, all kinds of cars, to see how they handle. "I drove some little foreign job home last night," he told me one day.

251

"It felt like I was on a platform between two motorcycles. I thought I'd get killed."

Iacocca saw the first clay model of the proposed first Falcon in 1956, and he was pleased with its lines, especially the Thunderbird-style roof. But the youthful appearance of that model was considered impractical by the executives of the period and a squarer superstructure was substituted for the T-bird roof line. There wasn't anything the 31-year-old junior executive could do about it. "Hell," he said later, "I could have cried."

Now that he could afford to be more critical of his predecessors, he told me bitterly: "They thought a guy buys a car purely to be able to get from here to there. They didn't understand that a guy wants to be *seen* going from here to there."

Ford wasn't supposed to do too well in 1959. The company had elected to stay with the old design. Chevrolet introduced a new model with big back fins. Even before the '59 cars came out, everybody was singing the blues. At the last minute, however, the Galaxie, top of the line, was awarded the Thunderbird roof line and engine. That year Ford was again Number One, for as car marketing manager, Iacocca leaped on the Thunderbird roof and sold it.

"It doesn't sound like much now," he said, "just a little thing, but oh, we clobbered them. It proved what I'd been saying all along. You can do something to convince people that you have a damn good car. I'd had some exposure to Mister Ford during those years, but I assume that it was that job that did it. Anyway, Mister Ford called me over at 10:20 A.M.—you never forget these things—on November 3, 1960. He said, 'We like what you are doing, but we have something else for you.' Then he said, 'How would you like to be vice president and general manager of the Ford Division?' I was flabbergasted."

"If you want to be in this business and not lose your mind,

you've got to be a little bold," Ford told him. "You're going to make some mistakes, but go ahead."

"I really think he took a hell of a gamble with a young guy," Iacocca said later. "I could have failed and embarrassed the hell out of him."

But he didn't. And he was bold. Only a couple of months later he and Ford were looking over the projected product program. It was, he told me, "pretty stodgy and every old lady in the country would love it, but the kids of America would tell us to drop dead."

He told Mister Ford that, too, and recommended that the product be recast. In the automotive business recasting a product takes three or four years and a lot of money, but he still argued for it.

"You better damn well get on with it, then," Ford said and Iacocca inaugurated his youth movement of which the Mustang has become the symbol.

The Mustang project started small. The original projection was for 180,000 cars. But Iacocca is an enthusiastic type of guy and he kept going back to Ford for more production. He got a commitment for 240,000 Mustangs at Dearborn, and then retooled the plant at San Jose, California, to raise the capacity to 360,000.

A *Newsweek* reporter finally gave him his objective. He asked Iacocca what he'd be happy with.

"What's the world's record?" Iacocca asked. They looked it up and found that the Falcon had sold 417,174 cars in its first year.

"I guess what I really want is to sell 417,175 Mustangs," Iacocca said.

He beat that number by 12,000. Furthermore, although the basic Mustang was priced at less than $2400, Iacocca talked Ford into providing more than 50 options for it. You could make it a luxury car or a hot-rod, take your choice. Most buyers took their choice. As accessories bring a high profit, the Mustang was even more successful than its record-breaking sales indicated.

Then came the Cougar. It, too, was successful, and continued what the marketing people hope will be a lasting trend in the head-to-head battle with General Motors. "This is where the Mustang did such a tremendous job for us," Gar Laux, then vice president of sales, said. "We started to win General Motors owners back. That was one of the great successes of that car—not just the numbers that were sold, but who we sold them to. I can prove it to you with the trade-ins. Cougar did it again. Fifty per cent of the trades on Cougar in '67 were GM cars. Fifty per cent! Great! That's the name of the game. The good gain we've got to take away from the competition.

"So now we have the opportunity to gain sales, hold our owners, make money. We've been kind of wishy-washy on this thing but now we've got a real strong track to run on. We've got to be dramatic, and we are. The '69 offering with the dramatic new Marquis is the first true medium-priced offering this company has ever had. People are gonna say, *I want that car*. The company's money is on the line."

Unfortunately for Laux's big dreams, the trend in '69 took in smaller cars as well as large, and the Marquis, though moderately successful, could not compare with the little Maverick as the big automotive news of the year. The first American sporty small car to buck the imports, it followed in the tradition of the Model T, the V-8, the original Continental, the postwar '49 Ford, the Mustang, and the Cougar, all of which preceded the competition by months if not years.

Ford could also offer, including its copy-cat cars like the new Marquis (BOP) and Mark III (Eldorado) a complete cross-the-board mulligatawny. Trucks, in which Ford maintained the number one position in the industry, also had the same exhausting range of something for everybody. Car sales were expected to drop in 1969 after the previous year's record, but management counted on its trucks, especially the smallest and the largest in the industry, to hold up the average.

Once I mentioned to Mister Ford that I'd just read a titillating report on an Elan. He looked blank and Ted Mecke explained that it was built by Lotus in England with a Ford motor. "Oh," Ford said, relieved. "Hell, I can't keep up with all of 'em."

The proliferation of models is so extensive that the people at the company don't even attempt to carry the full line in their heads. Walking through the lobby of the Central Office Building one day, I saw a snappy bright-red convertible and asked the executive I was with what it was. He looked at it, shrugged hopelessly, then reached in his inside coat pocket and pulled out two sheets of 8½ x 11 paper folded vertically in half: a list of the '69 line. "We all carry one of these," he said, running his finger down the list. "Hold on. That thing has got to be here somewhere." He found it: XL convertible.

Incidentally, the four-door Continental convertible was missing from the list. It was no longer available. This was sad news to me. Now it will become a collector's item and I'll never be able to afford one.

Back in the early Fifties, all Ford products were built on two body styles. Proliferation has brought about a situation so confusing that Chalmers Goyert, director of the central product planning office, has prepared a huge chart, in color, depicting the basic styles and the interchangeability within each so that Ford executives can figure out more easily what's going on. I told him it made me dizzy. "Oh," he said seriously, "if you looked at it for an hour or so it would become clear to you."

Without looking at it for an hour, I think I can give a simplified breakdown on what car is made on what frame. First of all, there are two different types of body shells, unitized and body-and-frame. There's a constant argument raging as to which is best for what. The unitized body, known as monocoque construction, holds itself together, in a sense. In the frame construction a less rigid body is put down on heavy rails. Ford uses unitized construction for its smaller cars, frame for the bigger models.

For the 1969 line unitized shells were used for the Maverick, Mustang, and Falcon-Fairlane. Body-and-frame shells were used for all other Fords (one shell) and Thunderbird. The Continental was a bastard, in a sense, as it contained less interchangeability. This makes a total of six body shells. Cougar used the Mustang shell, Montego the Falcon-Fairlane, all other Mercurys the basic Ford frame, and the Mark III the T-bird frame. Wheelbases, of course, differed within each category, as did overall lengths.

"As a rule the rear wheels stay in the same place in relationship to the passenger compartment," Goyert explained. "The front wheels can be moved back and forth easily. Let me point out that this tremendous range of shells is a critical element in profitability. The more proliferation, the more the costs go up."

Not all Fords please all people. I asked a dealer in a rural area what those funny-looking little things with wires on them were on the hood of the '69 Mustang Mach I. Keeping his voice under control, he said, "I think they call them racing-type hood latches." Then he suddenly turned purple. "Racing-type hood latches, for Christ's sake!" he shouted. "Who in the hell in this part of the country wants racing-type hood latches?" But after he simmered down he admitted that other models were getting "damn good acceptance."

My local Lincoln–Mercury dealer did a little poor mouthing at first. "We've done all right over the years," he said, "but that's because we've been in business a long time, featured service and have a steady come-back clientele. The company used to tell us the same old story over and over again—this year Mercury's bigger and better than ever. Then they'd send us something like that '58 job—oh, that was a real dog.

"I got to admit, though, that this time I believe. The Cougar was just great, and the new Marquis is a honey. I drove it to the football game the Saturday after it came out and so many people came up and asked me about it that I liked to miss the kickoff. At the District Dealers meeting there was more honest-to-God enthusiasm than I've ever seen. All these models are confusing as hell, and it's even worse with the Ford dealers—putting together one of those Mustangs would drive me crazy—but I got to admit that that's what people want. Seventy-five per cent of the cars we sell are ordered to personal specifications."

Defending the vertigo-producing variety of available automobiles, Lee Iacocca takes the offense. "It started back in 1961, when Mister Ford and I discussed the next three years in the car business. What we were going to try to do. And I must say he was a motivating force, because of his love of cars. He used to say, it's amazing, we don't have a four-speed box that's worth a damn. Well, now we do. He felt, somehow, over a period of time, we had gotten away from exciting automobiles. The Mustang proved you could have an exciting car and make money too—we made a killing with it.

"We're not going to depart from the normal four-door sedan market or the station wagon market, but I think we should have lots of different cars for lots of different people. What Ford Motor Company saw, Mister Ford saw, I saw, before anybody else saw, was the proliferation of cars that had to come because of the two- and three-car family. Everybody at first said, you guys at Ford are crazy. The industry guys said that. 'You're offering the public too much choice,' they said. But the die was cast and we didn't turn back. Back then we saw, in '65, about 13 million two-car families, and they're increasing a million a year. And I'll tell you this, a guy never buys two green two-doors. He doesn't buy any two models the same color, or the same size, big or little. What you usually see is the all-purpose family sedan that we've known for 50 years and then you see the compromise car. Like a Mustang. You can't go on a trip with eight suitcases in a bloody Mustang. Today with multiple car ownership a guy can say, well, I'll take a wagon and load the kids and the old lady and all the baggage in it when we take a trip, but then he sees a sporty Mustang, and he can still get the whole family in it to cruise out to the country club.

"We figured there was a great market for the second car and we wanted to make them exciting too. We were lucky. We didn't know that the long-hood–short-deck–low-slung top had the magic to bring in more than we thought, but we still knew there was a market there. And there's even more of a market today than there was then, and there'll be more of a market tomorrow than there is now. We know what we're doing here."

The 1968 sales figures reduce the Iacocca braggadocio to fact. It was the greatest year in Ford history. The company sold 4,744,002 cars, trucks, and tractors throughout the world, as well as other products, for a profit of $626,600,000. In the United States and Canada, the factory sold 2,669,128 cars. Whether they are the best or the worst cars in the world, I wouldn't know. I don't have one. My knowledge of Ford products involves the people who make them. I believe that Henry Ford, and Bunkie Knudsen, and Lee Iacocca, and Gene Bordinat, and all the rest believe in what they are doing, that they are driven not by terror and insecurity but by their pride in the name, their personal ambition, and their fondness for those March bonuses and stock options, to build cars that people will buy.

12

I DO OWE one obligation to Henry Ford II: I promised to repeat his opinion of Ralph Nader. I won't be starting any fight
here; it has been going on since 1965, but I don't like to
fan the flames. These two men, Nader and Ford, concern themselves with automobile safety every day. One of them has dedicated most of his life to developing an unparalleled expertise in
the field. The other has not only his own knowledge but a number of well-paid experts to advise him articulately and intelligently on the complex causes of the world's 200,000 traffic
deaths a year. I admire both of these men and would like to see
them on the same side.

Both are mavericks, both are dedicated, both have displayed extreme courage. Yet they are miles apart. Nader became
a maverick much earlier in his career than Ford did in his. The
son of a Lebanese immigrant, he was a Phi Beta Kappa at Prince-

ton and a nonconformist involved in a dozen quixotic projects. He continued them at Harvard Law School, where he got rid of his first and last automobile because he considered it unsafe at any speed.

Henry Ford II, at the age of 30, was throwing himself into the re-creation of a motor company; Nader, at that age, quit his law practice and went into automobile safety full-time on a national level as a government consultant. He resigned from that job to work without pay for Senator Abraham Ribicoff, chairman of a Senate subcommittee studying the issue, and his excellent research and presentation gave Ribicoff much of the ammunition for the hearings he conducted in 1965. In his time off from his uncompensated work Nader was working on his exposé of the automobile industry, *Unsafe at Any Speed*.

You can't help but admire a man who sacrifices a professional career to work without pay in an effort to save lives and prevent mayhem. I admit to some personal empathy with Ralph Nader, for I too tried to write about death on the highways. A couple of magazines permitted me to attack drunk drivers, a comparatively defenseless group, but not one of the many magazines for which I wrote regularly would touch a well-documented article, based on the research of prominent surgeons, which advocated such basic safety measures as seat belts, padded dashboards, doors which would not fly open on contact, and speed control. I gave up before Nader got started, but he didn't give up.

Unsafe at Any Speed was a best seller and Nader used the royalties to continue his crusade. General Motors hired private detectives who pried into his personal life. When two of the private eyes were caught trailing him, Senator Ribicoff brought James Roche, then president of GM, before the subcommittee where Roche publicly apologized to Nader.

Nader pointed out that the Ford management, after a

national conference on safety held in 1956 (when Nader was still in law school), came out strong for safety features. Fords were equipped with seat belts and other safety equipment since accepted by the entire industry. But leading the pack did not pay off. The campaign laid an egg. As someone said later, Ford sold safety, Chevrolet sold cars. Nevertheless, the campaign did have some beneficial effects.

To some degree, therefore, the Ford Motor Company and Ralph Nader were working the same side of the street. The company has always been safety-conscious in relation to the times. The best example I can think of in the case of the founder is something of an anomaly: he resisted hydraulic brakes for years because he felt that mechanical brakes were safer. As for Henry Ford II and safety, he said before seat belts were commonly accepted, "I think people are stupid not to strap themselves in." He considers shoulder straps a nuisance, but a worthwhile nuisance. He used them in Europe long before they became even optional equipment in America, and considered them more effective. The Ford Motor Company has long maintained a safety department, developing and testing safety features. One of the experiments of this department became a major bone of contention between Nader and Ford.

In his book, Nader said that the prototype of the Mustang contained eight safety features which were eliminated when the first model came out: a fail-safe dual braking system, head rests, roll bar, steering column with no rearward displacement, collapsible steering shaft, shoulder harness and belts, anchored seats, and bucket seats with lateral holding power. I made a note to ask somebody in the company about his statement.

Talking with Henry Ford about Nader, I found myself defending this voluntary ombudsman who had taken on the entire automotive industry. It seemed to me he had qualities a Ford could appreciate. After all, both Henry Fords have always had

261

a propensity for the man willing to work, and Nader not only knocked himself out, he did it on his own time. I asked Mister Ford, "Why do you pick on Ralph Nader?"

"I'll tell you why," Mister Ford said. "Because he doesn't know enough about what he's talking about, that's why. I didn't read his book and I'm not going to. And why didn't he go into driver training and stronger regulations on the people who drive these automobiles? This is a big industry that adds tremendously to the American economy, and the economy of the world. Where would we be without transportation, anyway? And this guy comes along and starts criticizing the automotive industry. Look, we make the safest cars that the American people will buy. If he knows so much about this, why doesn't he come out here and talk to us about it? As far as I know he never got anywhere near here, and he never talked to anybody that knows anything."

Mister Ford was getting pretty warmed up now. He was puffing away on a cigarette. "Look," he said, "I'll tell you what I want you to put in your book about Nader. You say, from me, he's full of crap."

I said I still thought Nader was a kind of a national hero, and Ford said, "Ha!"

I was groping. "Well what about the eight safety features that he said were in the Mustang prototype and then were eliminated from the production model?"

Mister Ford got upset all over again. "That's what I mean when I say he doesn't know what the hell he's talking about. That wasn't any Mustang. That had no connection with the Mustang. That was a thing we put together here long before we ever thought about a Mustang. It was an experimental car, I don't even remember what we called it if we called it anything, and it had no more connection with Mustang than Ralph Nader had. That's what I mean about the whole thing. He didn't know what he was talking about."

He drained a cup of saffron-colored tea, which he blends by pouring tea out of one silver pitcher, hot water out of the other. He must drink a gallon of the stuff a day. "Look, we could build the safest car in the world. We could build a tank that would creep over the highways and you could bang 'em into each other and nobody would ever get a scratch. But nobody would buy it either. We'd last about two months putting out stuff like that. The American people want good cars, good looking cars, fast cars, cars with power and styling and that's the kind of car we build. We spend a hell of a lot of time trying to make them better and safer and then some pipsqueak who doesn't know a thing about the industry comes along and tries to tell us how to do what we've dedicated our lives and billions of dollars to doing."

He glowered at me again and I figured I'd better drop the subject.

But I kept looking for somebody around the building who agreed with me about Nader. One morning in the executive dining room, Will Scott was sitting in Ed Lundy's chair— Lundy had come and gone early—and I found a mildly responsive echo. Scott, a brilliant, youngish man who has held several important jobs on his way up to vice president, had been automobile safety director for a time.

"I'll agree that Nader has made a contribution to the country," he said, "but I do disagree with him on some points. I've even said as much to Mister Ford."

One action of Nader's of which Scott and the entire company disapproved was his sending a letter to Ford and releasing it simultaneously to the press. Ford gave Scott the letter and told him to get rid of it. I happen to know that Scott keeps a special folder labeled Letters Never Received.

Another fellow sitting around the breakfast table got in the argument with the defense of higher-performance engines. I said I just didn't think anybody needed a 428-cubic-inch four-barrel ram air jet engine that would push the Mustang along at 150 miles an hour.

"If we didn't manufacture and make available a high-performance engine," this fellow said, "then people would just have their own engine modified at some specialty garage. If you want to buy a high-performance engine on a Cougar, say, it's going to cost you $1500 extra. Not too many irresponsible kids are going to pay that price. Another thing, it's part of a package. The faster you go, the more you need stopping power, so you've got to buy bigger brakes as part of the package. To keep from turning over going around curves, you've got to buy stronger suspension, another part of the package."

I said I still thought that manufacturing cars that blast along over the highway at 100 miles an hour is something like manufacturing guns, but I didn't get anywhere. People in the automobile business are in love with the cars they manufacture. They may not drive souped-up jobs themselves, but they like to look at them and identify with them.

One night, while having dinner with Ted Mecke, I asked him about the eight safety features Nader said were put in and then dropped out of the Mustang. He sighed.

"The whole thing was so complicated that if we told it like it was it would sound like we made it up, so we didn't say anything at all. Nobody would believe us."

"Try me," I said. "I'm a very credulous individual."

"Well, the safety department built this experimental little car that had all these features on it. They just happened to refer to it as a Mustang. Then the design staff built another car which was featured at Watkins Glen, and they called that Mustang II. We released stories and pictures on both of them. All this time the car that became the Mustang was in development—but it was referred to then as the Torino. See what I mean? Will Scott blamed the PR department for the whole thing. He said, 'If you weren't so damn eager to shoot off your mouths about every little thing that goes on around here you'd have never gotten in this mess in the first place.' "

I didn't find the story too hard to believe. Mecke is a pretty honest guy. As for Nader, it's the kind of conclusion that's easy to jump to.

The company maintains an intensive, extensive, and expensive automobile safety program. In an interesting little lecture I heard, C. R. Briggs, director of the program, pointed out that the United Nations estimates that 200,000 people die every year in automobile accidents, and 15 million people are injured. The estimated cost of accidents in the United States alone is $9 billion a year. In Great Britain the figure is 250 million pounds. With figures like that action is being taken in the direction of automobile safety all over the world. Investigations are being carried forward by private concerns and governmental agencies, and when weaknesses are found corrections are made.

The company has accepted the concept of governmental regulation, but as both it and its products cross boundaries, it feels that action should be international rather than national. Different governments maintain specifications that conflict with each other. Naturally, the company is interested in environmental condition differences all over the world. But it feels that if governmental regulations are going to increase, and they are, new standards should have meaning. They should be consistent with good low cost transportation achieved through a professional and scientific approach.

The governmental custom to which Briggs is most opposed is that of making regulations first and then seeing if they'll stand up. He calls it inexcusable. It places an unreasonable burden on the manufacturer and ultimately the consumer, because the manufacturer must include these unproven safety regulations in its manufacturing process. Furthermore, it has been the experience of persons expert in governmental operations that regulations do not get changed. Once a regulation is on the books, people lose interest in it. It's harder to change an existing law than it is to write a fresh one.

"We must have more background data, technical and scientific," Briggs said. "We've just about depleted the knowledge bank. The causes of accidents are not well known. Data is inaccurate. We need more research on the simple basic cause of accidents. This research is getting underway, both in the industry and outside, in universities and government laboratories."

At Ford, all of the safety research programs were drawn together in one building in 1966, and it is here that technicians derive new knowledge in regard to the strains and stresses of the automobile itself and human performance.

Safety includes both reducing the likelihood of accidents and reducing the injuries should accidents occur. In the area of impact dynamics, members of the staff study reports and photographs of accidents. They simulate crashes—two cars are banged up a day. They crash cars head on and sideways. They wrap them around posts. They constantly search for new materials which absorb energy. The new S-frame, which absorbs impact, is one result of the continuing studies.

Another innovation is a computer-operated braking system. The computer, about the size of a softcover book, prevents brakes from locking by pumping them up to four times a second. The device, called Sure-Track, was introduced on the Mark III and Thunderbird as optional equipment at $196. At first I thought this was a pretty frivolous gadget for two hundred bucks. Then my 16-year-old son John, driving a delivery truck after school, tried to beat a yellow light and banged into a taxicab. Although no one was hurt, it scared the daylights out of him.

"Pop," he said, still shaken up, "I jammed on the brakes but I kept right on going. There were tire marks all across the intersection."

"What happened," I said, "was that your wheels locked.

Only one part of each tire was on the pavement. The friction built up heat. You were sliding along on melted rubber. Didn't they teach you in school to pump your brakes, let your foot up and push it down again?"

"Pop," he said, "all I could think of was pushing on that pedal as hard as I could."

He wasn't the first and he won't be the last. Pumping sounds great in driving manuals, but it's not so easy to let up and push down again when you're pointed at another vehicle. Human impulses and muscles don't work that fast. Electronic pumping, also effective on ice, snow, or wet roads, no longer seemed so frivolous. I want one of those gadgets.

Another computer-operated gadget, ticketed for the future, is an antitailgating device. An infrared detector senses the distance between you and the car ahead and informs the computer, which in turn controls the accelerator and brake.

Nader was much harder on the Chevrolet Corvair than he was on any Ford product, but as a member of the automotive family, Mister Ford took his criticism personally. One morning he was scheduled to make a dedication speech at the opening of the new stamping plant at Woodhaven, Michigan. That morning Nader had criticized Volkswagen rear axles at a Senatorial hearing. Before the dedication ceremony, Ford asked both Allen Merrell, vice president for civic and governmental affairs, and Ted Mecke if they didn't think it was time somebody from the automotive industry, namely Henry Ford II, answered Nader's charges. Both strongly advised against it.

"Well," Ford said, "I'm going to do it anyway." At the conclusion of his remarks about the stamping plant, he spoke off the cuff for about five minutes. Blaming the situation solely on the automobile was unfair, he said. Ford builds safe cars and is constantly seeking to make them safer. Senator Ribicoff, he pointed out, when governor of Connecticut, cut highway deaths in that state by 50 per cent through regulatory laws not involving the automobile itself. The driver is the most important factor, because, "if you drive safely, accidents won't happen." Roads, licensing of drivers, and vehicle inspection are also important.

Then he got on Nader and his criticism of Volkswagen's rear axles. "Well, I say we've got jobs for rear axle engineers and, if he's that good, we'll be happy to give him a job. But frankly I don't think he knows very much about automobiles. . . . I think that if these critics who don't really know anything about safety of an automobile will get out of our way, we can go ahead with our job—and we have a job to do. We have to make our cars safer. As I said, we think they are safe today, but we have to make them safer still."

The surprising attack on a man who had criticized a competitor and the candid admission that cars could be made safer received a very favorable press. Henry Ford didn't set spies on Nader; he spoke out himself.

At the same time, quietly, Ford and his legislative assistants were veering from the industry's *laissez-faire* position toward a reasonable federal safety law. The Automobile Manufacturers Association had set up its own safety administrative committee to respond to the pressure for federal safety standards for motor vehicles. The Ford man on the committee was John Bugas and it fell to his lot to present the official statement reflecting the position of the industry. The statement would recommend to the Senate that the industry be permitted voluntarily to improve the safety of the vehicles it manufactured.

Both Ford and Arjay Miller were in Europe at the time the statement was drawn up, but Ford's man in Washington, Rodney W. Markley, Jr., vice president of the Washington staff, heard about it. The company's luxurious Washington office, with carpets so thick that a handshake is almost an act of double electrocution, must have had more than the usual amount of sparks flying that day. Markley, who refers to himself proudly as a lobbyist, bears little relationship to the popular stereotype.

268

He is a thoughtful, progressive, and analytical individual who discusses the automotive industry with startling frankness.

At the time of the Bugas statement, Markley told me, the image the automobile industry presented to the public was lousy. "There was an increasing public awareness of two things, air pollution and safety," Markley said. "In spite of these valid criticisms, the automobile industry in Detroit was continuing in its generic fashion, being dragged kicking and screaming into the twentieth century. Anyone could see that we were in for a hard time. But the industry's position was set in concrete, and the best its committee could come up with was voluntarism. In the face of current public attitude, I knew that it wouldn't go."

When Ford and Miller returned to Dearborn, Markley was there waiting for them. They discussed the proposed statement in meetings Friday, Saturday, and Sunday. Markley expressed his opinion that because of the changing public attitude, the automobile industry must accept some safety regulations. For sound, competitive business reasons, he advised, standards should be set by the federal government so that one company could not undercut the other. Rather than protesting against all regulation, the industry should draw up a model bill that would establish a sympathetic climate and set forth a preliminary approach. Presentation of the model bill would indicate to Congress that automobile manufacturers were now ready to shoulder some responsibility, long past due. It would set realistic lead times and standards.

It would be Markley's job—and he's good at it—to circulate among his friends in the Congress to gain support for the bill. In such operations, he told me, he is not averse to dropping the name Henry Ford II. "The name is magic," he explained.

The possessor of the magical name accepted Markley's suggestion, but Bugas was obligated to defend the stance of the committee to resist legislation with the plea for voluntarism. Finally Ford blew up.

"If you take this to the Senate committee they're going to laugh you out of the hearing room," he said.

The statement was revised. On April 5, 1966, Bugas took it to the hearing and defended voluntarism during the question and answer period. Senator Maurine B. Neuberger, a member of the subcommittee, sat quietly through the reading of the statement and much of the discussion. Then she said: ". . . I can't help but comment on it, because of your suggestion about the voluntary plan. The automobile industry has been able to have a voluntary plan since 1900. Only when pressure comes from Congress, and we think from the public through us about any of these problems affecting the general welfare, only then we get the sudden desire to 'let us do it'. . . . We've just had nothing but confusion as a result of self-regulation of industry. I just think it is humanly impossible for them to do otherwise. It is just going against the grain for us to put retarding influences on ourselves. So I say 'ha-ha' for any industry that comes along and wants to 'let us do it' . . ." Ford had called it right again.

After the incident in the Senate, the industry, in what Markley termed "a traumatic turnabout," took a more pragmatic stance and put forward new legislative proposals. The Traffic and Highway Safety Act that resulted was one it could live with. Now came the question of price increases reflecting the mandatory safety equipment. Senator Ribicoff, caustically critical, held another hearing on the subject.

GM had raised prices by $23 to $32 a car, reflecting the cost of the shoulder harnesses required by law. Nader claimed that the harnesses cost only $3, and Ribicoff charged the industry with trying to make money on safety. It's true that a couple of pieces of webbing and some hardware aren't worth thirty bucks, but more is involved. At Ford's, installation of shoulder harnesses required new dies to make the holes for the harness bolts, and three more men on each shift to install them. But automobile companies don't like to talk about costs in detail because the information could be valuable to competitors. Even an hour of touching doorknobs in Markley's electrified office would not torture an automobile executive into revealing the actual costs of individual components.

Senator Ribicoff, the irresistible force, was up against the immovable object. Washington, which enjoys a fight, was looking forward to the big showdown at the hearing. The first witness, representing General Motors, testified that GM would be unable to furnish the cost of items required by the new law, and Senator Ribicoff promptly chewed him out and called for the next victim. He was Arjay Miller.

To set the stage, it might be wise to explain the preparation any Ford executive receives prior to giving testimony before Congress. The procedure grew out of a casual remark Rod Markley once made to Henry Ford. He was describing the appearance of a top executive of a major corporation before a Senate committee. The executive brought with him a phalanx of subalterns, each with a briefcase. In response to each question asked by the committee, the executive would crook his finger and one of the members of his retinue would open up his briefcase and furnish the material for the answer. The point of the story was that there were so many attendants present that Markley couldn't find a seat in the hearing room.

Ford, however, did not think the story to be so much a laughing matter as an example of how not to testify. "That's not the way I'm going to do it," he said. "I'm going to get up there by myself, damn it, do the best I can, and stand on my own performance."

"That's fine," Markley said, "provided you know what you're doing."

Out of that conversation grew the standard procedure, pretty much a secret until now, by which Ford executives are girded for Congressional battle. It has produced performances that have been commended all through Congress for their smoothness and efficiency as well as for their valuable contribution. Legislators want more than facts and figures from technical assistants. Those they can get from the records. They want advice and opinions from the leaders they summon to testify.

Before making his appearance before the Senate Finance Committee in 1963, Ford attended other committee hearings to familiarize himself with the procedure. Markley, familiar with Senate protocol, gave him some pertinent tips. A common failing on the part of a witness is to permit needling questions to upset him and then to blurt out angry answers. To help him keep his cool, Markley subjected the chairman to a dry run in the Ford suite at the Shoreham Hotel. Markley and members of his staff fired questions, some of them antagonistic, at the witness-to-be. Next day Ford gave a virtuoso performance.

The pretestimony grilling sessions have been employed ever since. They may last for hours. In addition to Markley, the High Inquisitor, and his assistants, two moderators are on hand. Following the session, sometimes in the small hours of the morning, they give a critique of both the testimony and the demeanor of the witness.

"One executive got so mad after two questions that he stormed out of the room and went to bed," Markley said. "Next day he turned out to be a lousy witness. Another one also got mad at what he considered insulting questions, but we cooled him down, asked the same questions again, and made him answer them. The next day on the witness stand he was asked the very same questions which had made him blow his top the night before. He answered them calmly and satisfactorily. He looked good. The committee counsel asking the questions looked bad."

On the eve of his appearance before Senator Ribicoff's committee, Arjay Miller got "The Treatment." He testified immediately after the GM fellow while Ribicoff was still steaming. Thanks to the dry run, however, Miller was prepared for almost anything. He quietly and candidly explained that there was a difference between "what we know and what we're willing to tell." He proposed a carefully thought-out compromise: instead of making public its costs on safety equipment, each company would instead supply the figures to the Bureau of Labor Statistics. The Bureau would study the figures and arrive at an average cost for each feature. The government would have the information, the companies would have their little secret.

Senator Ribicoff was delighted. "I like your proposal better than mine," he said, and it was accepted. As an industry lobbyist told *Newsweek*, "Arjay took the pressure off all of us."

Markley, who as I told you is an unusual type of lobbyist, told me candidly that Henry Ford II makes his job in Washington much easier.

"For the first few years here," he said, "I was scared to death in this job. Mister Ford is totally unpredictable. He understands the value of precedent, but that doesn't keep him from changing his mind. There's none of this knee-jerk business about him. I was in a junior executive position here at the beginning, and I not only represented Mister Ford's business interests in Washington but I also saw quite a bit of him socially. I'd arrange dinners for him and of course I had to go myself. When he comes to Washington I have about two days of dealing with his insatiable curiosity about the national scene. He always greets me with the question, 'What's going on?' and that question usually takes several hours to answer. He has to be filled in on everything. Over the years though, I found that the only way to deal with Mister Ford is eyeball to eyeball. He's receptive to dialogue. You tell him what you believe, give him your best advice, and he accepts it.

"Well," Markley said, *"usually* he accepts it. During the period not so long ago when everybody was beating up on the automobile industry, the Federal Trade Commission chose to command some rather extensive documentation from the Ford

273

Motor Company on our warranty policy. Mister Ford didn't like that at all. He threatened to write a letter to President Johnson. Everybody told him not to do it. In Washington you go through channels.

"As for me, I have to work with the chairman of the FTC, and it would reduce my effectiveness for Mister Ford to go over my head. I didn't just plead with him, I got pretty forceful about it. I thought I had won the argument and then all of a sudden I got a copy of a letter Mister Ford had sent the president directly protesting the FTC action. The odd thing is that it worked. Everything seemed to smooth out after that. Next time I talked with Mister Ford I asked him why he had done it. 'Well,' he said, 'everybody else was against it so I decided I would do it.'

"Mister Ford has total recall, particularly about a thing like that. I'll present a course of action complete with facts and figures, and he'll say, 'That isn't what you told me last October.' So now whenever I recommend a course of action, he'll say, 'Dammit, Rodney, you told me to do it your way once before and look what happened.' "

After the Johnson Inauguration in 1964, the company gave a party to which cabinet members, Senators, Congressmen, all the big wheels in Washington were invited. Markley tried to arrange for Ford to alternate with Arjay Miller in the receiving line, but Ford wouldn't have it. He said he was going to stand in the line the entire time. Markley said it would be very tiring.

"I'm giving this party," Ford told him, "and a lot of people are coming to meet me and I'm going to be there." He stood in the reception line for four hours, greeting everyone personally, and frequently chatting with the visitors. The invitations had his name on them, and by God he was there.

For all his power, Henry Ford II is strangely self-effacing. Markley learned quickly that he wasn't supposed to hold his coat and run ahead of him to open doors. "He likes to think of himself as just another guy named Joe, which he sure as hell isn't," Markley said. "He's embarrassed by attention. One time the chairman of an important Senate committee who was also a great admirer of his grandfather invited him to come to his office in the Senate. When Ford entered the Senator jumped from his desk, greeted him effusively, and paraded him through his suite of offices, introducing him to everyone. Ford was embarrassed and ill at ease, and the Senator's insistence on referring to him as the son of Henry Ford didn't help things."

Just being able to throw the name Henry Ford II around would be enough, for it opens doors to Markley all over Washington. But more than that, Mister Ford permits himself to be used personally to back up his name. If Markley sets up a meeting, Ford goes to it. Furthermore, he helps. "He's got more political savvy, viscerally, instinctively," Markley said, "than most industrialists exposed to the Washington scene for many years have developed after years of study. He has some innate knowledge of the political animal. I don't know where it comes from, but I see it and I'm constantly amazed by it. I'm supposed to be a professional, but many times Mister Ford does a better job of handling politicians than I do.

"And yet I have to come back to that strange contradictory quality of self-effacement. Sometime ago we had a couple of hours to kill and I suggested that we go see Wilbur Mills, the chairman of the House Ways and Means Committee. I was rather proud of the suggestion, and wasn't at all prepared for his reaction to it—he was strongly opposed. 'What would Mills want to see me for?' he asked. 'He's a busy man. He doesn't want me hanging around bothering him.' I told him what I knew to be the truth, that Congressman Mills was interested in industry and what businessmen were thinking and finally Mister Ford, protesting all the way, permitted me to drag him out to the car. On the way a couple of times I thought he'd stop the car and get out of it. But we saw Mills in his office, and Mister Ford apologized for taking up his time. The next thing I knew, there they were, talking together on the same level. Mister Ford stayed two and a half hours. They both put their feet up on the desk together and talked about the automobile industry, about international trade, and touched on all the areas of the financial world and taxes. I'm constantly amazed at his knowledge of what's going on in the world. I ask myself where in the world does this blotter pick these things up? It's not so much an intellectual philosophizing as a tremendous knowledge of facts pertaining to his own area.

"One time I went out to Dearborn for a meeting. I was waiting for the elevator to take me up to the penthouse where I was going to stay when along came Mister Ford and insisted I come out to his house with him. About all I remember of the evening is the Ford art collection. He took me all over the house, showed me all the paintings, showed me photographs of paintings that he had loaned out to other people, and I was just overwhelmed by this man's knowledge and appreciation of art. I don't know what to expect from him."

One of the phenomena growing out of the increased national interest in automobile safety legislation is the press coverage of the recall of automobiles for mechanical defects. Seems like every few days you read about some company calling in thousands of vehicles. I had intended to make my own personal investigation into the recall situation, but a chance remark by Martin Hayden of the *Detroit News* saved me several days' work. Hayden was telling me of the pleasure it is to work with the Ford public relations department, under both Ted Mecke and his predecessor, the colorful Charles F. Moore, Jr. Ford stole Moore from Earl Newsom when he decided, with Newsom's blessing, to expand the public relations department in the company.

Hayden said that while the old company under Henry I had about the worst public relations department in the world—

"he thought the whole thing was insane and the way he ran it, it *was* insane"—the new company's PR department, under Mecke, is the best in the world with the possible exception of DuPont's. "Call Ted or one of his top assistants any hour of the day or night and you get an answer, and it's an honest one. If he can't give it to you off the top of his head, he says he'll call you back and he does. It's an honest, friendly, no-nonsense answer, too. If it's necessary to see Mister Ford personally, Ted gets us to him, and I tell you, when Henry says something, the whole world understands just exactly what he means."

Hayden had thought a story on the anatomy of an automobile recall would make interesting reading, and called the Big Three for cooperation. GM and Chrysler had turned him down completely, but Mecke said, "Sure, come on out." Hayden dispatched his automotive expert, Robert W. Irvin, who came back with a thorough story on the subject. The details were given for the first time, and, as far as I know, until now, the last. As I knew very well from reading Bob Irvin's stories that he had a much surer grasp of the technical end of the industry than I have, I asked Hayden if I could use the details of the story. He gave me a copy of it.

The recall Irvin investigated involved 46,812 1966 Lincolns, Mercurys, and Fords. It began with the arrival at a Ford chassis plant of a mislabeled shipment of steel from an outside supplier. The steel, destined for a part of the front suspension system, had actually been made for the fabrication of highway guard rails. When heated and cut into the proper size and shape, the steel became hard and brittle. One Thursday night, during the installation of coil springs on a Continental by a machine that exerts great pressure, the metal cracked. The quality control manager ordered a laboratory analysis that night which proved the steel to have the wrong specifications: it was too hard. A simple test was devised immediately to tell the difference between right and wrong: hit it with a punch and hammer. If you couldn't make a dent in it, it was the wrong steel. Company metallurgists and the manufacturer confirmed the diagnosis.

Of 12,000 pieces made from the shipment, only 2000 had gone out to the assembly plants. All but a few hundred of those were located, still unused. The parts were installed on test cars and given rough treatment that weekend, but deliberate efforts to break them were unsuccessful. It may have been the wrong steel, but it held up. However, it was decided to play safe. On Tuesday, word went out to all assembly plants to send out no more cars until the part in question had been inspected. At one plant the company hit an odd stroke of luck; assembly was shut down because of a power failure.

Examination of computer records showed that the defective parts could have wound up in a total of 34,198 Fords, 8614 Mercurys, and 4000 Lincolns. About 37,000 of these cars were checked—with hammer and punch—at assembly plants and in dealer inventories. Purchasers of the remaining cars were notified to bring them in for inspection. Dealers were given credit for a half hour's labor cost to check the part, a full hour to replace it. Total cost of the entire campaign ran about $130,000. New fail-safe tests were put in to make sure that such an occurrence could never happen again.

"Each one of these is a painful experience," Walter E. Sweigart, manager of the transmission and chassis division's quality control office, told Irvin. "Everyone I have been associated with has a deep sense of responsibility. We try to learn something each time."

Safety and air pollution are closely related in the mind of the public. In decreasing air pollution from the exhaust of internal combustion engines, Ford, as well as the industry as a whole, is either gunning ahead or dragging its wheels, depending on whose side you're on. Some conservationists believe that the automotive answer to air pollution is another form of power plant. Ford has spent millions during the Sixties in partially successful efforts to develop a long-lived battery to power an electric car. The company has also carried on its own research and development program in regard to a steam engine, and has a working agreement with the Thermo-Electron Corporation which is all steamed up about its engine that operates on temperatures of over 1000 degrees. It's my personal opinion, however, that despite all the money Henry Ford has spent on researching steam and electric power, their proponents will have to scald him or shock him before he'll give up his love for the internal combustion engine. "There is nothing as efficient in the world."

He says he doesn't see the electric car "as a feasible method of transportation in my lifetime." I'm sure he believes this to be a pragmatic approach, but I don't think he *wants* to see the electric car feasible in his lifetime. I doubt if Henry Ford II remembers that his grandmother used to take the street car to the garage where her little Baker electric was stored, and then proceed smoothly and noiselessly downtown in it, but I do believe that's what the electric car represents to him: a little car for grandmothers.

Ford is honestly progressive in regard to the betterment of mankind and he knows the value of decreasing air pollutants. His approach, rather than to do away with the exhaust pipe, is to eliminate the emission from it. From 1960 to 1968, industry technicians reduced hydrocarbon and carbon monoxide exhaust by about 60 per cent. The company also, according to its stockholders report, spent or allocated well over a hundred million dollars in the Sixties to decrease air and water pollution by its plants. The cost of air scrubbers for the towering smokestacks in the Rouge would take care of all the smoke pollution in most small cities.

13

TO A FORD HISTORIAN, the stockholders report with its justifications, explanations, and self-congratulations is a dramatic example of the company's transformation. The report is comparable to a river starting to run uphill.

Remembering his grandfather's acerbic relationships with his stockholders and his elaborate scheme to unload them, I find the current attitude of Henry Ford II to his stockholders a Ford contradiction. His scheme to acquire stockholders was far more elaborate than his grandfather's to eliminate them, and reflected paternal and avuncular influence. The actual circumstances of the change date back to 1936, when the Ford Foundation was inauspiciously and belatedly created.

As is par for the Ford course, the origins of the Ford Foundation trigger extreme reactions. Some think of it as a dirty-capitalist scheme to mulct the government of taxes and circumvent its laws. Others feel that it was a clever and praiseworthy retaliation against the confiscatory, soak-the-rich policy of the dirty-Communist New Deal. Whichever side you want to take, I can marshal arguments for the other, but a more reasonable centrist position can be justified.

Family foundations had long been in existence: Rockefeller, Guggenheim, Mellon, Rosenwald, Carnegie. Henry Ford, however, wanted no part of any philanthropy he couldn't control, and he didn't like the pernickety legal work that setting up a foundation would entail. Nor did he pass on any of his holdings in the company to his grandchildren through gifts, which in the Twenties would have been subject to far less tax.

The tax law of 1935, deliberately designed as a weapon against concentration of wealth and power, caught him unprepared. Inheritance taxes were raised to 50 per cent of everything over $4 million, 70 per cent over $50 million. The gift loophole was closed. If Henry Ford had died that year—he was 73—his heirs would have had to pay a hundred million or more in taxes. Even the Fords didn't have that much money lying around— if they did it was taxable—and the only way they could have raised it would be by selling stock in the company. Merely evaluating the worth of the shares—as was later proven—would have been an involved proceeding, for as a family-held company, there was no market value per share. Under those circumstances, after the Fords had sold enough stock to pay their taxes, they wouldn't even have stock left to keep control of the company. Ford would not only be public; it would be run by managers.

It was not until the death of Edsel Ford, eight years after the foundation had been set up, that the tax significance of the foundation was understood. At that time, incidentally, with his father showing positive indications of senility and Bennett and Sorensen synergistically depressing the operating capacity of the company, the value of each share would have been at rock bottom. Ford ownership of Ford would have been still further diluted. In the hiatus between Edsel's death and the filing of his will, many gloated at the prospective fall of the mighty.

The will, however, revealed an entirely different situation. In creating the foundation, the stock had been divided into two classes, voting and nonvoting. Of a total of some 3½ million shares, 3 million nonvoting shares went to the foundation while 190,000-odd nonvoting shares went to the family. That left only 172,645, but they were *voting* shares. And they went to the Fords.

Four years after the death of his only son, Henry Ford passed away. His last years had been peaceful and happy ones. He was proud of his grandchildren, and pleased with young Henry's direction of the company. On the afternoon of his death he and his wife had visited the River Rouge. At home, late that night, he called Clara to his side and complained of a headache. A spring flood had drowned out the private power plant and there were no lights, no heat, no telephones. He left the world as he entered it, by candlelight.

On his death the voting shares continued to remain in Ford hands, shared by Mrs. Clara Ford, Mrs. Edsel Ford, and the four grandchildren. Through the three pages setting up the Ford Foundation, therefore, the family retained 100 per cent control of the company. No share of stock was permitted to fall into private hands. The procedure was impeccably legal. And it made it possible for Henry Ford to rebuild the company. Without it, God knows where he or it would be today. If the Fords had had to sell control in 1943, the stockholders probably wouldn't have pulled the young officer out of the Navy. They might have brought in a Breech themselves to put the company on its feet. They might have let it continue under the control of Harry Bennett.

We could sit here dreaming about all the things that might have happened for another hour. But they didn't happen, and the Ford Foundation was the reason.

It was also the Foundation that was the reason for the Ford Motor Company's becoming a public corporation in 1956. By that time the Ford Foundation, which had started out peanut-sized, had grown to be the giant in the field.

Concomitantly with rebuilding the company, Henry Ford II was choosing personnel and directing the establishment of policy to make the Foundation a viable organization. To him, as to his father, philanthropy is not just a good deed but an intelligent approach to modern life. In a speech before the United Jewish Appeal in Chicago, he summed up his tripartite philosophy on philanthropy in one cogent paragraph:

"As compassionate individuals, we look upon poverty as a blight which deprives fellow men of life's enjoyment. As responsible citizens, we also see the poor as a drain on society who should be made into contributors to society. As businessmen we have a third view—the poor simply are not very good customers for our products, even the most basic necessities."

As Ford is an internationalist, that paragraph holds true for the world.

Henry Ford II does not run the Foundation; he and Benson Ford are currently the only Fords, and the only people connected with the company, on the sixteen-man board of directors. He has an influential voice on the board, for it would be difficult for him not to have an influential voice on anything with which he is connected. But that's as far as it goes. As a Foundation spokesman told me, "With a foundation of this size and respect you simply can't let one man's hobby horse influence too directly the activity of the entire operation." Ford has frequently been surprised, unhappily so, by Foundation activities.

In the late Forties and early Fifties, however, he spearheaded the organization of the Foundation and the determination of just what categories of service it was going to perform. The trustees unanimously accepted, in 1951, the report of a study committee that recommended five program areas: the establishment of peace, the strengthening of democracy, the strengthening of the economy, education in a democratic society, and individual behavior and human relations.

From the beginning of the new direction, Henry Ford knew that some of the Foundation's activities would be controversial; by its very nature the Foundation must embrace areas that are controversial. The Foundation concerns itself with problems, and by the very definition of the word that means controversy. Once the direction of the Foundation was established, its impact on the entire world progressed geometrically. In many of the emerging nations, its working delegations were larger than those of most countries.

As for wealth, it was loaded. With 88 per cent of the stock and the annual dividends of the Ford Motor Company, it was almost as big as the company itself, and the company was the entire source of the Foundation's operating capital. It had all its eggs in one basket, but it could neither count on the eggs—the automobile industry is cyclical; good years may be followed by bad—nor control the basket: the Ford family could withhold its income simply by not declaring dividends. Yet the Foundation could not sell its stock, and if it did, what would be the market value?

The only logical way out of the quandary was by diversification of assets, and the Fords began thinking seriously of means by which such diversification could be accomplished. The Foundation could not sell its stock to get money to buy other stocks unless its shares had voting power. This would mean public ownership of the company.

Sharing the Ford Motor Company with a broad spectrum of the people was not abhorrent to Henry Ford II as it had been to his grandfather. His father, influenced by Ernest Kanzler, had actually broached the subject many years before but had gotten less than nowhere; the issue was one of the major factors in the senior Ford's enmity toward Kanzler. But Henry II could see the advantages of public ownership of the Ford Motor Company. Though the company would no longer be a castle unto itself, public ownership could enlarge the team young Henry had put together.

But how should this be accomplished? Sharing ownership was one matter; abdicating control was another. Ford discussed the quandary with Charles E. Wilson, chairman of the Foundation's finance committee, in the fall of 1953. Wilson promptly suggested that the Foundation seek the advice of Sidney J. Weinberg, a senior partner of Goldman, Sachs & Co., and a financier of such repute that he was known as Mr. Wall Street.

"You can't have Weinberg," Ford said. "We want him as an adviser to the family."

Weinberg knew Mrs. Edsel Ford and had great respect and affection for her. He had met her son and liked him. When asked by Ford to advise the family, the already established relationship had a bearing on his decision, for Mr. Wall Street didn't need the money. He asked how long the job would take, and Ford said he had no idea. It took two years.

Weinberg's job was to work out a plan—acceptable to the New York Stock Exchange, the Securities and Exchange Commission, and the Internal Revenue Service—by which the company would go public but the family would not lose control, and by which the Foundation would be able to diversify its holdings.

Though Weinberg, a gruff-talking but warmhearted little man who rose to his present eminence from a $3-a-week start as a janitor's assistant, speaks modestly about his solution of the challenge, it's obvious that it was the high point of his more than sixty years on Wall Street. When he told me about it, his pride in being the architect of the plan was evident. He drew up about fifty reorganization plans in all. The procedure finally adopted was without precedent in financial circles. It was also the largest stock offering in history: $675 million.

286

Reduced to ridiculous oversimplification, the Weinberg plan set up three classifications of stock, Common, Class A, and Class B. Only Common and Class B carried voting rights, and Class B with 40 per cent of the voting stock was restricted to members of the Ford family.

"On stock as widely distributed as Ford Motor, 25 per cent is more than enough to retain absolute control," Weinberg said. He had provided a double cushion.

After it was all over, and Weinberg had received the fee estimated at a million dollars which he turned over to Goldman, Sachs, he also received the letter which hangs framed in his inner sanctum: headed simply, Henry Ford II, Dearborn, it is written in a large, plain hand.

Dear Sidney:

Now that everything seems in the groove and we are a public company, I just wanted to write our thank you for everything you did for the family to make this possible. Without you it could not have been accomplished, and we all (the family) are in your debt for the terrific job you did for us.

Words are hard to find to express how I really feel—so just accept our "thanks," please.

With best wishes to Helen and yourself,

Henry Ford

Sidney Weinberg spoke of Ford in phrases that may seem extravagant but didn't sound that way when he said them: "Henry's noble instincts and interest in social causes are not usually found in the scions of families of such extreme wealth and position. . . . I've seen too many young men in his position fritter away their lives. I must admit I'm prejudiced in his favor. I'm 77 years old and in 60-odd years of working on the inside of major corporations there is no man I've had more pleasure in working with than Henry Ford. If it hadn't been for the sheer delight of his company and my admiration for his intelligence and dedication, I'd never have stayed on the board after I reached 70."

Implementation of the Weinberg plan called for logistics as complex as its architecture. Blyth and Company was chosen to head the team of underwriters. Paul A. Conley, a Blyth vice president, was in charge of the operation.

"With a thing of this kind we must have a definite timetable, control it and work to it," Conley told me. "If I knew what the market was going to do tomorrow, I wouldn't be sitting here, so it stood to reason that the quicker we could get the job done the better. We set the date of the offering on January 26, 1956, and worked back from there. This gave us 80 days.

"A forty-three-page prospectus had to be drawn up and a million copies printed. Even the procurement of paper was a problem; there was a shortage of paper at that time. In a preparation of any prospectus, every word must be weighed, every comma. Full compliance with the regulations of the Securities and Exchange Commission is not enough. The prospectus must reflect business and moral significance as well as legal significance. Nothing germane to the issue can be omitted.

"To sell the shares we assembled the largest syndicate of dealers ever put together, here or abroad—over seven hundred —and allocated to each the number of shares it could purchase. To be left out of this offering would be a social blight. Throughout the period of preparation we had the full cooperation of Henry Ford and Ford officials including McNamara, Miller, Gossett and Yntema. Henry, though, was definitely the captain of the team. He is an astute man, with definite ideas of his own, but he listens to the advisers he hires. It was a pleasure to work with him.

"But the job itself was the most difficult I have ever worked on. When it was all over, I took off on a vacation. Went to Palm Springs for two and a half weeks. I had meant to play some golf, but I was so exhausted I couldn't stand up, much less walk around the golf course."

The price agreed upon was $63 per share, plus a commission of $1.50 to underwriters, for a price to the public of $64.50. During the period between the announcement and the sale, a buying fever developed. Some analysts felt that the price was pegged too high, and even a few of the underwriters confidentially told potential customers that $64.50 was too much money. But enthusiasm continued to mount. In an effort to avoid misleading the public, Henry Ford II told a meeting of underwriters two weeks before the stock went on sale not to get carried away.

"We at Ford Motor Company are businessmen, not miracle men," he said. "I think some people are indulging in wishful thinking about their chances for fast and fabulous financial gains. It's true that 1955 was the best year we in the industry in general ever had, but 1956 will not be as good a year as 1955."

One of the brokers present, on hearing that, turned to a Ford public relations man at the meeting. "My God," he said, "you people aren't going to let that get into the newspapers, are you?"

"It's already been released to the papers," the PR man said.

When the big day came the rush to buy Ford stock at $64.50 per share was like bargain day at Macy's. Keith Funston, president of the New York Stock Exchange, called it a landmark in the history of public ownership. One of the interesting features was the large number of purchasers who bought small amounts, often for their children or grandchildren. Ford had hoped for a broad-based ownership, and had sought to discourage brokers from selling large blocs of stock.

Short term speculators got burned, for the stock dropped after the sale. But those who held onto it saw it split and again approach the original price. Later offerings increased the number of individual stockholders to a high of some 400,000 before large purchases by institutions, pension plans, and mutual funds —a trend begun by the Ford pension fund—decreased the total number.

Henry Ford II seems to enjoy his role as head of a large public corporation. Stockholders' meetings are held in the Henry and Edsel Ford Auditorium in Detroit, and the large hall is filled. There are a lot of old people who look as though they have been loyally driving black Ford two-doors for years, and who sit quietly, listening intently to the proceedings. Special seats are reserved for the people named Ford; at the session I attended, both Henry's wife and mother were there.

A few days before that 1968 meeting, the company and the FBI received tips that attempts were going to be made to assassinate both Henry Ford and McGeorge Bundy, the new president of the Ford Foundation. Extraordinary security measures were taken at the meeting—guards were also placed at the Ford home—without any obvious appearance of increased security. Toward the end of the session, I went out a side door for a cigarette. Three uniformed guards were standing casually outside the door; when I tried to go back in, they weren't so casual. I'd be outside there yet if an official hadn't come to my rescue.

The one grating note was the inordinate amount of time taken up by the kind of people who seem to attend stockholders' meetings in order to call attention to themselves. For all his bluntness, Ford was patient with them. On two occasions, however, when individuals used the floor microphones to bring up extraneous issues, Mister Ford first politely asked them to keep their remarks to the point, and then, when his request was not heeded, gestured as if throwing a football to the technician controlling the public address system. The microphones went off in mid-sentence.

During the 1969 stockholders' meeting, the chairman was

criticized from the floor for his commitment to urban and social problems, with the implication that his involvement was politically motivated. "I give my time to my country, not to a party," he replied, and received a rewarding burst of applause.

Although the corporation is now public, the philosophy of the controlling Fords has remained the same. Management policy disappoints investors hungry for large dividends. Just as Henry I reinvested his earnings in new plants and equipment to build more cars and employ more people, so Henry II constantly reinvests corporate earnings. He has not bought vast acreage in Brazil for rubber plantations or American farmland to grow soybeans, but he has spent even more money on practical assets, such as his acquisition of Ford of England and of additional stock in Ford of Canada to bring total ownership to more than 80 per cent.

The company has gone into other, related industries. Perhaps the most natural was the purchase in 1961, for $28,200,-000, of a major portion of Electric Autolite Company. It is now the Autolite-Ford Parts Division, and it supplies replacement items such as spark plugs, batteries, and shock absorbers to dealerships, filling stations and neighborhood garages. Most filling stations carry replacement parts (known as the aftermarket in Detroitese), and Ford wants them to be Autolite. The division's new parts redistribution center built in 1969 is the world's largest industrial building: three million square feet, or 53 football fields. From this center, near Detroit, parts go out to 23 parts depots in the United States, and to other depots in other countries.

In 1956 Ford had bought a small operation on the West Coast and reorganized it as Aeronutronic Systems, Inc. (Some called it aeroneurotic.) When Ford acquired it, the company was built around a group of some twenty physicists and engineers. Within 15 years it had become the Aeronutronic Division of Philco-Ford, located in a plush modernistic plant in Newport

291

Beach, California. One of Aeronutronic Division's successful projects was the development of the Shillelagh missile.

Ford also maintains a scientific research laboratory, many of whose Ph.D.'s are engaged in basic research and operate on five-year contracts. Their projects may not even relate to direct interests of the Ford Motor Company. Ford justified the research lab's existence in a speech before the United Jewish Appeal, saying:

"Right now, few large companies feel secure enough to do without basic research as well—an activity which may have little relationship to today's products or profits. Ford Motor Company, for one, is committed to a strong program in the basic sciences. In the past ten years our Scientific Laboratory has grown into one of the outstanding industrial research institutions in the country and has been recognized for major contributions to world science.

"We do this not out of any sense of altruism but because it is good business. By maintaining a pool of talented scientists and engineers dedicated to advancing the frontiers of their respective scientific disciplines, we are hedging our corporate bets against technological breakthroughs that might revolutionize our industry and leave us behind."

One of the company's farthest-out ventures dealt with the pollution of our large lakes, especially Lake Erie. All bodies of water have always had a pollution problem—dead vegetable and animal matter—but the natural inversion of the strata twice a year due to changes in temperature takes care of it under normal conditions. The water simply turns itself over and provides new oxygen to the pollution on the bottom.

In many lakes, however, like Lake Erie, man has dumped in so much polluting substance that natural inversion is insufficient to clean it up. One of Ford's patent attorneys named T. H. Oster, with the encouragement of Mister Ford, worked

out a way to help nature along. He would install giant propellers, 100 feet in diameter, at points in lake bottoms to push
up the de-oxygenated water and suck in fresh water. "I'm a
great believer in slide rules," Oster said, "and my slide rule tells
me it would take eighteen of these propellers to equal the flow
of polluted water into Lake Erie from the Detroit River."

Oster's propeller-driven purification plan died as far as
Ford was concerned when estimates of the cost to turn the propellers by electricity came in. Oster, however, came up with a
cheaper source of power: the wind. Someday you may look out
across Lake Erie and see huge windmills spinning in the breeze.
They'll be turning even larger propellers on the lake bottom,
and, according to Oster and his slide rule, Lake Erie will be
alive and well again.

Almost as astonishing as this currently dormant project, at
least to financial analysts, was the actual acquisition by Ford of
the money-losing Philco company. In the late Twenties Philco,
then under dynamic leadership, started manufacturing radios,
the new national craze, on an assembly line basis borrowed from
the automobile industry. By 1930 it was the leading radio manufacturer in the country; you could buy a Philco radio then for
$195—tubes extra. Philco was already working on television and
by 1932 was operating an experimental television station. It
added a line of appliances. In 1955 it hit its peak, but from
then on all the lines on its chart pointed to the lower right-hand
corner.

The management had ignored the rise of the big national
outlets like Sears and the discount houses. Everything Philco
manufactured was under its own name and purchasable only
through dealers. But the American people had found other
places to shop; 20,000 dealers went out of business during that
period.

Philco attempted to meet the challenge by cheapening its

products, and then it didn't even have its famous quality any-more. In desperation it turned to making computers, but you don't just knock out a computer overnight.

Then Ford stepped in and bought the company for $100 million. Some thought Philco should have paid Ford that much to take it.

"It was a can of worms," Henry Ford told me.

I had visited the Philco headquarters in Philadelphia not long before, talked with several of the people there, and came away impressed by their attitude. It seemed that the people who had been there before Ford took over were now euphoric, and the men Ford had put in to run the place were pleased with their progress and confident about the future.

They loaded me down with facts, figures, and projects. The company was in 120 world markets. They were bringing out a new color TV line, as well as radio-phonograph stereo consoles, portable radios, tape recorders, phonographs, air conditioners, and a complete line of what the industry calls white goods—refrigerators, electric ranges, washing machines. Philco was furnishing the Post Office with address readers that could sort 36,000 pieces of mail an hour.

Philco was a prime contractor for the communications system in the mission control center in Houston which has the world's largest closed circuit TV. Twenty-six of its defense communications satellites were orbiting the world, and four huge dish antennas, 100 feet across, were picking up their signals. Philco equipment had flown around the moon; other equipment is *on* the moon. The company had designed, developed, tested, and successfully bid for the entire responsibility for the Shillelagh guided missile. It had more than 5000 civilian employees in Viet Nam as technical advisers.

Many of the more than 200 computers used by the parent company were Philco-built; from 200 locations in the United States and Europe you could call the Ford computer center in

Dearborn direct and, thanks to some 15,000 programs, get an answer to any conceivable engineering question in minutes. Philco was working on an electronic automobile stethoscope that would diagnose malfunctions in a car without operating on it. New plants in Taiwan were turning out electronic equipment. The white goods plant in Connorsville, Indiana, had been doubled in size and the new Lansdale plant near Philadelphia was producing a fantastic number of color picture tubes.

"We believe that the extrapolation of the entire field of electronics will approach automotive sales in the future," one of the eager enthusiasts said. "We see it as a $16 billion industry by 1980. TV is already the third major item people purchase after a house and car. The great future is in computer programming for the home. Push a couple of buttons when you get up Monday morning and the computer plans and cooks your meals all week, taking the food from the Philco freezer to the Philco oven and, eventually, what's left over to the Philco garbage disposal, without your doing anything but eating it. But that's far off. You may not believe this, but we've projected sales of a billion dollars in 1970, and we're hitting it in 1968."

Robert O. Fickes, president and chief executive officer from 1964–1968, went to Philco from the Norge Division of Borg-Warner. He quite frankly admitted that when the Ford headhunter first approached him at Norge, he didn't want to leave.

"I knew from the end of the business in which we were competitive with Philco," he said, "that there were some pretty good-sized problems, some of which I'd had at Norge. Well, one characteristic of Mister Ford is that he is a pretty persistent fellow.

"There'd been a great deal of talk in the industry about why Ford had bought Philco in the first place, and the speculation was that he wasn't interested in the consumer products business. He assured me that he had no intention but to stay with

295

consumer products and wanted to make it grow. I was convinced of Mister Ford's absolute dedication to the success of Philco. In four years the company spent $135 million in additional facilities. That's a pretty good demonstration of interest.

"We're improving our market penetration," he said. "The reason is that now we can deliver the goods. We've got the facilities and the manpower and direction to produce quality merchandise in quantity on demand."

Carl E. Lantz, the vice president–consumer products group, had been with Admiral, which also makes electrical appliances. "Looking at it from the standpoint of a competitor," he said, "I saw new strength and vitality in the company. We'd written Philco off. Now it was resurging, and it began to scare the hell out of us. The Ford name and reputation exists not only in the garage but in the home, it's familiar to everybody. I see in Mister Ford the desire to extend Ford products from garage into the home, and much further, into space and communications—into the universe! Pride is a tremendous factor in that man."

When I passed all this enthusiasm on to Mister Ford, he grunted sarcastically. "They're talking about their big sales figures and they make a lot of noise," he said, "but how about the profit? That's what I'm concerned about." He didn't seem too interested in his satellites orbiting the world or the computerized homes of the future. "Oh, they're fooling around with all kinds of things over there," he said. "They've got a lot of dreamers planning all kinds of things." When I said that for someone who spoke so sarcastically about the Philco operation he sure had put a lot of money into the white goods division, he said, shortly, "Maybe too much."

Then suddenly he snatched a paperbook of matches off the table and tore off half the cover. "They're building a radio this size over there," he said. His eyes lit up. "No bigger than that." For a couple of minutes he talked swiftly and enthusiastically about the application of such devices to cars and trucks, and the specific electric and electronic know-how that had come with the Philco operation. I got the impression that this was his real interest in Philco. Sure, he had put a lot of money into the consumer products end of the company, but his primary interest was in its adaptation to transportation.

A couple of months later I ran into Carl Lantz, who told me that Fickes had departed. The new president represented Bunkie Knudsen's first major personnel contribution to the company. He was Robert E. Hunter, formerly general manager of GM's Euclid division. I remembered that Knudsen had left GM because of a disagreement on matters pertaining to Euclid. I asked Hunter if he had been involved.

"Well," he said, "if my program had been carried out at Euclid I'd still be there. Does that answer your question? Knudsen knew me and called me to the attention of Mister Ford. So here I am. I like being with Ford. He's direct. He doesn't pull any punches. He comes right out and says what he's going to do, and does it."

Not long after that, I learned that Lantz was gone. Leo Beebe, Mister Ford's number one troubleshooter, had been sent in as vice president–marketing. The story was that the billion-dollar sales projection for 1968 had suddenly dissolved. It was up to Hunter and Beebe to make it reappear.

Ford executives told me that with Philco the Ford Motor Company probably acquired its last outside company, for Ford is so big that its lawyers advise that any further acquisition would be prohibited by the antitrust laws. Will Scott, vice president–corporate planning, said that there are any number of potential business arrangements that might otherwise be logical and sensible. Ford, for example, does not make a diesel engine. Some smaller companies do manufacture diesels, good ones, but not on a large scale.

"It would be logical to join hands," Scott said, "but antitrust, antitrust, antitrust. In a way, the very attempts by the government to maintain free enterprise probably are punitive to a large corporation that has capital, ingenuity, and desire to experiment, explore, test, try new things. Who's to say that we might not be able to bring greater success to some other industry with all our research and technical talent if we were to become a factor in that group? Who's to say? We might well advance the products and the techniques in the process. But I'm afraid that we're too large to be granted the freedom that does exist for smaller companies, solely because of governmental regulations.

"It's a damn shame. If we went into the diesel business we would have to make the investment ourselves, which is enormous from scratch, and if we're successful, we'll drive someone else out of business because we wouldn't make the market of the diesels get any bigger. . . . Someone else loses his shirt, or everyone loses a little bit. And we wind up with a manufacturing capacity that is maybe twice as much as necessary. It's economic waste."

Mister Ford is even more forceful on the matter: "I know a company building diesels, and I don't think it's for sale," he said, "but even if it is for sale, the government probably wouldn't let me buy it. At least that's what my lawyers say. I don't understand why in the hell I can't. The only way I can start building diesel engines is to start from scratch, which would mean penetration of an established market with a brand new thing. I don't know that it would work. But there are a lot of other phases of the transportation area that I could get into and would if they'd let me. I don't see why in the hell I can't buy Hertz. You got a thousand of these car rental agencies all over the country and they must be making money or you wouldn't see all these advertisements all over the place.

"But here you got RCA, a broadcasting company which manufactures television sets, and they can go out and buy a rental car agency, Hertz, and that's all right. Here I am, in the automobile industry, manufacturing cars, and I can't buy the damn thing. If I can't buy it, why do they let a television manufacturer buy it? It doesn't make sense."

Somehow or other, the company will expand. "Sure," Scott said, "we make 12,000 cars and a couple of thousand trucks a day. But Mister Ford is broader in his beliefs than that. We're in the transportation business; we're not just a manufacturer of cars and trucks. Where that will take us he doesn't pretend to project right now. I can't either. Nobody who will make a finite projection is even worth listening to anyway. But it's for that reason that we've got an operation like our transportation research and planning office. We're looking at things that are competitive to what we do. We're looking at transit, mass transit.

"What can we do to move people and move goods? Ideally we'd like to move them in the kind of things we make today. But if the kind of things we make today are not the best suited to the requirements that evolve over the years, I'll guarantee you that Henry Ford will be in the forefront of seeing that this company is reshaped so it can do the kind of things that will keep it pre-eminent in the transportation business.

"Ford doesn't make cars and trucks in a lot of places. So maybe we should. As markets expand and populations increase, as incomes rise in many countries of the world, the question that comes front and center is whether Ford should consider making a substantial investment to participate in a market that we're now in. A geographical market. We concern ourselves with that."

The director of transportation research and planning, which Scott mentioned, is Foster L. Weldon. The staff under Weldon's direction is studying the future development of the city in relationship to the transportation it will require. One projection is that the cities of the future will consist of a proliferation of special-purpose centers, extensions of the shopping centers we have today. The transportation system of the future, if cities develop in this way, must include a super network connecting the centers, with secondary networks feeding people into it. One of the systems that currently seems logical is an automated highway on which cars would proceed to one of the centers of the megalopolis, then get off and drive under their own power to their specific destinations.

The automated highway becomes necessary with the demands of increased traffic. Today a single lane of highway has a capacity of 1500 to 2000 vehicles an hour which is attained at a speed of about 40 miles per hour. Although both car and highway are designed for greater speeds, safety requires that the faster you go, the more space you must maintain between you and the car in front of you. Consequently greater speed actually reduces the number of cars being put through the highway pipelines. But on an automated highway a car would come under automatic control and less space and greater speed could be maintained. The combination results in an increased capacity to the factor of ten. Instead of 50 cars per mile, the automated highway would accommodate 500 cars per mile.

This is only one of many possible solutions, and the automation can be furnished in many different ways, but it gives an idea of just one of the projects that just one of many Ford staffs is working on. It is no coincidence, of course, that this projection would employ both a vehicle made by Ford and electronic controls made by Philco-Ford.

In Weldon's personal opinion, workable systems of this nature will be in effect in constricted rights of way such as bridges, tunnels, and airport accesses before 1980. Weldon also pointed out that Mister Ford is interested not only from a corporate viewpoint, but through his concern about improving the urban environment.

"Transportation is involved in social progress, cultural progress, everything that goes with making cities and living a better thing," he said. "Ford today has the technology to provide it; the problem is to define what it is."

300

14

THE SINGLE MOST vital ingredient of any successful enterprise is the manipulation of personnel. Ford himself says that in regard to people, if he can bat .500 he's doing okay. That means choosing and utilizing correctly every other person. Another comment of his in regard to personnel is worth repeating: "You can't just have 'em floppin' around here." His P stands not only for people, therefore, but for the way they are used in the organization and administration of the company.

Lee Iacocca, talking about his advancement in the company, unconsciously gave me an excellent example of a man who benefited from the organizational setup of the company—himself.

"I'll never forget the first time I had a guy work for me. My supervisor said, 'It's very simple. Because you're getting better, we believe you can multiply yourself through two people.' Then I got twenty people. And another fellow said suppose

I had a hundred thousand people? How do you motivate a hundred thousand people? So now I have 54,000 in this school —that's only salaried people—and 6900 dealers. That's what management is all about, multiplying yourself."

The organization plan of the Ford Motor Company has undergone constant change since Ernie Breech brought in the GM system in 1946. The major overhaul of 1968 retained only vestiges of that system, and as an entire department working under a vice president is constantly jiggling with organization, it will probably bear less resemblance to the GM prototype tomorrow. Unless, of course, they change it around again. Anyway, the degree of dissimilarity is immaterial to the independent thinkers at Ford.

As Neil Duff of the organization planning staff put it, "Back in 1953 when I first became interested in this, whenever we were discussing organizational improvement somebody would always ask, 'What are they doing over on the boulevard?' Today we couldn't care less about what they are doing over in GM headquarters on West Grand Boulevard. *We* know what *we're* doing."

E. D. O'Leary, vice president–personnel and organization, an executive trained in both law and accountancy who followed the strains of Breech's pipe out of Fisher Body, is pretty cagey about the fine points of the Ford system. He doesn't want to share its secrets. As an illustration, he whipped out an organization chart of a competitor and pointed to various blocs and lines. "They're in trouble there, and there, and there," he said. But where he pointed is off the record. "Let 'em find it out for themselves."

Nevertheless, one of the salient features of the Ford master plan can be definitely stated: it no longer clings arbitrarily to the old policy of decentralization. In some ways the Ford organization has come around full circle.

A quick example is in purchasing. A man who sells large

quantities of an essential product to all three automobile companies told me that doing business with each one is like dealing with three separate nations.

"With General Motors and its separate profit-sharing system," he said, "you have to deal with each division separately. Specifications for one may be very different from another, and may even change radically in a given division. We can spend a year defining the product to meet somebody's specifications and then find that we're in a whole new ball game and have to start over again. With Ford the standard for each division is set by the central purchasing department, the specifications are written down, and that's what we shoot for. On the other hand, it may take a year to get a decision out of the bureaucracy at the top. With Chrysler the situation is different all over again. There it's not what you've got to sell, but who you know to sell it to."

Back in the Twenties Henry Ford issued one of his pronunciamentos on organization:

"To my mind there is no bend of mind more dangerous than that which is sometimes described as the 'genius for organization.' This usually results in the birth of a great big chart; showing, after the fashion of a family tree, how authority ramifies. The tree is heavy with nice round berries, each of which bears the name of a man or an office. Every man has a title and certain duties which are strictly limited by the circumference of his berry. It takes about six weeks for the message of a man living in a berry on the lower left-hand corner of the chart to reach the President or Chairman of the Board, and if it ever does reach one of these officials, it has by that time gathered to itself a pound of criticisms, suggestions, and comments. Very few things are even taken under 'official consideration' until long after the time when they actually ought to have been done. The buck is passed to and fro and all responsibility is dodged by individuals—following the lazy notion that two heads are better than one.

"Now a business, in my way of thinking, is not a machine. It is a collection of people who are brought together to do work and not to write letters to one another. It is not necessary for any one department to know what any other department is doing—it is not necessary to have meetings to establish good feelings between individuals or departments. It is not necessary for people to love each other in order to work together."

Some twenty years later, Henry Ford II came along and said what he thought about organization:

"Organization is important. It is *the* important thing. Unless it is set up right, we know that we will have the pulling and hauling and canceling of instructions that are common to a poorly organized business. We know we have to have the proper organization to do the job right."

On September 21, 1945, when Henry Ford II became president, the company had an almost pathetically simple organization chart. Under the president were four directors: sales, personnel, engineering, and purchasing. The work was divided up by specialties, rather than by products. Twelve years later, after Breech had introduced and augmented the GM system, the organization chart reflected what corporate planners call Divisionalization: the work was divided according to product line, and each product, or group of closely related products, was established as a relatively autonomous business within the framework of the company as a whole. The Ford organization was broken down into four product groups—Ford, Lincoln, Mercury, Edsel—and eleven separate manufacturing divisions.

But now, on the organization chart set up in 1968, there is one big bloc called North American Automotive Operations under executive vice president Lee Iacocca. Under him is the product development group, the manufacturing group and the sales group. The Ford and Lincoln-Mercury divisions now simply serve as marketing agencies. Other divisions have been realigned and consolidated. The steel division had been tied in with the stamping division; now steel and glass are together under a basic products group. Just as Henry I's organization had a functional orientation, with Sorensen responsible for manufacturing and Davis responsible for sales, today Henry Ford II has returned to a functional orientation, on a much larger and more complex scale, with manufacturing, sales, and product development.

The intermediate step of decentralization was not obliterated by the swing back to functionalism. The general manager of the engine and foundry division, for example, still operates his own profit center. Through intracompany pricing, the executives up the line can evaluate his performance efficiently. But his operation is now oriented to an overall function rather than to an individual product.

Each division general manager works more closely today with the staff. If he wishes to install a drastically new technique or spend $50 million or so in fixed assets, he brings his plans up at a prior-review session with staff advisers. They can be more objective in judging the idea, and they may know something the manager does not know. He still has autonomy, for, within limitations, he can take off on his own even if advised against it. If his method pays off he's a hero; if it flops he'd better start reading the want ads in the *Wall Street Journal*.

The new functionally oriented organization at Ford represents the thinking of Henry Ford II himself.

"As a result of Mister Ford's interest," O'Leary said, "the company today is in a fine organizational state. I don't say that it is set. Looking back at some of the mistakes we made in reaching this point, I can't understand how we could possibly think they would work. Maybe we are making a similar mistake somewhere today. But basically, I think it's sound. Further, our pattern is a model for all industry and has great influence on other industries because our people are frequently being hired away from us and take their expertise with them. One thing they can't take with them, though, is Henry Ford. One of the things that annoys me is the myth I hear constantly that Henry Ford runs this company from the Riviera. That's nonsense. He works with a lot of people, he knows a tremendous number of people, he knows a number of individuals in this company closely and he works as hard, if not harder, than all the rest of us."

The philosophy of the new Ford Motor Company was set forth in Policy Letter A-1 sent out over Mister Ford's signature in March, 1968. Five pages long, it sets forth in simple language the duties of the line management, operations, the central staff, and the committees. On every executive's desk, or on his bookshelf, is a copy of the bulging authorities manual that implements the policy letter. The manual spells out who has the authority to do what in the various areas of capital assets, fiscal matters, product development, purchasing, pricing, sales, marketing, organization plans, and it gets down to the nuts and bolts of what a man can do and what he can't do.

It's referred to constantly. When Colombia, one of the emerging nations, informed the company that it could either manufacture an arbitrary percentage of parts in Colombia or get out, the decision had to be made whether to conform or depart. Who should make this decision? Should the problem be sent to the highest level, the board of directors, so that this high-priced group could thresh out the problem of building a plant in one small country? The authorities manual had the answer. It states that the executive vice president of the overseas automotive operation is empowered to spend up to $5 million on capital assets. That amount would pay for the construction and equipment sufficient to manufacture the percentage required. One individual could make the decision to keep Ford in Colombia.

"The company competes in two markets," Henry Ford II once said. "One is the market for our products, where our success is a matter of record. The other is a market for people. I've often pointed out that our progress depends essentially on our ability to attract and retain talented men and women, and that this is a function of our business we must perform extraordinarily well."

The company has an elaborate system for evaluating its personnel. Mister Ford is dedicated to building up personnel strength for years ahead. One of the most important operations in this goal is the personnel review. At regular intervals the performance of every salaried employee is reviewed by his superior, then the two review it again together. Criteria of performance, of course, vary with the position. An executive involved in the production of hardware is measured along different lines from a member of Markley's staff in Washington, Mecke's PR department, or O'Leary's organizational planning staff. Evaluation of the performance of staff personnel can become pretty subjective.

One method of judging performance is by objective. The superior and his subordinate sit down together and jointly establish a goal: what it is, how long it's going to take to get there, and what it will cost in terms of time, manpower, and money. After the goal has been decided upon, the progress of the individual in accomplishing it can be checked. Executive vice presidents report constantly to the president, and the process continues down the line. These sessions can be embarrassing. "This is what you said you were going to do, why didn't you do it?" Yet these personnel reviews provide motivation, for they result in merit increases in pay and bonuses and sometimes in departures.

Personnel reviews are subject to further review by higher levels, for sometimes an unfavorable report on a subordinate can reflect unfavorably on the superior. A man who receives a rating of only satisfactory may be shifted to another department and given another chance. After all, he wouldn't have been hired if someone hadn't perceived some potential there. A man has to strike out two or three times before he is cut off the roster, and then the amputation is made as painless as possible.

As someone who viewed the corporation from the outside put it, "Henry Ford has a surprising amount of sympathy for the corporate slob. His grandfather didn't understand the problems of the men who worked on the assembly line. Henry tries hard to understand the problems of a minor executive in this huge operation."

The rewards are great for the man who produces. There are 28 pay grades for salaried personnel. The salary range for Grade 1 is $5191–$7672 per year. Salary range for Grade 28 is $181,000–$272,000. I was surprised to learn that when Arjay Miller was vice chairman of the board he was not in the top grade; only Ford himself and Bunkie Knudsen made it.

At Grade 11, salary range $16,020–22,464, the annual bonus becomes effective. The bonus can amount to 100 per cent of the annual salary, or even more. It's possible for a man with a salary of $45,000 a year to wind up with close to $100,000.

Bonuses of over $15,000 are reviewed by the supplemental compensation committee of the board of directors. Sidney Weinberg, who was chairman of the committee when I talked with him, was still impressed with the amount of compensation in the automotive industry. "We have to pay these large sums to keep our men," he said. "Local society has a lot to do with it. You've got a couple of women playing bridge at the country club, and if one of them knows the other one's husband makes $100,000 more a year than her husband, she's going to needle him to get more. We figure the records carefully in determining bonuses. Henry has a big book this thick"—he held his hands three or four inches apart—"and he's familiar with every name in it. Henry himself always protests at accepting his bonus, but we force him to take it to keep the entire scale up. Being a Ford doesn't automatically mean you get a bonus. A couple of years ago an executive had been sick. To give him supplemental compensation would mean the destruction of the equitableness of the structure. He didn't get it."

When executives reach Grade 16, $29,000–$40,000, they become members of the executive roll, which entitles them, among other privileges, to the use of a company car, Continentals included. From Grade 9 up, personnel can lease a company car or two. The rates aren't bad; a Cortina runs about $26 a month, including company maintenance. That's less than a dollar a day. For a Continental you'd have to pay about $3 a day. The company, incidentally, does not lose money on leased cars; they are kept in excellent repair and bring a good price on the used car market. Other fringe benefits include Blue Cross, accident and health insurance, life insurance and participation in the pension plan, all except the contribution portion of the pension plan at no cost.

Company employees are entitled to invest up to ten per cent of their annual income in Ford stock or government bonds and the company itself adds 50 per cent to the total investment. That is, you can buy $150 worth of stock for $100. You don't draw dividends, but they accumulate for capital gains and are re-invested. Go to work for Ford at the age of 22, quit at 52, which you can do with the special consent of the company, and you can easily have $100,000 subject only to capital gains taxes, plus pension and paid up life insurance. If you stick it out to the mandatory retirement age of 65, you'll be that much better off.

Mister Ford, incidentally, in the early spring of 1969, said he sure as hell is going to retire at 65, if he's still around. Did that mean he had any definite intentions of leaving earlier? Apparently not. I repeated to him the comment of someone who had observed him in action. "Henry Ford II has totally committed himself to his responsibility," this fellow said, "which makes him a complete idiot in my book."

Ford grinned, but only for a split second. "Well, I like it," he said defensively. "It's the most interesting business in the world. It's exciting and challenging and if it wasn't I'd just get out of here. I'd walk away from it."

"You couldn't do that," I said. "What would happen? Who'd hold it together if you left?"

"We've got a board of directors," he said. "They could find somebody. That's their job."

In the meantime, he was doing his. Though he occasionally grumbles about it, he gets to work early, like everyone else, and usually stays late. His working hours include portal-to-portal time, for he sits in the front seat of his chauffeur-driven Continental, which is equipped with a reading light, and goes through his papers with his own filing system. He tosses unimportant memos over his shoulder into the rear seat to be thrown away, puts matters requiring future action in the glove compartment, and shoves urgent documents in his coat pocket.

He travels constantly. Though he's mildly fond of golf, he hadn't played for over a year when he was asked about it in the summer of 1968. And although his brother Bill, as owner of the Detroit Lions, could conceivably have gotten him a ticket to a game, he hadn't seen them play once the previous season. He was either working, traveling, or exhausted.

Since then, even with the new organization policy and the addition of the new president, Bunkie Knudsen, Ford has had no chance to coast. The increasing involvement of government in the automotive industry, on all levels, and the continuing trend to proliferation of car models require extra effort.

Though the company is interested in educating its workers, and pays tuition for some at the nearby campus of the University of Michigan, most of its bright young men come in through college recruitment. In 1968 Ford recruiters visited 205 colleges and universities throughout the United States and hired 1550 graduates. The company has its pet institutions; J. Edward Lundy told me that in a recent graduating class from the Carnegie-

Mellon University Graduate Business School there was only one man he didn't want. But Ford has its problems in recruiting. As the price tag on graduates, particularly holders of advanced degrees, goes up, the company sometimes finds itself paying a larger salary to an untrained recruit than to one of last year's crop. Recruiters don't get involved in bidding for star graduates. They offer only the going rate today; tomorrow's potential is the major Ford selling point. Straight-A students are not always the pick of the crop. A graduate who has worked his way through college, sacrificing top grades but gaining dependability and discipline, may be the first-round choice. Nor are trainees selected exclusively from business and engineering majors. I was surprised by the range of expertise which fill the pipelines to the future. Trainees in government and international affairs are coming in, for example. And would you think that an automobile company would want music majors? It seems they make excellent computer programmers.

Holding trainees is as important as hiring them. "You have to keep watching the people you bring in," O'Leary said. "You have to motivate them with opportunity and compensation; you've got to keep them happy. If you let them wander around with nothing to do, or if you don't advance them along the financial line, you're going to lose them. They'll quit on you."

Fortunate indeed is the young executive who comes under the wing of J. Edward Lundy, who has a deserved reputation in the company for helping and encouraging his protégés. Will Scott, hired by Lundy as a finance analyst in 1948, says, "No one in America today can rival him in the development of personnel. His boys are scattered through industry. He culled them, sifted them, cultivated them, developed them—they are in key places today. He has brought in young men who didn't have the best possible grades, but they had something of value which he was able to detect. He gives you a brief psychological analysis, then works with you, helps you, advises you."

311

Lundy, a crew-cut, soft-voiced man with the poise and confidence his salary-plus-bonus income of $390,000 in 1968 helps acquire, was modest about his own contribution, but proud of his protégés. He did discuss the Ford training method, which doesn't just turn its trainees loose to look over other people's shoulders, but gives them challenging projects with a definite completion date.

Lundy trains his people so well that the company can't hold them; it can't leapfrog them over other capable people to the positions and salaries they are offered elsewhere. Just recently, he said, they had lost a a 28-year-old junior executive who became vice president of a big corporation.

"We hated to see him go," Lundy said, "but we wished him Godspeed. Mister Ford doesn't want to stand in the way of a young man leaving for career betterment. His personal policy, and the policy of the company, is that if you talk someone into staying on against his wishes, both the man and the company will regret it for the rest of his life."

Lundy mentioned an executive who left his $18,000-a-year job with Ford for $50,000 elsewhere. A $27,000 executive was lured away by a guaranteed income of $500,000 spread out over three years. Lundy made up a list of 53 graduates from his department for me. Three have become presidents of other companies, forty-two vice presidents. Some of the companies benefiting by the transfer include American Bosch, Pullman, Irving Trust, Texaco, Seiberling, Chrysler, Westinghouse, American Motors (president *and* vice president), Olin Mathieson, Xerox, Goldman, Sachs, North American Rockwell, Celanese.

The opportunities are particularly challenging in the overseas operations. The company likes to develop its foreign personnel, but Europeans don't seem to like to leave home. Frequently a top job will open up in one European country which provides the opportunity for a man to move diagonally upward from his position in his home country. Almost as frequently,

a European suited for the job won't take it. Americans, however, are mobile; they'll go anywhere. When Ford of Finland,
for example, needed a treasurer, a German in a lower echelon
position was offered the job. He didn't want to leave home. An
American was moved there from Portugal.

Americans don't seem to mind working hard, either. In
addition to their company duties, which are demanding, they
are also expected to take part in civic and community activities.
Government—federal, state, and local—has a broad effect upon
business today. Taxes, tariffs, labor, air pollution, zoning, safety
regulations, schools—all affect business. Industry is making a
painful adjustment to this harsh reality and has not reacted
wisely in all cases. To provide direction from the top, Ford was
the first major company to set up a civic and government affairs
department with a vice president in charge. Not so long ago, it
was customary in industry to ignore politics. Today the company encourages and expects its employees to get involved in the
processes of government.

Henry Ford II, when he first brought up the subject of
increased involvement, received a little static from the executives
at the meeting. "Look," he said, "I'm sitting in the captain's
chair, and I say, get involved." There was no further argument.

How a Ford executive finds time to participate in local
affairs is a question I can't answer. Working with John Sattler in
the public relations department at Dearborn, I noticed that he
always stuffed papers, magazines and reports in his briefcase
on leaving the office. It was usually around 6:30 or 7:00; most
executives wrap up the day's activities after normal quitting
time. John reads the morning papers at night.

John's department includes special events, which involves
everything from the tours hundreds of thousands of people take
through the plant each year to the entertainment of VIP's; stock-
holder and investor relations; educational affairs; getting out
seventeen publications including the 1,600,000-circulation *Ford*

313

Times, and being nice to me and Arthur Hailey, who was also poking around the company. He makes frequent trips to New York and other parts of the country. He was responsible for Ford's exhibits at the 1968 HemisFair exposition in Texas, and made the arrangements for the second annual meeting of the National Alliance of Businessmen in Washington. Before his arrival in Dearborn, John was in charge of Ford public relations in New York; he was referred to frequently as "Mr. Ford." He handled all the myriads of jobs that came up including the $35 million Ford exhibit at the World's Fair, and he helped out with the Fair in general, for which he and the company won an award. On the side he worked his way up through the chairmanship of various committees of the Public Relations Society of America to become national treasurer and president of the New York chapter. He was a director of the Advertising Club of New York, and an active working member of a dozen other groups including the Overseas Press Club, Publicity Club, Greater New York Council of the Boy Scouts, and Greater New York Safety Council. When he left New York for Dearborn his friends gave him a send-off that was heard all over Manhattan.

"I've seen a lot of changes in the company since Mister Ford took hold," he said, "and I want to stick around and see some more."

Another Ford executive who commented on the company's growth was Gene Bordinat, who, with his artistic eye, looked back upon his years with the company as a series of still photographs.

"I'm grateful for my good fortune in coming to the company at the time I did," he said. "Mister Ford had just taken over and it was just beginning to grow. It was volatile, exciting, dangerous. It was the best of times and the worst of times. Heroes were made and bums were made, and sometimes they were the same. You could actually see the company grow, and I had the opportunity to grow with it."

Will Scott told me that in actuality the Ford Motor Company going into the Seventies was only about 20 years old. "The first of those ten years it operated on the momentum built up by the first Henry Ford," he said. "Henry Ford II and Ernie Breech were re-creating it, making it a viable organization for the future. Since the late Fifties it has become the unique, world-wide organization it is today. It represents the best of two men, both named Henry Ford."

Men of social conscience

15

ONE EPITHET YOU can't apply to either Henry Ford is *stingy*.
Wary, maybe, or choosy as to the object of their generosity, but
close-fisted, never. A generation before the development of
the fine art of giving for the sake of tax deductions, Henry I was
giving away a third of his net income. He had his own peculiar
method of selecting his recipients, but once he latched on to a
cause, he poured in the money.

His son and grandson have been more orthodox in their
giving, but they have continued the tradition. As for the family
as a whole, its contributions through the Ford Foundation are
incomprehensible. I'll never forget the expression on Sidney
Weinberg's face when he leaned forward across his desk and
told me, "This family has given away *four billion dollars!*" Weinberg, economic adviser to both Republican and Democratic ad-
ministrations, has been involved with billion dollar corporations

and is one of the few people I know who has any idea what four billion dollars means. If he's impressed, I'm impressed.

To give one interpretation to the old quotation, "For the gift without the giver is bare," a contribution even more significant than money is commitment. Anybody can write a check or buy a box of Girl Scout cookies, but how many of us put our names, our reputations, and our time into those causes in which we totally believe? The Fords have. They've stuck their necks out a mile, practically had their heads lopped off as a consequence, and have then come right back and right out on another limb.

One day in the summer of 1915, Henry Ford and a newspaper reporter friend of his named Theodore Delavigne were rambling around the grounds at Fair Lane, talking. Ford said he'd give all the money he had to stop the war in Europe. Delavigne, of course, said, "Can I quote you?" Within two minutes he had permission not just to quote him, but to make up the quotes. Delavigne wrote an antiwar diatribe containing five columns of purple prose, all attributed, sight unseen, to Henry Ford. Ford the elder didn't mind at all. Of his mother's three brothers, one had been killed in the Civil War and one had received injuries which shortened his life. Mrs. Ford had nurtured in her son an abhorrence of war, and no pacifist polemic could be too strong.

In 1915 the American attitude was largely against involvement in the European war, and letters approving Ford's position poured in. People poured in, too, and one of them was Rosika Schwimmer, Hungarian, Jewish, radical, suffragette, and pacifist. Her intensity was the major factor in Ford's decision to commit himself and his money to what Delavigne had said for him in print. He leased a Norwegian ocean liner, the *Oscar II,* and sent out invitations to a list of prominent Americans to go with him to Europe. "We'll get the soldiers out of the trenches by

Christmas," he told the press. He proposed a general strike on Christmas Day all over the world, including the battlefields.

War supporters, including members of the as-yet-unnamed military-industrial complex, and the people who don't like to get involved, ridiculed the peace crusade. Ford's own pastor, Dean Samuel S. Marquis, tried to talk him out of going to Europe. "It is right to try to stop war, isn't it?" Ford asked. Marquis agreed. "Well," Ford said, "you have told me that what is right cannot fail."

Not all of the responsible Americans Ford invited to accompany him agreed to go along, and quite a few nuts took their places. On the way across the Atlantic the pacifists began fighting among themselves and the 50-odd reporters on board reported the skirmishes to the world. By the time the ship arrived at Oslo, Ford was ill and exhausted.

Five days after his arrival, before he had really said or done anything, he was hustled secretly out the back door of his hotel and returned home. The group he had led continued on at his expense and did at least elicit from Germany an offer to talk things over. The Allies refused. The boys did not get out of the trenches by Christmas. Ford's peace ship had made an unnecessary trip. As a pacifist, Ford was a flop. But when the war was finally over, and the Ford Motor Company went seriously after the European market, the survivors remembered the name. Because he had tried.

Actually, the Neutral Conference for Continuous Mediation went on throughout the war and was one of the forerunners of the League of Nations. Ford continued to pay all the bills for the group, even after he returned home.

Henry Senior also supported President Woodrow Wilson in his unsuccessful effort to put America into the League of Nations. In 1953 his grandson carried the Ford spirit of internationalism several steps further as a member of the United States

Mission to the United Nations. He had been appointed by the Eisenhower administration he had supported, and some considered him merely a dilettante. But though he was only an alternate delegate, he took seriously his participation in "The Other State Department."

One of the many Ford legends concerns the Thanksgiving morning in 1953 when Henry Ford II replied to harsh criticism of the United States made by the leader of the Russian mission, Georgei Petrovich Arkadyev. The most common version has the entire U.S. delegation off eating Thanksgiving dinner when Arkadyev sprang a surprise attack. Ford, conscientiously present, leaped to his feet and turned the tables on the Russian delegate with a powerful blast of inspired rhetoric. It didn't happen exactly that way.

The General Assembly meets on Thanksgiving but it usually adjourns after the morning session in courtesy to American custom. David Zellerbach, chairman of the Economics Committee to which Ford was assigned, was not present, but Ford and the staff were. No one expected anything of moment to happen, and, in anticipation of an easy day, Forrest Murden, a member of the delegation, had on the previous night given himself cause for a galloping hangover.

Arkadyev had been speaking for several minutes before Murden realized that the Soviet delegate was taking advantage of Ford's presence to make an attack on the United States using Henry Ford II as the symbol of American imperialism and exploitation.

Ford was squirming in his chair. "What next?" he whispered to Murden.

"I'm afraid we're going to have to reply," Murden said. He began making a quick outline of Ford's response, determining the points which would have to be answered. He needed technical information on some of the points and got up to get it from the appropriate experts of the delegation.

Ford looked at him with an expression that suggested panic. He had never made a speech at the UN before. "Where are you going?" he asked.

"I'm just going to get some facts," Murden reassured him. "You stay here and listen."

The Soviet delegate was an old hand whose characteristics Murden knew well. He was confident that Arkadyev would use the same old Russian arguments, and so Murden wouldn't miss anything while he was out. As it was, it took him a little longer than he had anticipated—and Ford was an anxious man when Murden finally slipped back into the seat beside him. Arkadyev finished speaking, and the two men quickly discussed Ford's reply and how the facts and figures Murden had obtained could best be utilized. Then Ford got up to answer, armed only with outline and notes, and it was Murden's turn to be anxious.

"I've seen other delegates develop lockjaw under the pressure of lesser crises," Murden told me. "Some have actually gotten up and run out."

Ford, however, spoke cogently and lucidly for about ten minutes. About 60 delegates were present, and several hundred sightseers in the gallery, but he delivered an unruffled explanation of the American position. It was a solid, creditable performance.

The session adjourned. Somewhat later Zellerbach dropped in. "I guess you had an easy day," he observed innocently. Ford and Murden exchanged a smile and said nothing.

The days Ford put in at the United Nations were long and grueling, and often ended with social functions which required his attendance. The World Series was played in New York that year, and Dan Topping, then owner of the New York Yankees, invited Ford and his wife to join him in his private box. On the UN agenda the first day of the Series, however, was an elaborate luncheon hosted by the Pakistani delegate. Ford asked Murden if he could see the ball game.

"No sir," Murden said, "you can't go." Ford attended the luncheon.

As the session drew to a close, the American delegation wanted to have a get-together, but there was only $30 left in the budget. Ford gave the party himself at his suite in the Pierre, and, on the spur of the moment, invited everyone—including guards, secretaries, switchboard operators. It was planned as a 6:00 to 8:00 affair, but at 8:30 Ford asked Murden, "Why don't we roll up the rug?" Ford likes to dance. The two men got down on their hands and knees, rolled up the rug, and the party went on until 3:30 in the morning.

Full exposure to the inner workings of nations buttressed Ford's international understanding. People in the Ford foreign department refer to the company as multinational rather than international, and think of themselves as citizens of the world. Answering the critics of the United Nations, Ford has said, "It's a lot better to talk than to fight."

While he was an alternate delegate, he stood up to Secretary of State John Foster Dulles with the recommendation that Red China be included in the United Nations, and he hasn't changed his mind. He's in favor of trading with China, and every other nation as well.

"When you talk to people," he says, "you can at least get a feel of what's going on in their country."

He was referring there to the self-survival necessity of knowing what the potential enemy is thinking.

He has been in the forefront of those helping friendly nations build up their own untapped resources through industry. In 1964 his friends Senator Jacob Javits of New York and Forrest Murden developed the idea of using private capital to help boost the economy of Latin America by investment in local industries that the normal sources of capital would ordinarily not be interested in. Ford was the first to put in his check, for $500,000. Other industries, American and European, followed his example. Within five years the organization known as ADELA, from the Spanish for Atlantic Community Group for the Development of Latin America, had committed more than $50 million to 74 projects in 18 countries, and had created 20,000 new jobs. ADELA was not expected to show a profit; but it was successful in getting Latin Americans to use their own energy and resources to help themselves and their communities.

Both Henry Fords have demonstrated full acceptance of their responsibility to their own country. But the elder Ford's negative views in the closing years of his life have tended to obscure his positive involvement in government in earlier years. His staunch support of President Wilson in 1916 was a factor in Wilson's reelection, and Wilson personally persuaded him to make his unsuccessful campaign for the Senate in 1918.

Though there was a strong grass-roots Ford-for-President movement prior to the 1924 election, he stopped it by announcing his support for Calvin Coolidge. There's a strong possibility that he himself realized his inadequacy for the job. In the early days of the boom he expressed his idea of the presidency as something like his role in the Ford Motor Company: he'd just wander around the various government agencies and talk to people. Apparently he found out that a little more office work would be involved.

As for Henry Ford II, he dismissed any governmental aspirations in 1969 with a simple declarative sentence, "I'd be a lousy politician." He may have sized up the situation pretty well in that remark. From what I've seen of his accomplishments and the way he works, I think he'd make a great chief executive. But he'd never get elected. He'd be a terrible campaigner. He gets bored with his own speeches and he's too blunt.

He's also completely unpredictable. He was a strong Eisenhower supporter, and apparently a loyal Republican. During the 1964 presidential campaign, Lyndon B. Johnson visited Detroit. Ford went to the airport to meet him, ostensibly as a courtesy by a leader of the Detroit community. Allen Merrell, a personal friend of Ford's and the company's vice president for civic and governmental affairs, drove to the airport with him. Merrell told me that on the way they did not mention politics, and he had no idea that Ford was even considering supporting Johnson.

At the airport Ford went aboard President Johnson's plane to look it over, and chatted briefly with Johnson, then emerged. A reporter for the *Detroit Free Press* routinely asked him what he thought of Johnson. Without hesitation, Ford said, "Mr. Johnson is doing an excellent job as President. I've heard him say many times that he is for all the people, for business, for labor, for the general public. I agree with what he says."

This off-the-cuff answer led to his becoming chairman of Businessmen for Johnson and threw him slambang into the Democratic party for the first time in his life.

Two years later, when G. Mennen "Soapy" Williams, former governor of Michigan, was running for the Senate on the Democratic ticket, it was naturally assumed that Ford, now a Democrat, would support him. Instead, he said, "I wouldn't support Soapy Williams for dogcatcher of Grosse Pointe Farms."

In 1968 he supported the Democratic candidate, Hubert H. Humphrey, from the beginning. His brother Benson, incidentally, was chairman of a large fund-raising dinner for the Republican candidate, Richard M. Nixon, while the youngest brother, William Clay Ford, was chairman of Michigan Businessmen for Eugene McCarthy.

After Nixon was elected, Henry Ford gave a party in Washington two nights before the inauguration. A group of students lounging around outside the club where the party was held saw him arrive and started a cheer, "Ford for President!" An astute politician in the atmosphere of goodwill immediately preceding the Nixon inauguration would have brushed it off with a mean-

326

ingless comment. Ford, instead, shouted: "Save your vote for Kennedy in 1972!"

In short, it would be impossible to keep Henry Ford II from talking himself out of winning the election. He's a lousy politician.

When it comes to efficient organization in the service of his fellow man, however, Ford is superb. He emerged as the acknowledged leader of American industry in attempting to alleviate one of our greatest domestic problems.

Ford grew up in a family predominantly blind to the color of a man's skin. His grandfather was a friend and benefactor to American Negroes, in his own, personal, individually philanthropic way. He wasn't strongly affected by the misery of people he didn't see, but when he saw it, he did something about it. And he saw it in two widely separated Negro communities, the Detroit suburb of Inkster, and the rural area around Richmond Hills, Georgia. Inkster, when he stumbled across it in the early Thirties, was a bankrupt community without police, electricity, garbage collection, or sewage. Its banks had closed. Many of its houses were only half finished, but people lived in them anyway, surrounded by their own garbage. The Georgia area was in even worse shape. The landowners had deserted their plantations following the Civil War, and in the ensuing generations the population existed without sufficient food, with little or no education, and without hope. The elder Ford brought to each not charity, although he fed the hungry and set up centers which sold food at cost, but opportunity to work. The residents of both communities, availing themselves of the chance to improve their own lives, proved Ford's contention that people prefer the rewards of work to the handouts of charity.

Henry I was the pioneer in equal opportunity in the automotive industry, at least in the Detroit area. His grandson inherited the policy, but in his first years with the company he did not greatly enhance it. He was busy with his career. But as he was rebuilding the company, conditions were developing in the community that no responsible industrialist could ignore. Owing in part to the hiring policies inaugurated by the Ford Motor Company, the Negro population in Detroit grew from a mere 5 per cent in 1920 to almost 50 per cent in the Sixties. As some half-million whites fled the inner city for the suburbs, the blacks, 700,000 strong, spread into some of the most strategic real estate in the metropolitan area.

One of the answers to those who predicted ethnic revolt was that the influx of a new group had been faced before in Detroit history. The city had welcomed unskilled European peasants in years gone by, and had seen them assimilated into the community.

"But though those who held this view could see that there was a real difference in color between the European peasant and the American Negro," an observer of the scene told me, "they could not see, or did not want to see, the potential consequences of this difference. Sure, the immigrants could climb their way up the ladder and be assimilated, but the vast majority of Negroes could not. They're black, they stand out, they remain at the bottom. No matter how hard the black man works, society proves to him day in and day out that he's still a nigger and he's stuck with it. Some of them just give up and quit trying. But whether they quit or whether they strive, the anger and resentment remain, and build up like pressure in a boiler. The pressure spreads throughout the entire community. When it lets go, look out."

Though you don't find many bleeding heart liberals in industry, the Ford Motor Company happened to have one in William H. Schoen, Director of Urban and Community affairs. Schoen had joined the company in 1951 after serving with the U. S. Department of State and the Department of Commerce.

"I'll never forget the first time I saw Mister Ford at the

UN," Schoen told me. "I expected to find some pompous fellow and here was this pleasant man in his shirtsleeves stuck in a tiny office trying to lower his window blinds. I started enlightening this backward businessman and he just knocked me right over. I came out of that session feeling that I had been trying to tell the score to a man who knew it a lot better than I did. I remember thinking, this guy's too good to be true. He was a tremendous hit with the other delegates and became one of the most effective members of the U. S. delegation. From that time on, I've never doubted his capacity to think and act."

Schoen had been given a copy of Gunnar Myrdal's *An American Dilemma* on his twenty-first birthday, and was acutely aware of the pressure building up in the Negro population. He was not close enough to Mister Ford to discuss noncompany matters with him. However, particularly after the burn-baby-burn riots in the Watts area of Los Angeles in 1965, there were some stirrings within the company of the need for somebody to do something, and Schoen took on the part-time assignment of looking into urban relations. He began to see vast areas in which industry could play a more vital and effective role in narrowing the gap between the races.

While Schoen was making his study, remote from the throne, somebody with no company-ingrained inhibitions was moving right in on Henry Ford II. Having been exposed to the zeal, charm and charisma of Whitney Young, Jr., myself, I feel almost sorry for Mister Ford. He never had a chance.

During the Time–Life tour of Europe in 1966, it was natural for Ford to seek Young's company. Both are tremendously likable guys. Ford is a hard-driving executive, Young an equally effective crusader who has turned down a half-dozen vice presidencies in industry to continue as executive director of the National Urban League, but both relax with equal intensity and thirst. Just as young Henry had been raised without prejudice, so young Whitney had been raised with prejudice—for the Ford

Motor Company. The senior Young had voluntarily left a $300-a-month position with the company in 1919 to become a $68-a-month teacher in a Negro school, but he never forgot, and never let Whitney forget, that Ford had given him, a Negro, the opportunity to work as an electrical engineer.

Whitney Junior had been plucked from the faculty of Atlanta University by the Urban League, sent to Harvard for a year, and named executive director in 1961. He took the job with the proviso that the League, considered by many blacks an Uncle Tom, white man's organization, take a more militant position. Young marched in the big demonstrations of the mid-Sixties but he also furnished efficient direction to the League, brought in donations and grants to make it financially strong, and greatly increased its efforts and its successes in its goal to improve the black position through employment and advancement. He talks bluntly, candidly, and reasonably.

"Business cannot function in an all-black city in a climate of tension and hatred," he has said. "We will either help Negroes to become constructive, productive citizens—or they will become destructive dependents."

During the European tour, Ford would frequently sneak away from the celebrity seekers, asking, "Where's Whitney?" Young was a man he could be comfortable with.

But Young is also a man to take full advantage of an opportunity. "We're at a perilous stage in our country," he told Ford, "and we can't leave the solution to our problems up to the kooks. Who are going to be the prophets, we or they? It's people like you, responsible businessmen, and people like me, with an organization respected by both business and the nation as a whole, who've got to take charge now. We can't let a crazy bunch of irresponsible people take over. You've got to come in with us. You've got to lead."

Ford, who can be strangely shy, demurred. "Aw, hell . . ." he'd begin.

"Listen," Young would interrupt. "I'm going to make you the white Moses. You're going to be known in history as the businessman who turned this critical period of black and white relationships around."

They maintained their open, natural friendship after the tour was over. One day Ford dropped into the League's office in New York and told the receptionist he'd like to see Mr. Young. He was told Mr. Young was busy. He waited patiently, then tried again. Still busy.

Ford took the phone and was put through to Mr. Young himself. "Whitney," he said, "this is Henry, and I'm staging a sit-in down here until you let me come up." The Ford sit-in didn't last long.

That Christmas, 1966, Whitney got a handwritten note from Ford. It read:

Dear Whitney—

It has been a great privilege for me to get to know you. You are a great guy and run a wonderful organization.

This being the holiday season I enclose a check which I know you can put to good use. Spend it any way you wish.

All the best to you and all your family for Christmas and the New Year.

Best regards,
Henry

The check was for $100,000. "I'd never held that much money in my hand before," Whitney told me. "I just sat there and looked at it."

In the company, too, Young's missionary work was beginning to pay off. Mister Ford was taking a stronger position on hiring Negroes and promoting them to positions of importance. He met with resistance. Arjay Miller, for example, then president, had no prejudice against Negroes, but he opposed preferential treatment based on anything but ability. Ford brought Young out to Dearborn to talk informally with a select group of about 35 top executives of the company.

"That's like Henry," Whitney told me. "He's so smart, so human, realizing that you don't ram things down people's throats. You get in someone else to explain the issues. I didn't talk long. I just said that there were two reasons why I was there. One was my respect and affection for Henry Ford personally, and the second was that I owed my father's debt to the Ford Motor Company for opening up its gates to him as a professional man. I told them what I tell all businessmen, to give Negroes a chance to prove ourselves. Don't expect us to produce all Lena Hornes and Ralph Bunches. Just remember there are some dumb white people too."

When he finished, Arjay Miller broke in spontaneously. "I had some doubts," he said, "but now I know that we're not doing enough and we should do more." Whitney estimates that 50,000 jobs resulted from that one trip to Detroit.

Young is a more forceful speaker than Ford, and I commented on it to Whitney once. "Yeah," he said. "He's not comfortable up there, and he doesn't have a good speaking voice. But you ought to hear him when he really talks from the heart. I prevailed on our friendship to get him to speak to our national meeting in 1967. It was one of the most moving addresses I've ever heard."

It's too bad Ford didn't have his pal on his payroll in 1957. I think Whitney Young could have sold the Edsel.

In the summer of 1967 what Henry Ford called "the anguish and despair that come with being poor, being black, and living in the ghetto" reached the bursting point in Detroit. The bloody riot was the most costly in American history. It changed the thinking of the Ford executives who were dragging their feet on human relations. From the upper stories of the Central Office Building in its peaceful oasis in Dearborn they could look to the east and see smoke from the burning inner city rising into the gray sky.

"Let me tell you," Allen Merrell said, "when you look out the window and see your city burning, it does something to you."

This feeling, incidentally, is not restricted to Detroiters. "You can always tell when you're talking to businessmen from cities which have experienced riots," an interested observer in Washington told me. "They're different. They know they've got to bite the bullet."

Even as the city burned, Bill Schoen and a small cadre of Ford PR executives wrote a comprehensive program called "How Industry Can Help Detroit" and it was sent upstairs to Mister Ford. Setting forth the premise that "the Detroit community can no longer look to government alone to meet these deep problems," the program began with a plan to organize industry action to clean up after the riots. It ended with specific long-range proposals to turn the power of corporations on unplanned and ill-defined poverty and welfare programs, on lack of coordination, destructive rivalry and overlapping, undefined goals, and lack of statistical data. When Ford attended a meeting of Detroit leaders called immediately after the riots, he took the copy with him. He had something positive to offer.

Out of the meeting grew the New Detroit Committee. Its 39 members included the most prominent members of the white community, men like Joseph L. Hudson, Jr., of the department store family; Lynn Townsend, chairman of Chrysler; James Roche of General Motors; Henry Ford II and Walter Reuther; as well as Negro leaders. Staff members and secretarial help were loaned by companies and institutions. Five Ford executives were released on immediate loan to the committee.

The New Detroit Committee unfortunately suffered from characteristic ills. The white members found it hard to empathize with the people who had tried to burn down the town. Negro members, ranging from moderate to militant, were divided not only from the white members, but among themselves. There was no firm chain of command, as in the Ford Motor Company. Incompetence and hesitancy met militancy and self-interest.

Henry Ford, accustomed to demanding positive progress from responsible executives, almost exploded with frustration during some of the time-consuming, unproductive sessions. His own men made mistakes. On one occasion he seconded a motion with the assurance that it would go through. It received only three votes. ("Did he chew my tail out on that!" Bill Schoen told me later.)

He could not get positive answers to direct questions. On receiving one vague, rambling reply, he blew his top. "I wouldn't take this crap if you were working for me," he snapped. "If you were working for me you wouldn't be working for me anymore."

To get some idea of how to deal with the committee problem, Ford asked the advice of an expert. "I've been called in by a lot of industrialists," Morton Coleman of Pittsburgh, an unusual combination of idealistic social worker and practical politician, told me, "but I found Ford a new breed. Most people have skimmed through a report or two and talked with somebody a little bit, but Ford had read all the reports and was thoroughly familiar with the situation. For the first time I could skip my preliminary lecture and start even. I was a little wary of this great industrialist at first, but in a couple of minutes he demonstrated a frankness and honesty which put me at ease. No pomposity, no sham. In working with Ford I've found that he studies the issues thoroughly, becomes knowledgeable, then acts quickly, decisively, almost impulsively. This man is providing leadership in Detroit.

"In spite of everything, the city is far ahead of most others in community relations. That doesn't mean it has solved the major problem in America of holding our communities together. You're close to having two armed camps in Detroit. Like all other cities, Detroit suffers from a lack of interpretation of the Negroes' needs to the white community. You've got to do a selling job. If the Mustang had been promoted like race relations, it would never have gotten out of the showrooms."

One of the great successes of the New Detroit Committee was the beginning of a dialogue between the schisms. Ford was the leader in making an effort to understand the position of the extremists. He talked with everybody. One of the members of the committee was an 18-year-old black high school leader named Norvel Harrington who later became a leader of the Black Panthers. In an effort to understand the angry youth of Detroit, Ford talked with Harrington alone for two or three hours, trying to reach a common ground.

Ford did not rely on newspaper stories for information of what the militant groups were planning and saying. He sent Bill Schoen to cover a meeting of the black establishment movement. Newspaper stories the next day were full of incendiary quotes from the speakers. Schoen, however, reported that aside from the hostile rhetoric thrown in for emotional effect, he had not heard one statement that night that he could not endorse. Their principles were the same as those of George Washington Carver and Booker T. Washington, whom Henry Ford the Elder admired: black people can work with other black people better than white people can.

A powerful leader of the black militants in Detroit was the Rev. Albert Cleage, pastor of the Central United Congregational Church, also known as the Church of the Black Madonna. Left out of the New Detroit Committee, Rev. Cleage organized his own group to combat it. Most of the white members of the committee, and some of the black, thought of Cleage as a kind of horned devil and were scared stiff of him. Ford suggested meeting with Cleage to find out what he had to say. After the horror died down, the question of protocol arose: who would meet whom where?

"I'll meet him anywhere he wants me to meet him," Ford said bluntly. The two men sat together in a little Sunday school room in the basement of the church for three hours.

"Some of us who thought we knew Henry Ford almost had the feeling we were seeing a stranger during those days," Allen Merrell told me. "The way he sought out people with whom we thought he had so little in common, and the way he accepted them and understood them and interpreted them to us—well, he was like another man."

One of the Ford people assigned to the New Detroit Committee was Levi Jackson, the junior executive from Yale. I'd heard some snide remarks about Jackson—ornamental Negro, Uncle Tom, and worse. Jackson was quite frank about his acceptance of his position.

"I've always lived in a white man's world," he said. "I've rarely been discriminated against. I came to the Ford Motor Company instead of into professional football because I fell in love with the place and I've tried to do a good job as a person, not as a Negro. When Mister Ford asked me to work with the New Detroit Committee I was reluctant at first because I had no experience in race relations, but I said I'd be happy to go if he wanted me to. At the time I guess you could call me an unconcerned moderate. Now I'm very concerned. For the first time in my life I've had a constant exposure to race relations and I've begun to think about it. For example, when I have an appointment with a man I haven't met before, I look for the sudden expression that frequently comes over someone's face when he sees I'm a Negro. I looked for it when I met you, but I didn't see any reaction at all. But I guess you knew, didn't you?"

"Gosh," I said, "that's terrible. Here you've been going along all your life as just another American citizen and now all of a sudden you're different, you're a Negro."

"Don't feel sorry for me," he said. "This is the best thing that ever happened to me. It forced me to realize who I am.

Instead of subconsciously playing down the fact that I'm a Negro, now I have pride in what I am. I shave much better every morning. I'll tell you something else. I used to be satisfied with my position here. Now I realize that there are only three Negroes in the whole company who are in Grade Eleven, and that's as high as any Negro has gone so far."

It was the new Levi Jackson, the man who knows who he is and is proud of it, who walked up to Henry Ford and handed him his proposal that the Ford Motor Company hire the hard-core unemployables. Out of that proposal came the famous blue letter which revolutionized Ford hiring methods. Ford ordered his plant managers to stop screening people out and start screening people in. As a result, thousands of reliable workers who would otherwise still be living from hand to mouth are now producing Ford products, taking home paychecks and paying taxes.

Henry Ford II has himself carried his beliefs out into the nation. Early in January, 1968, Henry Ford received a call from the White House asking him to come and see President Johnson. The President announced the result of the meeting in his first special message to Congress of the year. He proposed a major industry-government cooperative program to find jobs in private business for the nation's hard-core unemployed. To administer the program, a nationalized projection of the new Ford hiring practices, he established the National Alliance of Businessmen. Its chairman: Henry Ford II.

The President did not mention that Ford had driven a bargain with him. Still fretting over the frustrations of the lack of firm line of command in the New Detroit Committee, Ford had agreed to take the job only if he could name the executive director.

For that job, Ford went back to his Navy days, and tapped his old chief, Leo Beebe. At 11:00 P.M. Thursday, January 18, Beebe was sound asleep in his home in Toronto. He'd had a

337

hard day as vice president of Ford of Canada, and he'd gone to bed early. The phone rang. It was Mister Ford. "Can you come down and see me tomorrow?" he asked.

Beebe walked into Ford's office in Dearborn at 8:30 A.M. the next morning. Ford outlined to him briefly the mission of the National Alliance of Businessmen—to put 500,000 hard-core unemployed to work over a three-year period—and said it needed an executive director. "You're it, if you'll do it."

Beebe went back to Toronto, cleaned up his desk, and was in Washington Monday morning, ready to go to work. He had no office, no secretary. He met with what few people had an idea of what was going on, then began drawing up organization charts and directives. That Friday Ford came to Washington. Working until early Saturday morning, they wrote that Beebe calls the complete bible of the organization, setting forth its policy and directives clearly and unmistakably. Ford partici-pated to the point of changing a semicolon to a comma. At noon Beebe presented the program to the President, Ford, and the 15 board members—all prominent industrialists.

After the luncheon the board met all afternoon and into the night. J. Paul Austin, president of the Coca-Cola Company, was vice chairman, and from beginning to end Ford consulted him on every major decision. During the next few weeks Ford kept in touch with Beebe constantly by phone, calling from Europe on a couple of occasions, and spent another full week-end with him in Washington. Another weekend was spent with President Johnson on his ranch in Texas.

On Thursday, March 14, Ford again appeared in Wash-ington to go over the preparations for the kick-off meeting that Saturday. By this time Beebe had an office. He sat at his big desk, a huge American flag behind him, while Ford sat in a straight chair at his side. They were at it until late Friday night, and for four and a half hours straight Saturday morning. The agenda had been carefully prepared by the staff, but Beebe, knowing Mister Ford, anticipated last minute changes. ("He just wants to do things his own damn way.")

Sure enough, when the meeting began the next morning, with 1000 beautifully printed agendas carefully placed on the chairs, Ford began the meeting by idly commenting that it wouldn't do any good to look at the agenda: *he* certainly didn't.

I don't think the rearrangement made much difference; it was an inspiring meeting. I remember a few little vignettes. Secretary of Labor W. Willard Wirtz, mentioning Beebe in his speech, suddenly stopped, looked up, and ad libbed, "who is the best thing that ever happened in this town." Mister Ford had picked the right man.

Carl B. Stokes, Negro mayor of Cleveland, told a personal anecdote to illustrate the forbearance which must be shown to men who have not had the opportunity to get used to working. A high school drop-out, Stokes had gotten a job on an assembly line, but couldn't keep up. The foreman told him harshly that if he couldn't perform he was through.

"I thought then and there that the whole world was against Carl Stokes," Stokes said. But an older man showed him some of the little tricks necessary to the operation, and he stayed on.

It was the turning point in his life. There could be similar turning points in the lives of hundreds of thousands of men in the years to come.

After the opening meeting, Ford attended similar sessions in several of the 50 regional and city offices of the NAB. He made a total commitment to the program. It was never publicized, but I know that he cancelled an African safari that he and Cristina had been looking forward to with eagerness.

"This is too important," he explained. "We've got to get this whole program off right, and I can't take off now."

Yet he was strongly advised by his Washington representative, Rodney Markley, not to take on the job in the first place. "I thought its chances were nil, and I told him so,"

Markley told me after the program was underway. "Anyway, it scared me. He could fall flat on his face. It amazed me when he accepted it, but now I understand. The challenge was so great, the opportunity to really do something so big, he had to do it. His conviction on this was phenomenal. I've seen a lot of businessmen take on a job like this, then assign somebody to it and forget it. I told him if he wasn't going to do it right, then not to do it at all. You know what he told me? He said, 'Look, I want to tell you something. I feel deeply about this, too. I'm going into it with all I've got.' "

All over the country, the nation's most prominent industrialists made personal visits or telephone calls to thousands of employers securing pledges to hire the hard-core unemployed. When a year later, he turned the chairmanship over to President Nixon's appointee, Donald McIntosh Kendall, chief executive of Pepsi-Cola, Inc., Henry Ford could report that NAB had placed nearly 146,000 people in jobs with 12,500 firms and that 88,000 were still on the job. On the average, these men had been jobless for six months during the year preceding their employment. Though one of the provisions of the program was for the government to pay for training new workers under certain conditions, two out of three job placements were completed with almost no cost to the taxpayer.

"We demonstrated that—given a high level of employment in the economy," Ford said in his farewell address, "the business community has both the determination and the ability to absorb substantial numbers of disadvantaged people into productive employment. We showed that private initiative can be harnessed to broad social goals. We showed that businessmen and government officials can work together harmoniously and fruitfully."

There's a good chance that Markley was right, and that the goal of 500,000 in three years could never be reached. Some critics—a minority—caviled at the number still on the job. But even if there were less, the total swing from marginally employed and people on relief to wage-earning taxpayers would be impressive. More important than numbers, however, is the effect of the program itself.

The NAB under the leadership of Henry Ford II and Leo Beebe has had more far-reaching results than the employment of a certain number of people. Actively led by hundreds of blue-chip business executives—President Nixon invited only chairmen and chief executive officers to the second meeting— the NAB has influenced community relations throughout the nation. Big corporations are no longer located exclusively in big cities. Their plants and their influence today extend across the country, into areas once hidebound by reactionary provincialism. Though the hard-core unemployed are by no means all one color, the NAB program can't help but benefit racial tolerance and understanding.

The dialogue Ford fostered between disparate elements of society in Detroit has continued, and is spreading throughout other communities. This may represent only one small step toward the eventual solution of the problems of our cities, but that step has been taken. Henry Ford II has not only proven the economic feasibility of hiring the disadvantaged, but has made it fashionable.

As his friend Max Fisher says of him, "Henry Ford II, the leader of the new breed of businessmen, makes it possible for others to join him. Other businessmen have told me that only Ford could pioneer in this great area of human relations, because his name is on the door. Well, now he's done it. He's paved the way. The new breed will follow him."

Aided to some degree by an offer of a prestigious government position, Levi Jackson was jumped *two* grades, to the private salary roll. The company *did* practice what it preached.

It's ironic that during its years of equal opportunity the company has existed in a community almost completely restricted to whites. The mayor of Dearborn, Orville L. Hubbard, told me in the spring of 1968 that Dearborn is no different from the suburbs of other large cities. "Look at Detroit, Chicago, Washington, any number of cities," he said. "You got niggers all crunched up together with white suburbs around them. Ten, twelve thousand of 'em come into Dearborn every day to work and if they've got any problem I haven't heard of it."

I said I'd read that only one Negro family lived in Dearborn, and there must be a reason. He said I couldn't believe the "damn newspapers." Shortly after my talk with the mayor I learned that the one Negro family had moved out.

Hubbard has promised police protection to any Negro family who moves to Dearborn, and Ford officials have admitted to me that Hubbard has a record of keeping his promises. He had furnished the city a clean, efficient government since his election —opposed by Harry Bennett—on a clean-government platform in 1941. In 1948 he and the company, this time under Henry Ford II's direction, had another battle over a housing development, and Hubbard won again. He said there was nothing personal about it. His son is named Henry Ford Hubbard.

"My motto is Be Nice To People and that includes young Henry," he said. "I always liked Henry."

Young Henry, when I talked to him about Dearborn and its mayor, did not return the compliment. The Ford Motor Company in 1967 paid $21 million in taxes to Dearborn, representing 54 per cent of the city's income, and the all-white pattern of the city Ford supports galled him.

"I've about given up on the whole thing," Ford told me. "I can't lick him and I'll be damned if I join him."

16

IN CONTRAST TO his grandson's involvement with hundreds of industrialists in a major issue involving a major national crisis, the elder Henry Ford liked to play his own cards close to his own vest. He didn't like to work with committees even when he was chairman. He proved it in 1910 when a group of Detroit doctors and laymen concerned over the need for improved hospital facilities in the city named him as chairman of the fund-raising committee. Four years later, during which time he never got around to calling a meeting, the money the members of the group had put up originally was gone and the buildings they'd started were abandoned. A newspaper printed the story of the fund-raising flop with the name of the chairman of the finance committee in big type.

Henry I reacted in his own characteristic way. He gave the contributors their money back and built the hospital himself.

Furthermore, he ran it himself. He didn't think much of the medical profession in the first place—if you ate properly and got plenty of exercise how could you be sick?—and being charged $1500 for the removal of Edsel's tonsils was like having liniment poured on the irritation.

The Henry Ford Hospital treated everybody and charged everybody, rich and poor, the same. His doctors worked on salary. They were prohibited from charging extra fees, nor could they treat outside patients. For a time they were required to punch a time clock, but not even Henry Ford could get away with that. He made a large segment of the medical profession hopping mad, and yet, through his application of some of the ideas just emerging, such as the clinic method of diagnosis of a patient by several specialists—its detractors naturally called it an assembly line—he made his own peculiar contribution.

He may have been the world's worst committee chairman but the Henry Ford Hospital, into which he put $15 million as well as some crazy ideas, has long been regarded as an excellent medical institution. It has also, under a board of trustees headed by Benson Ford, maintained its tradition, today fully accepted by the profession, of a closed, salaried staff.

For a while Henry Ford I maintained an orphanage, taking a personal interest to the point of having Christmas dinner there each year, but after World War I he turned it into the Henry Ford Trade School. Boys came to it from all over the country and from other parts of the world to learn mechanical trades. The curriculum didn't leave much time for books, for, as Ford said, "What's the use of knowing a lot if you can't do anything?"

Ford made contributions to other schools and colleges, but nearly all of them were work schools in which all students were required to work as well as study. Ford liked the idea of work. On the mantel over the huge fireplace at Fair Lane was chiseled the motto: Chop your own wood and it will warm you twice.

The Berry schools in Georgia, operated on the work-school principle, received millions from Henry Ford, and he and Mrs. Ford visited them regularly. According to one story the relationship began when Martha McChesney Berry, founder of the schools, received a token contribution of one dollar from Ford, used the dollar to buy peanut seeds, and made a nice profit. Just one Ford gift to the Berry schools was the Ford quadrangle, a complex of six handsome buildings.

Ford's greatest gift to education grew somewhat haphazardly out of his own nostalgia, and his aversion to book-learning. In his late fifties, he began taking an interest in the old farmhouse he had fled from as a boy, and began its restoration. He spent happy days combing the backwoods of Michigan for the exact type of woodburning stove that had stood in the parlor. Ford had so much enthusiasm that he couldn't restrict it to one house, or one period, or even one category. By 1920 he had his professional scavengers out scouring the world for an assortment of things. Some of his acquisitions were huge, like the giant Newcomen engine he found rusting away in England, and some were tiny, like the needles of early sewing machines. Out of the acres of junk an order and theme developed. He had once told an interviewer that "history is more or less bunk," and like many another casual statement he dropped during his lifetime, it brought ridicule and derision. Well, he'd show them. Instead of portraying history in dull school books, he'd show it the way it was, in three-dimensional objects. He bought hand tools and steam engines, buggies and automobiles, the finest antiques and the crudest farm tools. He bought and brought to Dearborn whole houses, too: the laboratories of his hero, Thomas A. Edison, at Menlo Park, New Jersey; Luther Burbank's office at Santa Rosa, California; the Wright Brothers' bicycle shop at Dayton, Ohio; even an English stone cottage, complete with several hundred feet of stone wall.

In the restoration of his own home he'd had workmen dig through the trash heap in the backyard and had been rewarded with shards from which the original china could be reproduced. He also had Edison's and Burbank's trash heaps sifted. Burbank's widow drew the line when he wanted the skeleton of Burbank's pet dog dug up and shipped to Dearborn. He got stung badly on occasion, too, as with the house in which Stephen Foster was supposed to have been born; actually Foster had never set foot in the place.

For all the helter-skelter of the assembly, the collection and the theme came together to form one of the great showplaces of the world. Ford called it the Edison Institute and had the inventor there for the dedication on October 21, 1929, the fiftieth anniversary of Edison's invention of a practical electric light. It was a ceremony of Fordian proportions. President Hoover went to Dearborn for it. That night Ford arranged to have the lights cut off all over America. When Edison reenacted his first demonstration, they all went back on again. Hoover introduced Edison on a national radio hookup. Edison burst into tears. Then he made a little speech, concluding: "As to Henry Ford, words are inadequate to express my feelings. I can only say to you that, in the fullest and richest meaning of the term—he is my friend."

Today the Edison Institute is composed of the Henry Ford Museum, 14 acres of fascinating Americana, and of the rest of Greenfield Village, 260 acres and nearly a hundred buildings in all, including the museum. Though the whole idea was considered an outrageous opposition to the basic tenets of education, Ford had the last laugh. Today, it is visited by a million and a half people a year. Similar operations, like the Rockefeller restoration of Colonial Williamsburg, have been developed all over America.

Henry Ford I spent about $30 million out of his own

pocket on this one monument. Henry E. Edmunds, Ford archivist, says that never has one man spent so much money for the pleasure of others, but Ford had a ball doing it.

The museum and village not only demonstrate to school children how this country was developed, but help visitors understand us better too. I went through the museum and Greenfield Village one day with the Harvard International Fellows. That night, a government official of West Germany and another from Pakistan told me it was the most interesting day they had spent in America.

Tucked away in a corner of the museum are the Ford archives—five library levels of catalogued documents containing the records of the industry, the company, and the individuals connected with it. The vast collection ranges from personal notes scribbled by Henry I when a child to voluminous business records. When Clara Ford died in 1950, the 56 rooms in Fair Lane were found to be packed with tons of material her husband had stashed away. A team of archivists spent years sorting it all out. The archives are now open to any interested person.

Meanwhile a team of historians under the direction of the noted historian Allan Nevins was beginning work on the official history of the company underwritten by a grant to Columbia University. In all, a total of 44 books and hundreds of magazine articles had been written on Henry Ford, many containing wild inaccuracies. Earl Newsom, during his early days as public relations consultant to Henry Ford II, had become concerned over biased accounts available to the public, and convinced the young president that a scholarly history would serve a beneficial purpose. The grant was the result, and it in turn resulted in three large volumes by Nevins.

The history of the company is so rich that several spin-offs dealing with specific phases of its activity over the years have also been published. Material for more can be found in the Ford archives, at the Edison Institute.

What could have resulted in a far greater undertaking than the Edison Institute was Henry I's proposal following World War I to take over the largely abandoned dams and plants on the Tennessee River and create a Ford version of what was to become, years later, the Tennessee Valley Authority. His plan was for a 75-mile-long city in which people would live and work in a hydroelectric paradise on the banks of the Tennessee. A majority of both houses of Congress, farmers, and labor were all for it and it nearly went through. However, conservation-minded Senators who didn't want to give the river away blocked the Ford program, and the river was unharnessed until the TVA came in.

In retrospect, maybe it would have been unwise to turn the whole thing over to one man, especially one so unpredictable as Henry Ford, but the accusations of attempted robbery made against him at the time were not justified. He was not greedy.

Another program which Ford, in his ingenuous way, sincerely believed would be beneficial to his fellow man was unfortunately far more successful. For 91 consecutive weeks in 1920 and 1921 his personal newspaper, the *Dearborn Independent,* hammered on the theme of anti-Semitism. The paper itself had a limited circulation, but Ford's articles were compiled, translated into many languages, and circulated throughout America and Europe. Rabbi Leo M. Franklin of Detroit, who had been a close friend of Henry Ford's and regularly received a new car from him, returned the 1920 gift with the explanation that Ford had "fed the flames of anti-Semitism throughout the world."

Almost a half century later Max Fisher, warm friend of Henry Ford II and prominent in both national and local Jewish organizations, sadly underscored the effect of the campaign. "You have no idea," he said, "how this seeps through the Jewish community, even through the generations. Today, here in Detroit, people still feel it."

Ford's attacks against the Jews seemed to have grown out of the Peace Ship episode, when he apparently became convinced that "the international Jew" began the war and refused to permit it to end. One of Ford's right-hand men during that period was a Prussian martinet named Ernest G. Liebold who may well have influenced him. It seems clear that Ford did not begin the campaign out of racial hatred but rather as a naive, paradoxical attempt to persuade American Jews to remold themselves in a Ford-approved image. He even accepted the discredited *Protocols of the Learned Elders of Zion,* which claimed that the Jews were out to conquer the world, but withdrew his endorsement in 1927.

For no known reason, the series was discontinued after two years. In 1924, however, he began another series attacking a Chicago attorney named Aaron Sapiro who was active in organizing farm cooperatives. The *Independent* accused Sapiro of representing "Jewish international bankers" in an attempt to defraud American farmers and control American agriculture. Sapiro brought a million-dollar suit against Ford for defamation of character. Ford settled the case out of court and published a complete retraction of all his anti-Semitic utterances and a personal apology to Sapiro. The *Independent* published no more anti-Semitic articles, and that year, 1927, ceased publication altogether. There were no more printed attacks on Jewry, but as Ford entered his seventies he frequently made anti-Semitic remarks and expressed a fear of some Jewish conspiracy against him.

People who knew Edsel say that he had no prejudice whatever, nor did Eleanor Ford. This was the heritage they passed on to their children. "I've discussed his grandfather's anti-Semitism at length with Henry," Max Fisher told me, "and I'm convinced that Henry just simply doesn't understand it. It is not in him to comprehend intolerance. He gets so much of this from his mother. She's a fine person, a woman of many qualities, of culture, of strength."

"Do you think maybe he's reacting to his grandfather's anti-Semitism?" I asked. "Does he have a feeling of guilt?"

"There may be, to some degree," Fisher said. "There can't help but be. However, that's not the reason he is what he is. Henry just likes people. He likes interesting people, people from all walks of life. On the cruise we took through the Aegean, we had a lot of time to just lie in the sun, relax, and talk. We had long conversations. One time we got into a very intense argument. I insisted that Henry was a sensitive person, and he insisted that he's not sensitive at all, that he's just an average guy. He got mad about it. But I still say he's one of the most sensitive people I've ever known. Here, I'll give you an example."

The background of the story Fisher told me deals with a suit brought by the stockholders of the Chrysler Corporation in 1961 against L. L. "Tex" Colbert, Chrysler's president and chairman of the board. "Innuendoes were being made that Colbert was anti-Semitic. Henry was a good friend of Colbert's, and he believed the rumors to be false. He came to me—I'm pretty well known in the Jewish community of Detroit—and said to me, 'Look, this is wrong. This man is being persecuted for something that isn't true.' He asked me to talk to Colbert myself, size him up, and if I agreed with Henry, to let my friends know my opinion of him. I arranged a meeting with Colbert, discussed the whole matter with him, assessed him, examined him, and I became convinced that he was a fair and square man, without prejudice. I did pass the word along and I think I helped put to rest some of the false rumors about him. Tex and I became fast friends, incidentally. His office is right next door. I want to stress the fact that Tex Colbert at that time was a competitor of Ford's, but Henry took it on himself to help clear this thing."

The Aegean cruise took place about the same time as the

brief Arab-Israeli war of 1967. Fisher, who has been an adviser to the Israeli government since the state was born, was naturally deeply concerned. As a former president for several terms of the national United Jewish Appeal, he is familiar with fund-raising and helped organize the Israeli Emergency Fund. Naturally, as he was emotionally involved, he discussed the situation with his friends, but he deliberately refrained from taking advantage of his friendship with Ford to ask for a donation.

"Here," Fisher said, "let me show you something. Nothing has ever been said about this and I wouldn't want you to use it without Henry's permission, but just take a look at it."

I later obtained grudging permission from Ford to reprint the short note handwritten on his personal stationery:

Dear Max:

Enclosed is a donation to your cause. I had meant to do this much earlier, but I feel that, with the continuing problems we discussed the other evening at your house, you will continue to need substantial funds. . . .

All the best,

Henry

"There was a check for $100,000 enclosed," Fisher said.

Another of his grandfather's shortsighted and callous attitudes for which Henry Ford II atones in his own way was the failure to contribute to local charities and worthwhile causes outside his orbit of personal interest. During the transition from the Model T to the Model A, thousands of Ford workers were laid off. Many could not find employment elsewhere and the situation in Detroit reached the crisis stage. The elder Ford ignored pleas from the city welfare department and charitable organizations.

His wife and son contributed large sums to the Detroit Community Fund at that time and through the years. Edsel also contributed heavily to the Detroit Symphony and the Detroit

Institute of Arts. It was Edsel's contributions that made possible the polar flights of Admiral Richard E. Byrd. In 1924, when Byrd made his first request for funds for the flight, many of the well-known explorers of the day believed that exploration of arctic regions by plane would be impractical if not impossible. After the successful flight over the North Pole, in which large areas were surveyed for the first time, Byrd said he could never have made it without the help and encouragement he received from Edsel Ford. He named the plane *Josephine Ford,* after Edsel's daughter. Edsel was also the first and major contributor to the Byrd antarctic flights of 1928–1929 and 1933–1934.

Henry Ford II, though showing a strong tendency like his grandfather to make his major contributions to areas in which he can commit his personal efforts as well as his money, has also, like his parents, been active in community organizations. During the hectic summer of 1945, when he was attempting to gain control of the company, he was serving as chairman of the major industry unit of the Detroit Community Chest. After he assumed the presidency of Ford, his company worked much more closely with the organized charities of Detroit. It participated in four annual campaigns, the Community Fund, Red Cross, American Cancer Society, and March of Dimes.

Early in 1949, when Edgar Schmidt was with the Community Fund, Henry Ford II came to a meeting with a suggestion. He had heard that one of the big steel companies had combined all the campaigns into one, and he proposed that the idea be adopted not only by the Ford Motor Company, but throughout Detroit.

"By running four campaigns we're spending four times as much time and effort than if we staged just one big campaign once a year," Ford said. Further, the four-campaign operation resulted in inequity, for although the Community Fund supported some 100 agencies, under the current setup the four campaigns were more or less equal.

"Mr. Ford's conviction and enthusiasm convinced us," Schmidt told me. "With his cooperation and direct participation we contacted the cream of the Detroit business and industrial community—GM, J. L. Hudson Company, Burroughs Corporation, Michigan Bell—as well as the labor organizations, and got their support. Mr. Ford himself approached C. E. Wilson, who was chairman of the American Red Cross at the time, and got them to go along with us. He did more, in his nice gracious way, to sell the new concept in the community than we did.

"It wasn't any easy wedding, as the annual roll call of the Red Cross was normally quite successful, and concessions had to be made to enable the Red Cross to keep its identity, but it wound up a rousing success. In 1948, as I recall, we had raised some $5 million a year for the Community Chest, and in 1949, through one big campaign, we increased that figure to about $9 million a year. Word got around and people came in from all over the world to see how we did it, how we got people to go along with us, the arguments we used. Today the United Givers Fund concept is in operation in over 2200 cities in the United States. It's the perfect solution to the problem of staging a myriad of campaigns and it all started in Detroit with Mr. Ford's suggestion."

The United Foundation in Detroit is the most successful UGF in the country. Though in many communities corporate gifts amount to over 50 per cent of the total, in Detroit corporate giving is less than 30 per cent because of the large donations made by individuals, with members of the Ford family always in the forefront.

Henry II is not the only Ford active in the United Foundation. Benson in particular always played a leading role. One of the company executives told me that late one day, long after quitting time, he went into Benson's office to find him coatless, surrounded by papers. A large batch concerned the United Foundation, which he headed that year. He looked up and

353

sighed. "They tell me I'm worth $100 million," he said. "What the hell am I doing here?" Then he laughed and went back to work.

The same year the United Foundation began, the Ford Motor Company Fund was established with a grant from Ford Motor Company to disburse in an efficient and stable manner funds for charitable, scientific, literary, and educational purposes. The Fund has received subsequent grants from the company through the years. The money is invested in a diversified portfolio. Thus, in 1967, a year in which profits were low, the fund was still able to disburse a total of more than $6.5 million. The largest single bloc of contributions in 1968 was under the heading of social welfare, $3.25 million.

All of the other Ford individual and company donations combined, however, represent only a small portion of the expenditures of the Ford Foundation, which in 1969 possessed $3 billion of the total of $20 billion owned by the 30,000 foundations in the United States. The Foundation became a national and international force, and no longer just an agency interested primarily in Detroit and Michigan institutions, in 1951, when the program devised by the planning committee established by Henry Ford II went into effect. Since that time, it has brought about benefits to humanity of which its original founder would have been inordinately proud. It has also brought monumental headaches to his grandson. In a sense Henry Ford II brought them on himself. Nobody paid any attention to the Ford Foundation, not even the Fords, until the vast profits of the Ford-Breech re-created company began rolling in. All of a sudden the Foundation had to start getting rid of that money.

The new Foundation got off to an unusual start when its first president, Paul G. Hoffman, who had successively headed Studebaker and the Marshall Plan, decided to locate it in Pasadena, California. It promptly became known as Itching Palms.

Hoffman, used to hopping all over the world and emitting ideas like a geyser, couldn't stay in one place or with one idea long enough to create an efficient organization. When he took off, with the Foundation's permission, to campaign for Eisenhower in the spring of 1952, Henry Ford spent a week a month in Pasadena minding the store.

"I found there was no coordination—no contact even—among the four associate directors," he said. "Each one was trying to run his own show, all by himself. There was no teamwork. I tried to build a cohesive, functioning team, as I had at Ford, but I didn't get very far."

Hoffman was permitted to resign ostensibly because Foundation headquarters were moved to New York and he preferred Pasadena. According to one account, however, Ford lowered the boom on him at the Eisenhower inauguration, saying, "This is the end, Paul."

Hoffman became chairman of the Fund for the Republic, of which Robert M. Hutchins, former president of the University of Chicago, was president. Many of the early troubles of the Foundation were brought about by the activities of this tiny offspring. The Fund for the Republic, as Hutchins expressed it, was actually "a wholly disowned subsidiary of the Ford Foundation." The parent body had given it $15 million and turned it loose. Julius A. Stratton, former president of the Massachusetts Institute of Technology and chairman of the board of the Ford Foundation when I talked with him in the spring of 1969, explained the thinking behind that procedure.

"There were four or five other groups established in the same pattern," he said, "but you never hear much about them. Okay, you set something up. Now, do you intervene in its activities, censor its statements, and if so, how much? The decision was made, and I think it was a wise one in spite of all that's happened, to fund these operations and turn them

355

loose as separate entities. Unfortunately, in the case of the Foundation and the Fund for the Republic, it has been impossible for the public to differentiate between the two.

"I know that much of the controversy has brought anguish and distress to Henry Ford. He didn't always agree with the program of the Fund for the Republic, yet he was forced to face the consequences. I watched this man when I knew he wished he could separate himself entirely from what was going on, but he had the courage and the toughness to stay with it. He has not agreed with all the Foundation has done, either, but he has never imposed his will, never treated the Foundation as a captive group. The board has had some heated discussions, let me tell you, and Henry has on occasion been on the losing side. But even though they may have hurt him and the company, he has lived with the decisions of the board."

The Fund for the Republic came into being during the period when Senator Joseph R. McCarthy was spearheading a widespread movement against subversion and suspected subversion in the federal government. One of the Fund's allocations was $25,000 to the American Bar Association to investigate the uses (and abuses) of Congressional committees. Proponents of the House Un-American Activities Committee and the McCarthy subcommittee chose to interpret this grant as a direct attack. The $25,000 figure was overlooked and the attention put on the $15 million in the Fund. Since the total allocation of the two Congressional committees was only $250,000, the committees were made to seem like David vs. Goliath. Furthermore, because of the confusion between the Fund and the Foundation, the public was left with the idea that there was plenty more where that $15 million came from.

The powerful right wing columnists and commentators of the day, especially Westbrook Pegler and Fulton Lewis, Jr., attacked both Fund and Foundation continually for months. The American Legion and other patriotic groups condemned the

Ford Foundation as a result. Among its many projects, the Fund for the Republic also showed an interest, in a small way by to-day's standards, in racial inequality. Consequently, show windows of a few Ford dealers in the deep south were smashed. Repercussions reached Dearborn, and some company officials attempted to pressure Henry Ford into taking action against the Fund. He resisted.

Some Ford dealers also questioned the Foundation's international program, suggesting that the organization which their sales supported spend less time and money abroad and more helping them sell Fords at home. Indeed, a quick look at the annual report of the Ford Foundation shows what appears to be inordinately large staff in areas like Africa and Southeast Asia. Spokesmen for the Foundation, however, point out that in contrast to America and Europe, where expertise in, say, agriculture, already exists, in the developing nations the Foundation must find and develop administrators and technicians. In some areas its work is as basic as demonstrating that iron-tipped plowshares are superior to plain wooden ones, and that rotation of crops is sound agricultural procedure.

The whole idea is for program officers to work themselves out of their jobs by training local people to take their places. Actually the Foundation has had its greatest successes abroad. In 1968, for example, thanks in part to the patient work of the Foundation's representatives, harvests in India, Pakistan, and the Philippines exceeded those of the best previous years by almost 40 per cent.

While helping emerging nations feed their starving millions, the Foundation is also active in the area of family planning so that the increased production will go around.

Most of the billions spent by the Foundation have gone into causes that have occasioned little adverse comment. It has influenced the increase of salaries of college faculties, for example, provided scholarships for thousands of deserving high school graduates, and sponsored the arts. Its support of educational TV has been more controversial.

Following the theme that the Foundation should treat problems that no one else seems to be concerned with, it has brought about changes in attitude in many areas previously overlooked. There had long been public apathy to the plight of the aging, for example, although one-tenth of the people of the United States are over 65. Study and individual casework in the field of geriatrics by the Ford Foundation have resulted in a much greater interest in the problems of the aged. Another comparatively ignored area was the study of business administration on both an undergraduate and graduate level. The arts and sciences have long been considered more glamorous, and the Foundation has contributed to them, too, but its activity in developing schools of business administration has made them more respectable in the academic community. The Foundation has even supported a small war against heroin pushers. In cooperation with the Urban League it chased dope peddlers out of a New York City high school in which 50 per cent of the students had sampled the stuff.

Adverse criticism of the Foundation simmered down appreciably over the years until two isolated incidents, each representing a pitifully small proportion of the Foundation's total expenditure, occurred during 1968. One was the division of some $131,000 in travel-study grants among the staff of Senator Robert F. Kennedy following his assassination. The other was the effort to increase the interest of the parents of disadvantaged children in school activities.

Many parents undergo without complaint the ordeal of the PTA. I had to drive five miles to see my eighth-grade daughter Sue give a two-second performance as the fainting sister, cousin or aunt in *H. M. S. Pinafore*. The other fathers were there too, squirming in the hard bottomed chairs. But in the Ocean Hill–Brownsville area of Brooklyn, few parents, father *or* mother, showed up even if their child was valedictorian in the commencement exercises. Of the total $4.2 million allocated by the Ford Foundation to New York schools and colleges, $59,000 was earmarked for the Ocean Hill–Brownsville project designed to bring about greater parent participation in the education process. The project was *too* successful. The parents' group demanded what they considered more meaningful courses in subjects pertaining directly and uniquely to black children. The teachers resisted the call for an abrupt change in the curriculum.

"Before we knew it," a Foundation spokesman said, "we were eyeball deep in a school strike."

In the hysteria of the situation, the issue of anti-Semitism became involved. Anti-Semitic literature, most of it later traced to one fanatic, was passed out in the neighborhood. The striking United Federation of Teachers reproduced the crudely mimeographed sheet in an unfortunate effort to maintain the unity of the teachers, most of whom happened to be Jewish. Press and radio gave full coverage to charges and counter-charges, and suddenly the entire Ford Foundation found itself under attack. Even the New York headquarters of the Ford Motor Company received protesting telephone calls. The issue of anti-Semitism obscured the basic issues and made the whole thing twice as hard to resolve.

Only after the strike was over, with the children back in school and neighborhood tempers abated, could a clear view of the events be taken. In the March 12, 1969, issue of the United Federation of Teachers' paper, Harriet Goldstein, chairman of the federation's chapter at the school involved, calmly reviewed the tragic episode. "Anti-Semitism was never the issue," she wrote, "and it's destructive to black and Jewish relations in general to overemphasize it."

The Ocean Hill–Brownsville episode threw the city of New York into an uproar; the revelation that eight members of Senator Kennedy's staff had received travel-study grants ranging from $6390 to $22,000 threw the Congress of the United States into an uproar. The grants were first publicized during the House Ways and Means Committee hearings on tax-exempt foundations in April, 1969. McGeorge Bundy, president of the Foundation, spent four hours on the stand defending them. The virtual presents of cash were hard to defend; I've heard fervent admirers of the late Senator Kennedy criticize the grants ("It's the tax-payers' money!" they said) and one of them told me that Senator Edward M. Kennedy also voiced disapproval. One national columnist speculated that the issue would be the ultimate factor in bringing about Congressional action on tax-exempt foundations.

Henry Ford II, according to an inside report, was also displeased, particularly with Bundy. Stratton, speaking calmly in retrospect, explained that the grants were made during the emotional period immediately following the assassination. The Senator's aides were grief-stricken and at a loss, and the grants gave them time to pull themselves together. The awarding of individual grants for travel-study purposes by the Foundation is not unusual, and most have produced sound results. However, it was obvious that Stratton himself, after thinking it over, agreed that the action, however well intentioned, had been unwise.

The Foundation is really not that easy to get money out of. Benson Ford, who was able to get a grant for the Henry Ford Hospital when the Foundation was still a more or less local operation, told me that he had been unable to secure additional money for the hospital which bears the name of the man who made the Foundation possible. The youngest brother, William Clay, who was a close friend of the late President Dwight D. Eisenhower, attempted to obtain a grant for the Eisenhower Medical Research Center in Palm Desert, California. "I couldn't get a cent," he said.

The Foundation took a new, dramatic direction in September, 1968: it began making what it termed social investments within the philanthropic process. Of the 2,000,000 self-employed persons in the United States, only 3.2 per cent that year were Negroes, for blacks find it hard to get credit, management training, or business information and counseling. And it is difficult for Negro and Puerto Rican would-be entrepreneurs to secure capital to establish their own businesses. Yet the creation of jobs and income for those most in need of them fall clearly within the province of the philanthropy.

As a result the Foundation has invested in minority-run enterprises, and in opportunities designed to benefit minorities. It has purchased $300,000 worth of common stock in Progress Enterprises, Inc., of Philadelphia, a profit-making enterprise that grew out of $10 monthly contributions by members of the Zion Baptist Church. The Foundation invested $1 million in the Mutual Real Estate Investment Trust, which purchases apartment houses outside of Negro concentration areas for integrated occupancy. It has put up seed money without which Federal Housing Authority mortgages could not be completed and for insurance bonds for Negro building contractors. The Foundation funded the Council for Equal Business Opportunity which provides management training and services such as advertising and accounting to black operators of food stores.

"Our new thrust clearly represents the participation of Henry Ford," Stratton told me. "He has always been interested in the Foundation, of course, but now he is showing more personal involvement. He is knowledgeable about this phase of our operations, and directly concerned. The board is also concerned —we went into it only after free discussion and complete agreement. We know we are headed for some risky operations but we're committed and we're going to continue along these positive, constructive lines. We're glad to have Henry with us all the way. These meetings used to be pretty dull. Now they're always exciting."

Men who love life

17

ON THE NIGHT OF JANUARY 1, 1885, the Greenfield Dancing Club gave the social event of the year, the New Year's Ball. Henry Ford, the young mechanic, was dancing in a quadrille with his cousin Annie as his partner when he noticed the girl opposite him, and for one of the few times in his life, for he loved dancing and was good at it, he missed a beat. When the dance was over Annie introduced him, and then had to remind him to take her back to her seat.

The girl was Clara Jane Bryant, one of ten children of a prosperous farmer. She was both pretty and smart. Henry was soon taking her for buggy rides during the summer, sleigh rides in winter, and writing poorly spelled letters ending in flowery poetry in between. After a time she began going out on his timber-clearing jobs with him, bumping along on the engine.

The Bryants sent out handsome invitations to the wedding

and served supper to all the guests after the ceremony. Henry was 24, Clara 22.

They lived for a time in a small cottage, but Clara put her husband to work almost immediately building a house to her specifications. Assisted by a carpenter, and surely with Clara supervising, he built a solid home in excellent taste. She must have been happy in it—but then he moved off to Detroit so that he could learn how to build a gasoline engine. She didn't protest. That was the pattern of their life. She ran the house, but she believed in him, and those of his many pursuits she did not encourage she accepted. How else could anybody live with Henry Ford for 59 years?

His automotive activities would have driven most women crazy. In the early days he and his mechanic friends trooped in and out of the house at all hours of the day and night. She helped him when he took over the kitchen sink on Christmas Eve to run his first engine; and when he finished up his first vehicle, the quadricycle, after a solid work stretch of 48 hours, she was there at 2:00 A.M. to watch him knock down the wall of the tool shed and sputter off into the misty night.

Even in the 1890's, when most men stayed home, Ford traveled constantly to see what other automotive pioneers were doing. She stayed at home with the baby. Henry went off fishing and hunting a lot, but he also loved picnics and visits back to the home place, and fortunately Clara did too. She watched him risk his neck in Detroit's first automobile race, and make a Don Quixote of himself with the Peace Ship. Clara didn't even complain when he made one of his rare invasions into her domain with his dietary ideas. Not every woman would go along with a meal composed entirely of soybeans, including ice cream. For a time Ford was convinced that the sharp points on the crystals of granulated sugar damaged the digestive system. One of his chemists, after hearing of the new Ford health fetish, added a few drops of water to a little pile of sugar; the crystals, sharp points and all, dissolved. Ford wouldn't speak to the chemist for weeks after that. The interesting thing is that Clara, who as a good housewife also knew that sugar dissolves, let him discover this culinary phenomenon somewhere else.

Far from attempting to hold him back in his whims, she went along with him with equal enthusiasm. She, too, enjoyed the simple pleasures of life. Together they walked the fields around Dearborn observing wildlife, especially birds. When a robin built her nest on the screen door of their cottage, and Henry Ford decreed that their uninvited visitor remain undisturbed while she raised her family, Clara was careful to use only the back door. She cooperated in his attempt to prove that birds migrated south in winter to find water. They installed electric heaters on all the drinking stations of their feathered friends at Fair Lane, but the birds still went off and left them. The Fords liked birds; whenever he came home he announced his arrival with a birdlike whistle, and, wherever she was—sewing room or rose garden—Clara whistled back and came to greet him.

A chance remark could send her husband off on an activity tantamount to a career. Restraint was not in the Ford vocabulary. One afternoon when she heard the children coming home from school she quoted a rhyme from the McGuffey Reader of her own school days:

> Hear the children gaily shout
> Half past four and school is out.

Neither Clara nor Henry could remember the rest of the verse, and there was no McGuffey Reader in the house to refresh their memories. In the next few years Ford spent thousands accumulating an outstanding collection of McGuffey Readers. The nostalgic recollection of his own school days was a prime factor in the creation of Greenfield Village and the school established within it.

One evening when Ford was 60 years old, he and Clara had

some friends in and somehow the conversation got around to the dances popular before the foxtrot. Nobody could remember all the patterns and the calls. Clara remarked wistfully that it had been years since they had done any dancing. Lord knows how much that remark cost. Ford assigned his staff to find somebody familiar with the old dances. A dancing master named Benjamin B. Lovett was tracked down in Massachusetts, and Ford went there himself to interview him. The acid test was whether Lovett know a step called the ripple, and when he passed it, he was imported to Dearborn for a Halloween party in the old barn. The weather turned a little chilly that day so Ford had steam heat installed for the occasion. He knocked some walls out of the engineering laboratory and laid special flooring to create a ballroom, and kept Lovett on as the company's dancing instructor.

A group of musicians was hired to be on hand whenever Ford felt like dancing, and from then until World War II there was both dancing and live Muzak day and night at the factory. If the Fords felt like dancing, they simply summoned a group of executives and their wives to join them. You couldn't get out of it; no matter how hard you'd worked that day or intended to work the next, no matter whom you were entertaining, you came, brought your wife, and danced until midnight. One day a visitor who had a business appointment arrived to find Mrs. Ford sitting on a table in the ballroom, clapping her hands and tapping the leg of the table with her foot, while Ford himself was simultaneously dancing a jig and playing a jew's harp.

Ford organized dancing classes in Dearborn until at one point there were 22,000 public school pupils attending. He extended the tutelage to the college level, and courses in square dancing became a part of college curricula, with credit, in schools from Missouri to Smith. Today hundreds of thousands of Americans participate in this unique American art form, and U. S. service personnel have introduced it to foreign countries.

All square dancers should pause during the next do-si-do and give thanks to Henry Ford for his revival of their terpsichorean delight.

Henry I was also a physical fitness nut. He was wiry and strong. He boxed, wrestled, and roughhoused with his buddies during his early days in Detroit. He suffered from a delicate stomach and lumbago for a few years following his first success but, at least in his opinion, his diet cured one, his chiropractor the other. He not only strode about the open country in Dearborn, but went on lengthy camping and hiking trips with his cronies, Edison, Harvey S. Firestone, and John Burroughs.

Because some of his friends were interested in golf he built an excellent course complete with clubhouse and pro, but then his interest waned; all of life was a game to him and he really didn't need to walk around hitting a ball. When he was in his sixties, a newspaper photographer started to snap a picture of him on a new bike but the plant police interfered. Ford winked at the photographer and nodded to the back gate. Then he sneaked away from his own guards and demonstrated his technique, one hand, no hands, while the photographer snapped away.

But running was his favorite exercise. A guest on board the Ford private railway car noted early one morning that the train was running slowly. Curious, he went back to the observation platform. Ford was running along behind the train, getting his morning exercise. About the only thing he really enjoyed about his yacht, the *Sialia,* on which he spent a couple of million dollars and also got seasick, was running around the deck. He always ran from his car to his office, until, one morning, at the age of 79, he slipped and fell. His doctors had warned him, but he had to find out for himself that he was no longer young.

He loved pranks. He personally whittled out wooden croutons for Firestone's soup. He went through an elaborate procedure to substitute a cheap watch for the prize possession of one of his executives, and then, accidentally on purpose, smashed it.

Some of his jokes were downright cruel. To get rid of an executive who lived in a company-owned house, he had the sewer stopped up. With Clara, his jokes were sweeter. She asked him to stop by the store on the way home to buy some pie tins, but he kept forgetting. After being reminded on several days, he showed up one night with a carful of pie tins. He had bought out the store's entire stock.

Money never seemed to intrude in Henry's and Clara's relationship. The Fords were never really poor. Even when he was working for $90 a month, and occasionally forgetting to cash the paycheck, they lived fairly comfortably, went to the musical comedies that came to Detroit, and enjoyed their Sunday picnics.

During the Twenties and Thirties the press generally agreed that Henry Ford was the richest man in the world, and there were even some printed speculations to the effect that he was the richest man who had ever lived. Newspapers had fun speculating on what he could do with his money. In 1926, for example, it was estimated that he could buy General Motors, the New York Central, and United States Steel. Yet Clara, emptying his pockets at night, frequently found checks that he had forgotten, sometimes for more than $100,000. Every morning an envelope containing $200 in new bills was placed under the inkwell on his office desk. After his death many unopened envelopes were found lying around the house. But when he attended the first day sale of a commemorative stamp in honor of Edison in Atlantic City he had to borrow two cents to buy one stamp for himself.

Clara Ford was just as bad. She insisted on darning his socks—Harry Bennett would run into a store and buy Ford a new pair which he'd put on in the car. But she spent a fortune on her rose garden—she wanted a hill in it—and she frequently suggested contributions for her husband to make. One time, for instance, when they were in the rustic dining room of one of the Berry schools, she observed to her husband that the girls had to work awful hard to keep the old building clean, and suggested, "Don't you think they deserve a new dining hall?"

"Why don't you give them one?" Ford asked. The dining hall turned into the six-building Ford quadrangle.

Clara was capable of stepping out of her role in the home under extreme provocation, as when she told her husband to make peace with the union. Why she permitted her husband to dominate their only son is a mystery. It may have been that she didn't fully realize what he was doing. There was little if any shop talk at Fair Lane. Though Edsel did call home every night, because of his unusual loyalty to his father he may simply never have told her. Family get-togethers were pleasant; Ford loved his grandchildren and gave them parties and presents. As for learning about the father-son relationship from her daughter-in-law, the two were friendly, but not close. When Eleanor Ford did come to her in 1945 with the plea to support her son, Henry II, it was Clara Ford who made her husband resign as president and agree to their grandson's taking his place. After that she reverted to her role as The Believer and lived with her husband in harmony and love for his remaining years on earth.

In almost six decades of marriage, she took an active part in company decisions on only those two occasions, and rarely, if ever, attempted to restrain the exuberance he poured into his myriad of activities. There is no indication that he enjoyed even the most fleeting dalliance with any other woman.

A little more than fifty years after Henry Ford fell for Clara Jane Bryant at the social function of the year, his grandson Henry met a girl under equally gala circumstances, an

Atlantic crossing on the *Queen Mary*. Her name was Anne McDonnell and, like Clara Jane Bryant, she was a member of a large family somewhat higher in the social scale. She was one of 14 children. The McDonnells weren't richer than the Fords, but they were multimillionaires and members of New York society. They had a three-floor apartment on Fifth Avenue— one floor was for the servants—and a huge home at Southampton, on Long Island.

Young Henry courted Anne for four years, driving down from Yale in a convertible, and they were married in July, 1940, the year he did not finish Yale. The ceremony was observed by some 750 spectators, including 50 photographers.

Before marrying into one of New York's most prominent Irish Catholic families, Henry had received instruction from Monsignor Fulton J. Sheen, a Catholic teacher and philosopher, and had been baptized into the faith. Sheen also performed the marriage ceremony, and the union was blessed by Pope Pius XII. Following the wedding, a reception was held in a pavilion joining the house. Henry's grandfather, spry and nimble, danced with the bride.

Again like Clara Bryant Ford, Anne McDonnell Ford went with her husband to Detroit, but Anne did not leave her life behind. The young Fords kept an apartment in New York for weekend visits and a house on Long Island for summer vacations. Anne accepted her role as a member of the Ford dynasty. When her husband traveled throughout the southeast visiting Ford dealers, she accompanied him.

Like Edsel Ford, however, Henry made a clear separation between the Factory and his home. Both his daughters recall that business was never discussed in the family. Anne's duties as a member of the Fords of Detroit were more civic and social. Her mother-in-law, Eleanor Clay Ford, was revered in Detroit for her broad spectrum of activities—Community Fund, Institute of Arts, Detroit Symphony—and Anne made a successful effort to follow her example. She was the leader in bringing the New York Metropolitan Opera to Detroit and was involved in many civic activities.

Henry I had built Clara's second home with his own hands. Henry II showed a similar interest. The young Fords' first home was a wedding present, but later they bought a large Georgian mansion overlooking Lake St. Clair and remodeled it to their own tastes. Mrs. Marion Morgan, an interior decorator with McMillen Inc. of New York, lived with the young couple for several weeks while they planned the modifications and furnishings, and the three of them discussed the project for hours every night. Mrs. Morgan also decorated several apartments and two places in Southampton for the Fords, and she knows them well. She was always impressed with Henry II's taste and courtesy, and by the intense interest he showed in his home.

In planning the new house, he was interested not only in the overall motif but in the details, even in the hinges and knobs on doors and drawers. He was particular about the shower spray and the arrangement of the light over the washbasin. He devoted many hours, over a period of months, to the creation of his bed. It was built around an antique headboard found in England. Mrs. Morgan found a beige damask of the George I period to recover it with. A four-poster bed was designed and built to go with the headboard. She found a beautiful piece of needlework which was made into a canopy. He, of course, examined both the damask and the needlework before approving them.

One night after the servants had retired, he went into the kitchen for a late snack. Suddenly he shouted, "Anne, come here!" She and Mrs. Morgan hurried out to the kitchen to find Henry inspecting a silver knife with a speck of dirt on it. He went around the kitchen pulling drawers out of cabinets and emptying the silverware and cutlery onto the big table in the middle of the kitchen to be cleaned and polished properly by the household staff next morning.

He also spent a great deal of time and thought on the library. The walls were of pine which came out of an old New England home; the wood had aged to a soft beige. The furniture, all of which he approved, included a superb red-lacquered secretary, and a Chippendale chair.

"His taste runs to a sense of appropriateness," Mrs. Morgan told me. "It's not soft, not hard, rather it applies to whatever the situation demands. He wants a bedroom to look like a bedroom, a library to look like a library. You have to work with him closely for a long time to realize how truly sensitive he is. He has a tremendous amount of feeling and sympathy but one of his weaknesses is that he doesn't always put his best foot forward. He doesn't let you see the real Henry Ford. Instead he tries to act bluntly and insensitively. But after having been associated with him for so long, I couldn't help but break through some of that armor. And you know what, I like the guy."

Though he has a reputation as an art collector, Mrs. Morgan says that he is not so much a collector as a person who just likes to live with nice things. But Ford himself disparaged his own interest in painting. "I used to buy a painting every now and then," he told me, "but not anymore. The price is out of sight. I was in London at the time of the sale of that famous Monet for a million four hundred thousand dollars, but I didn't even bother to attend the auction. I'd heard it was going to run over a million and I wasn't interested in anything at that price."

His friend Nate Cummings, a world-renowned collector of paintings of the Impressionist and post-Impressionist periods, told me that on their cruise in the Aegean they talked a great deal about art. Ford displayed a thorough knowledge and impressed Cummings in particular with his awareness of the use of color by the Impressionists and post-Impressionists. Talking about auctions, they learned that they had bid against each other on several occasions. "He bought a Renoir I wanted badly," Cummings said. "I went to London expressly for the auction of that Monet, but the bidding got out of my range, too."

One of the stories art lovers like to tell about the elder Henry Ford concerns the attempt of the famous art dealer, Lord Duveen, to sell him several paintings. He had excellent reproductions of several works of art bound into three handsome volumes, with a scholarly text describing each painting on the facing page. Duveen called at Fair Lane with the volumes. Henry looked at them, then called to his wife, "Mother, come in and see these lovely pictures." It took him some time to understand that Duveen was making him a present of the three volumes, and eventually Duveen had to explain almost bluntly that the idea was to sell him the originals. Then Ford was really perplexed. "What would I want with the original pictures when the ones right here in this book are so beautiful?" he asked.

The old man didn't concern himself with integrity in art. He had an artist named Irving Bacon paint a 17-foot canvas of the Golden Jubilee of the electric light. The Edsel Ford family could not be present at the ceremony because one of the children had a contagious disease, but Ford had all six members painted in anyway. Clara didn't like one of the women present and Ford had her painted out. The harassed artist was constantly taking people out and putting others in according to Ford's changing whims.

His son Edsel, a patron of the arts and himself artistic, had a strong respect for artistic integrity. He underwrote the cost of the Diego Rivera frescoes in the Detroit Institute of Arts, with no limitation on the renowned Mexican Marxist's freedom of expression. When Rivera completed the frescoes in 1933 one panel, considered by some to be sacrilegious, caused bitter controversy; the *Detroit News* stated editorially that the murals ought to be whitewashed from the walls. Edsel backed up Rivera completely and the frescoes, unchanged, are today considered among the world's finest.

Henry Ford II, reminiscing about his adventures in art one day, told me of a visit he had made to the village of Saint Paul de Vence in southern France. He struck up a conversation with a villager who turned out to be the mayor. When he learned that the mayor's wife painted, he politely went to see some of her work. Though hardly masterpieces, some of her paintings had an appeal, and he bought two or three for, he recalled, about $30 apiece. He brought them back home and had them framed and hung. Later an appraiser came in to check the value of his art collection and saw the paintings of the wife of the mayor of Saint Paul de Vence. She had signed them with her name, which happened to be Delacroix. "He valued them at $10,000 apiece," Ford said.

If the young Henry Fords of the 1890's had few money problems, certainly the young Henry Fords of the Forties and Fifties had none at all. The couple's annual income was in the millions. Though in contrast to his grandfather Henry Ford II was acutely aware of the company's cash flow, he retained a strange naivete about money per se. Just as his grandfather showed a complete lack of interest in speculation about his personal fortune, all Henry Ford II had to say about his omission from the 1968 *Fortune* list of America's richest men was, "No comment." He and Anne had absolutely everything they wanted. They traveled extensively, maintained several lavish homes, and were able to indulge themselves in their collecting hobbies—he in the field of art, she in the area of French furniture and clothes. Like his grandfather, Henry Ford II had to protect himself from panhandlers, even of the $100,000 variety. At the UN one day, David Zellerbach made the mild suggestion that Ford contribute to a charity with which Zellerbach was connected. "I don't carry a pen," Henry said. Then he grinned at Zellerbach, who was also a man of wealth. "I notice you don't carry a checkbook, either." They laughed in mutual understanding and that was that.

Ford makes substantial personal contributions, as his friends Whitney Young and Max Fisher have attested. Sidney Weinberg told me that his personal donations are made in orderly fashion at the end of the year in keeping with his deductible allowance. The identity of the recipients is his own business.

Forrest Murden told me that one day at the UN he mentioned the new Broadway show, *Tea and Sympathy,* and idly commented that he wished he could see it. Tickets were hard to get at box-office prices. A couple of days later Ford casually dropped a pair of tickets on his desk. "Somebody gave me these," Ford said, "but Anne and I are tied up. Maybe you can use them."

Murden said he certainly could. "It took me a couple of days to realize that nobody had given him those tickets," Murden said. "It was a gracious way of handling it."

One day Murden and Ford happened to be leaving the office at the same time and Ford offered to drop Murden off at his apartment. On the way Murden mentioned that it sure beat the subway. Ford opened his mouth to say something, hesitated, then blurted: "How much does it cost to ride the subway?"

It was Murden who first took Ford to P. J. Clarke's, the New York pub where he can be just another member of the Clarke club. His friend Pat Doyle says that he electrifies the place when he comes in, but he still has some degree of privacy because a lot of celebrities hang out there. Ford has his own ways of handling people who push too hard. One fellow who wheedled an introduction to Ford handed him his card and said, "Drop in and see me sometime when you're in New York." As Ford was leaving someone else came running up, introduced himself, and said he'd like to get together sometime. "Sure," Ford said, "here's my card," and handed over the one that had just been presented him.

"I'll admit I've been studying this man, trying to see what makes him tick," Pat said. "I've been on the *News* for 23 years and I've known a lot of big shots. But Henry Ford is the most real, most honest, unpretentious and unassuming person of all the millionaires, big shots and big wheels I've ever known. I have respect for him—a hard respect."

In talking with people who know Henry Ford II socially, I can see a close parallel in the ebullience and zest for living of the two Henry Fords. But Anne Ford was no Clara. She was strained and uncomfortable in the company of the Ford executives, for example. She was particularly ill at ease with Ernest Breech and his wife, who had a warm, earthy sense of humor and liked to tell stories dealing with outdoor privies in the Ozarks. There is almost no social contact between Ford and the top echelon of the company.

Their social life was mostly in New York. As many of Ford's friends have told me, when he works he works hard, and when he plays he plays hard. As the evening goes on and the glasses are refilled, he becomes an extrovert, joyous, dynamic, the center of activity. Just like his grandfather, he loves to dance, and although it may not be a gavotte or a ripple, he throws the same enthusiasm into it. He can turn on a tremendous amount of charm.

"I remember one particularly tough day in New York," Jack Davis said, "when Henry and I were at sales meetings, receptions, dinners, and so on, all day long, right up until 11:30 that night. We were going back to Henry's apartment in a cab when he said, 'Let's go over to the El Morocco and see what's going on.' The last thing I cared about was what was going on at the El Morocco, but I went along. We went in, got a table, and had a couple of scotch and sodas. I noticed Henry's eye keep straying over to a table where two couples were sitting. One of the women was particularly good looking. 'Boy, that's a cute girl over there,' Henry said. 'I wonder if I could get her to dance with me.'

" 'Look,' I said, 'you don't know whether that girl is married to that guy she's with. Besides, there are two men. You're liable to get your head knocked off.' Henry just grinned and said, 'I'll bet you ten bucks I can get her to dance with me.' I gave up and put ten dollars on the table. Henry put his ten down on top of it, got up and walked over to the table. I have no idea what he said to them, but you could tell that he was turning on the charm and pretty soon they were all laughing together. After a couple of minutes the girl smiled, gave a little shrug, got up, and Henry took her in his arms and started dancing. They whirled by my table, and without breaking step or changing expression, Henry reached out, grabbed the twenty bucks off the table, put it in the girl's hand, and they danced on."

At parties in Southampton, Ford loved to lead the orchestra. One of his favorite songs is "When the Saints Go Marchin' In." One night at an outdoor party, he led the orchestra. He beckoned them to follow him and they did, single file, still playing "The Saints." He led them to the swimming pool, jumped in the shallow end, and started wading across. They all followed, still playing.

Another night when the Fords were hosting a party at Southampton Henry suddenly disappeared. Anne, worried and embarrassed, sent people out to look for him. They found him on the National Golf Links, driving his new car hell for leather over the fairway.

When they went out to parties, Anne, raised in a strict household, always impeccably dressed and perfectly groomed, ate just so much and no more, drank just so much and no more, and always wished to leave at just the proper time. That made absolutely no sense to Henry Ford II. If you're having a good time, why stop? If the party's good, why leave? Sometimes Anne went home alone, which took the edge off things. Sometimes she dragged him with her, which took the edge off even more.

"I'll tell you one thing," Jack Davis told me, "nobody named Henry Ford likes to be bossed around."

Were the Fords a loving, affectionate couple? Someone who knew them well told me that Henry was openly affectionate, or tried to be, while Anne was restrained.

I'm afraid the consensus among friends of Henry's is that Anne was, or attempted to be, a restraining influence on Henry Ford in all the areas of enjoyment of life. If he complained, I haven't heard it. And though he may have danced with a girl on a bet, Forrest Murden, who traveled with him throughout Europe and Latin America, often when Anne was not along, assured me that there were never any other women.

In April in Paris, 1960, the Ernest Kanzlers gave a party at Maxim's. The list of guests included more men than women— Anne, by this time, accompanied her husband very rarely on his business trips—and the Kanzlers thought of a friend from Milan who always brightened up a party. Her name was Maria Cristina Vettore Austin. She was 33, and divorced from her British husband, Robin William Melville Austin, the president of a sugar company in Montreal. Daughter of an Italian physician, she had been educated in a convent and had studied art at the Accademia de Belleas Artes. She was at home at "21" and Le Pavillon in New York as well as in St. Moritz and on the Riviera. Though a member of the chic, glamorous European jet set, Cristina was known for her unaffected naturalness. She was happy and uninhibited, fun to be with and talk to. Her own amusing frankness encouraged her companions to confide in her. To many she was beautiful, to others she was, well, Cristina.

She arrived in Paris the day before the party and met

Henry Ford II just briefly. It was long enough to make such an impression that he asked to be seated next to her the next night. As she told me many years later, "Then the romance began."

To Henry Ford II, Cristina was a warm, encouraging, tolerant companion, as well as a beautiful woman. For a time their meetings were secret, and then rumors began appearing in Rome and Paris newspapers. Eventually they spread to the United States. The staff of the *Detroit News* discussed the question of reporting the rumored liaison, and decided against it. "It takes a hell of a lot of manpower to run down every rumor," Martin Hayden of the *News* told me, "and we didn't want to print anything that wasn't factual."

Other newspapers were less careful. Cristina told me that it was because of the publicity that they stopped seeing each other. Max Fisher, a close friend of Ford's and a man of perception, said it was much deeper and more complex.

"First of all," he said, "you must realize that this was a period of excruciating torment to Henry. A great deal of soul-searching led up to that decision. This man loves his children, feels close to them, and he didn't want to lose them. And I think I saw what a lot of other people did not see, and that was Henry's own insecurity with himself—a possible guilt complex. He wondered what had he done wrong, how had he contributed to the failure of a marriage. Further, this was more than just domestic trouble. Henry represents the company. Marital difficulties, scandal, even the possibility of a divorce would not affect only an individual named Henry Ford, but the entire company. He just couldn't haul off and break up a marriage, just like that. I tried to help him understand that a man must find his own happiness in his own inner emotional security, and that he could accomplish nothing by berating himself. A man deserves to have a mate."

Cristina was no secret in the Ford home. Anne and the three children moved to New York, taking a duplex apartment on Fifth Avenue. It was so big, a visitor reported, and had such a long center hall, that it seemed like a bowling alley.

One of the many stories printed about the move to New York said that the mother and children felt rejected and that Charlotte had a nervous breakdown. "I suppose we did feel rejected, in a way," Charlotte said, "and I'll admit that I was upset over it. But I didn't have any nervous breakdown."

It was a tough period for everyone. The three Ford women were frequently seen in the right places and their presence dutifully reported in the society pages. All were on the list of the Ten Best-Dressed Women in America. The mother, small and slim, was sometimes referred to as looking more like a sister. But someone who saw her often during that period said she looked terribly thin.

Still there was no thought in the children's minds that their parents would separate. For one thing, all were good Catholics. So the announcement came as a great shock. "They called us in one evening and told us," Charlotte said. "The whole thing was done so formally. We were just not prepared for it."

Almost four years after the party in Maxim's, 23 years after the wedding, Anne McDonnell Ford received an uncontested divorce. A little more than a year later Henry and Cristina were married. It was a quiet ceremony in the Ford hotel suite in Washington, with only the judge who performed the ceremony and two witnesses present. The announcement was not made until the next day. A representative of the company delivered the announcement and a photograph of the couple to the *Detroit News*. Ford had remembered the *News'* refusal to print the rumors.

The couple left immediately for London. The paper dutifully reported that Cristina was wearing a crepe wool dress by Trigère and boarded the plane wearing a coat by Norman Norell. A spokesman of the archdiocese of Detroit stated that Ford remained a Catholic bound by the laws of the church, but could not receive holy communion.

Charlotte and Anne received a telephone call from their father, telling them of the wedding and tendering an unusual invitation. Would they join him and his bride during their honeymoon in Switzerland? Recalling the invitation, Anne told me that they both thought it a little odd. The wedding itself had been expected, for their father had said at the time of the divorce that he would probably marry Cristina in about a year. But the suddenness, and the telephone call informing them of it, did come as a surprise.

"Charlotte and I," Anne said, "expected to sit in our rooms by ourselves the entire time, but it turned out to be one of the nicest times we've ever had together."

As for Charlotte, she said, "It was one of the smartest things Daddy ever did."

Cristina proved to be irresistible even to her husband's daughters. "Daddy's life has changed completely since the divorce," Charlotte said.

Anne went into more detail. "Cristina draws him out, makes him talk," she said. "I think it's good for him, and I'm very happy for him. Mother never pressed him to talk business, and we kids certainly didn't. Now I guess he's reacting."

The way the two girls speak of Cristina and her idiosyncrasies, she obviously quickly became a fully accepted member of the family.

"She lives in complete disorder," Charlotte said, laughing. "She carries all her correspondence around with her in a great big bag, and it takes her hours to find whatever she's looking for. She must have letters in there that are years old. Daddy pokes fun at her all the time."

Cristina Ford is warm, beautiful, disarming, wise, but more than anything else, she impressed me as being a wife in the full sense of the word. She had a difficult remodeling job to do. One of her first goals was to get him to slow down. "He tried to do everything, he burn himself out," she said. "I want him to do less and do it longer, until he is 75."

She painted an almost unbelievable picture of Henry Ford, of his coming home from the office, having a drink, relaxing, then dinner, "just the two of us," watching TV, and going to bed. "We are many times in bed at 10:30."

Pat Doyle had told me that he liked to picture Henry and Cristina alone in the evening, lounging on the living room couch. I thought Pat had lost his mind; he wasn't describing the Henry Ford I had heard about. Later I mentioned to Charlotte, a little cynically, what Cristina had told me: drink, dinner for two, in bed at ten thirty. Charlotte looked at me wide-eyed. "But that's what they do do!" she said. "That's exactly what they do."

Cristina had a new swimming pool and cabana built in hopes that she could get her husband to take a swim when he came home. She loves to go on long walks, and is occasionally successful in getting him to accompany her. More often, she said, sadly, "I see it do me no good to nag him. I like to get him to put on a little shirt and sporty pants and relax. It's good for him. You know"—her eyes crinkled up as she threw out an Americanism—"recharge the batteries."

Often he would come home tired and concerned over something that had happened at the office. She'd try to draw him out, get him to talk about it, get it off his chest. "He was not used to this, it was my hardest work," she said. "I think before all he heard was gossip and talk about clothes. Nobody was interested in *him*. I am interested in him. I want him to be happy. He has great responsibilities. This is important. I don't think I care for a man who has not these responsibilities. But he must be encouraged, he must be comforted. He must do these great things but he must not have to do them all alone. I must help him. This is *my* responsibility. This is why I stay home and do not run around getting my picture in the papers. I could be chairman of this, chairman of that. But Henry tell me that he is doing enough for both of us, and I should take care of *him*. So I do. I want to be ready for him when he comes home."

But though Cristina was dedicating herself to making a home for a tired man during the week, when play time came she was right there with him. She loves to entertain, travel, and be with her husband no matter where and no matter how late. She shares his enjoyment of that exotic taste delight, a big hamburger with plenty of onions.

Pat Doyle has joined them often at P. J. Clarke's, long after midnight, and watched them, happy for them, as they cuddled like teenagers. "They're not putting on an act, either," he said. "She bawled the hell out of him one night because he was kissing her too hard on the neck. One night I told him I'd appreciate knowing when and if they were going to have a baby so I'd be first with the story. He gave me a smile, grabbed Cristina around the waist tight enough to make her wince, and said, 'For the present, Pat, I'm her baby.'

"In Cristina, Henry Ford has found somebody who supports him completely. She understands him, pushes him, she's with him. Here's a woman who understands his driving force and wants to augment it and help him. That's her life."

Cristina also tried valiantly to get her husband to cut down on smoking—successfully when she's around. He smokes Benson and Hedges DeLuxe, the short ones that cost more than the long ones, and asks photographers not to snap him when he's smoking. "I'll catch hell from my wife."

Nate Cummings, who was 71 when the Cummings, Fishers and Fords went on a cruise together, said, "Oh, that Cristina, she's a charmer. She brought a great big hamper with her that contained sausages and cheese and 12 bottles of wine made on her family's farm. Homemade wine! We all kidded her about it, but you know something? It was good. I love to watch her and Henry together. He beams when she's around, his whole attitude changes. She looks after him the way every man hopes his wife will. She doesn't nag, but shows her concern and her love for him openly. She worries about his waistline and when he reaches for another helping she says something gentle, like 'Are you sure you want it?' and he's so pleased that she cares about him that he'll gladly do without."

Her friends include celebrities of the entertainment world, jet setters, and President Johnson. Frequently over the weekend the big house at Grosse Pointe is full of European nobility. But she's just as pleasant to Ernie Farkas, one of the company chauffeurs who frequently drives her around.

"She doesn't talk like rich people do," Ernie said. "She talks like a friend, like she's one of us. She's one of the nicest people I know. We talk about exercise and diet and children and gardening. She likes to raise her own vegetables, but I don't guess she does much of that here. We talk about making soup, and the vegetables we like in it, and we talk about making wine. You never know *what* she's going to talk about, she's so spontaneous and pleasant."

The story ended happily for both Henry and his first wife. Charlotte told me that her mother and father came to be on the best of terms. After the divorce Anne Ford met a handsome Los Angeles lawyer named Deane G. Johnson. They were married in Charlotte's apartment with only a few close friends in attendance. They purchased a Regency type house in Beverly Hills, and the new Mrs. Johnson furnished it with the exquisite French furniture which she had selected, then removed from the big house at Grosse Pointe.

18

ON EDSEL FORD'S 21st birthday, in 1914, his father took him to the bank, had the vault opened, and showed him one million dollars in gold. That was his birthday present. Less than five years later Edsel was given another present, the presidency of the Ford Motor Company. They were not merely presents, but, in a sense, the payment of a debt. Edsel had lacked a full-time father. During much of Edsel's boyhood, Henry Ford was building automobiles.

Edsel Ford's children suffered no such neglect. They had a happy home life. Their father played football and baseball with them. The two oldest boys had a regular tennis game with their parents: Henry and his mother took on Benson and his father. The only handicap the third generation of Fords had in being born wealthy was their protection against kidnappers. Even that has been exaggerated over the years. Hotchkiss alumni have told me that Henry Ford II had a bodyguard in residence, and Ford himself told me that he knew there was one around, but he never actually saw him.

I have become accustomed to the Fords' lack of knowledge about themselves. Benson, for example, was positive that his grandfather had never flown in a plane whereas we know that he not only flew, but his first pilot was Charles A. Lindbergh. So I asked the former headmaster of Hotchkiss, George van Santvoord, about the Ford bodyguard. The answer: in the first place, the bodyguard didn't exist, and in the second, Henry must have seen him.

To explain that confusing sentence, van Santvoord said that Edsel Ford received a threatening letter, and reported it to the FBI—not to Harry Bennett. The FBI arranged for one of its agents, a pleasant young college graduate, to come in and look the situation over. As cover, he assisted in the alumni department and helped coach the Hotchkiss swimming team. It didn't take him long to determine that the school, in the tiny community of Lakeville, Connecticut, provided probably the world's safest sanctuary from kidnappers. Both the Fords and the school accepted his evaluation, and he went on back where he came from. He was not a bodyguard, and Henry must have seen him.

The three children of Henry Ford II, unfortunately, did not see as much of their father as he had seen of his. He rarely got home before 7:30, and it was necessary for him to travel constantly.

Charlotte looks back on her childhood wistfully. "I just didn't see much of my father," she said. "He was always away, or coming in from work after we had gone to bed. We had a Christmas tree and presents, and birthday presents and all that, but looking back on it, I think I'd have been happy to have less presents and more parents."

Anne expressed the same view, though less strongly. She

does remember traveling to Europe with her parents, flying over in the old Stratocruisers. Both girls went off to boarding school in the eighth grade. Young Edsel, several years younger than his sisters, also went off to boarding school, first Hotchkiss and then The Gunnery.

As each of the girls reached 19, she was given not a million dollars in gold, but debuts which were $250,000 knock-outs. Charlotte's party was held at the Country Club of Detroit, fitted out in an eighteenth-century motif by a Paris designer. For the 1270 guests there were 5000 finger sandwiches, 2160 scrambled eggs, 100 pounds of corned-beef hash, 480 bottles of Dom Perignon (1949), and 720 bottles of liquor. The Meyer Davis orchestra flew in from New York to play, and Cholly Knicker-bocker, the Hearst columnist, called it THE party of the century. Charlotte wore a St. Laurent strapless dress. The father of the debutante had more fun than anybody, leading the band and singing "The Whiffenpoof Song." At 6:00 A.M. he did a high-kicking jitterbug and finally went home.

Anne's debut was equally sumptuous. Two summerhouses were set up on the grounds of the Grosse Pointe estate. On the walls were arches of red and white roses, 50,000 of them, each in its own container. Again Meyer Davis played, featuring a song for the occasion, "Man, That's Anne." Anne designed her own dress, and her hairdresser was flown in from New York. Ella Fitzgerald was the vocalist. As she started to sing the crowd failed to quiet down and the father of the debutante shouted, "Dammit, shut up!" Then he added, "Now I'm going to catch hell from my wife."

Anne, normally the quiet Ford, was particularly effervescent at her party. It must not have been easy, because her father had confided to her the night before that he and her mother were separating. The night following the debut, both parents made the official announcement to the three children.

Anne's party was in the summer of 1961. Seven years later,

curious as to her feelings about an event that struck many people as a rather frivolous expenditure, I asked Anne if she thought it was worth it. "Well, Daddy said it provided work for a lot of people," she said. "Actually neither Charlotte nor I had any choice whatsoever about debuts. They aren't any fun at all. First you have to get ready. Then all you do is just stand in line and receive people. Do you mean would I want my daughter to have one? No."

Henry Ford II understood his two daughters, and the differences between them. "He has an uncanny ability to put his finger on the personality traits of people, their characteristics, and size them up," Anne said. She had become seriously involved with someone whom she didn't name, and her father had a talk with her about him. "He told me that he wasn't going to interfere with my marrying this man if I insisted upon it, but that he did want me to know of certain faults and weaknesses, and he enumerated them. He asked me to think about them before I went ahead and got married. I did think about them, and I stopped seeing him."

"Was your father right?" I asked.

"One hundred per cent," she said.

Charlotte's case was different. In Switzerland, when the two girls were enjoying their father's honeymoon with Cristina, Charlotte began a romantic encounter. The man was Stavros Niarchos, one of the richest men in the world. He was 33 years older than she, and had been married for 18 years to his third wife, with whom he had four children. That summer Charlotte and Niarchos saw more of each other, for his yacht was moored near the Fords' yacht on the French Riviera.

A close friend of Henry Ford told me, "Henry tried to cover up his true feelings about Charlotte and that man. He made jokes about it, and tried to treat it lightly, but I could see that it was really bothering him underneath." Ford knew better than to try to tell Charlotte what to do, and helped arrange the marriage.

Charlotte and Niarchos were married in Mexico in December, 1965, and flew to St. Moritz. Columnists pointedly commented on the fact that Niarchos' wife and children were also at St. Moritz and that he was frequently seen with them over the holidays. The reason for the seemingly strange arrangement was simple: Charlotte wanted her husband to be with his children at Christmas.

Their baby, Elena, was born and Charlotte and Niarchos were divorced a year later. All of this, of course, was reported at length by the press. In the spring of 1969, a story in a major magazine recounted the affair, and then said that Charlotte and Niarchos were seeing more of each other since the divorce than they had during their marriage. I asked Charlotte about it. She told me the whole story.

First of all, she was honestly and sincerely in love with Stavros Niarchos. She is not sorry she married him. When I asked her whether her belief that she had been lonely as a child could have had anything to do with her falling for a much older man, she looked at me sharply, then replied, "It may just have."

Why did they break up? "He drove me nuts," she said bluntly. "My ex-husband is not a happy man. He can't relax. He has no office, his office is with him wherever he goes. I found out that he was married to his Telex machine. That was all that mattered to him. It's as simple as that."

Strong implications were made that the Ford girls spent all their time buying clothes.

"I don't spend 15 minutes a day, not 15 minutes!" Charlotte said. "I've got a lot more to do than to waste time buying clothes. I'm fortunate in having an innate taste for clothes, and I don't have to spend a lot of time to look presentable." (Anne said practically the same thing, adding that anyone who thinks primarily of clothes leads a pretty shallow life.)

Anyone reading about Charlotte would get the impression that she chases around all day doing nothing. She's actually a busy girl. She has done extensive work with the Police Athletic League, appearing on radio programs, working in the centers, judging art shows and other contests. She has also long been active with the Skouras Center for Creative Arts, training producers and directors. In 1968, she, like her father, fell under the spell of Whitney Young, Jr. "One night at a party he asked me, 'Why don't you work with us?' " She embarked on a program working with children in Harlem.

"This is pretty difficult," she said. "You have to work your way in slowly, to get the trust and confidence of these children. I'm working with them on a personal basis, having them in my home, and exposing myself to them, trying in my own small way to narrow the gap between blacks and whites."

Another story that has made the rounds is that Charlotte stayed with the children of the late John F. Kennedy while their mother married Aristotle Onassis.

"There's not an ounce of truth in it," she said. "After the assassination of the President, I used to take Caroline out for walks about once a week. That lasted about a year. Stories like this make me so mad. Why do people print these things when they don't know what they're talking about? I'm here, I'm available, I have a telephone. Why are you the only person who ever bothered to ask me the truth?"

Out of all the anguish of her short marriage, Charlotte has gained a charming daughter and has drawn closer to her father. "I see more of Daddy now. He's a lot more affectionate with my child than I think he was with me, and I love to see them playing together. And I'm so proud of him. He's aware of the change in our times. He knows he's Henry Ford. He believes that our form of government, our way of life is the best—it has certainly been good to us—and there is really nothing he can do but work hard to defend and protect it. I'm only sorry that he has to drive himself so hard all the time.

"At least if he works hard, he rests hard, too. I remember weekends after long periods of work when he'd sleep until two or three o'clock in the afternoon. I was in Nassau with him and he slept practically all the time. You don't hear about him when he's asleep. It annoys me when European friends tell me that Americans don't enjoy life. Well, Daddy is one American who does. He has the facility for really getting away from the office, for relaxing completely away from his work. And he deserves it."

The Christmas before Charlotte and Anne went to Switzerland with their father and Cristina, Anne went to a tree-trimming party. There she met a dark, lively young man named Giancarlo Uzielli. "I've never dated anyone since," she said. "He's the most gregarious man I've ever known, the most fun to be with. You know it's so funny, thinking of my great grandfather's hatred of Jews, of international bankers, of Wall Street financiers. Now I'm married to one!"

Uzielli, who was born in Italy but came to America as a small boy, is indeed Jewish, works in Wall Street and is an expert in the field of international investments. He has been described as a descendant of the Rothschild family, but the relationship is remote. He's proud of who he is, and although he is certainly delighted to have a wife like Anne and a little boy like Alessandro, he'd prefer to see his name in the *Wall Street Journal* than in the society columns.

"I was absolutely terrified of Henry Ford," he said. "I'd only met him briefly, and here I had to go to his apartment and go through the formality of asking his daughter's hand in marriage. Really, I was scared to death. But the moment I walked in Mr. Ford put me right at ease. He said, 'I know why you're here, and anything that my daughter wants is all right with me.'"

One of the problems of the marriage was the fact that Uzielli was divorced, and Anne, of course, was a Catholic. However, all the Fords believe that divorce today no longer bears the stigma of old, and Anne and Uzielli went ahead and got married. Anne's parents were present both at the ceremony and at a party in Delmonico's Crystal Room the day before. Some 445 guests drank 100 magnums of Piper Heidseck, 1959. There was music by the Wild Ones for frugging, and by Emory Davis, the son of Meyer. Both Anne and her mother wore dresses designed by Oscar de la Renta. Cristina was in a green brocade which, her husband said, came from Grosse Pointe. It was a happy party. Ford danced with his former wife, and Cristina danced with just about everybody. Henry Ford was still going strong when the happy couple left at 3:00 A.M to rest up for the wedding the next day.

While his sisters and parents were getting married, young Edsel was finishing up at The Gunnery, class of 1968. That summer he had the American boy's dream job, working with Carroll Shelby souping up the Shelby version of the Mustang. In the fall he began college at Babson Institute in Massachusetts. Young Edsel displayed a knack all through school of getting along with people. "He's the manager type," Anne said. "He's awful smart— that's what makes us all so mad! He could do so well. Instead he turns on that charm and just scrapes through."

Father of a college student, Henry Ford II turned his extra-business attention in the spring of 1969 to the future represented by college youth. In a time of extraordinary ferment in America he chose a typical Ford approach. Instead of decrying the spreading spirit of rebellion, as might be expected of a corporate executive, he looked upon it as a reaffirmation of the human spirit, a demand for independence, and an attack on tyranny of all kinds.

"Throughout the world," he told students at Vanderbilt

University, "ordinary people, especially young people, are deciding that they have had it with the way things are. . . . This trend holds great hope of building a better world, a more pleasant environment, a more just social order and greater freedom for the individual." He classified conformity, pretending that things are better than they are, right along with a hippie-type withdrawal, as negative choices. Revolution just isn't possible, and would lead only to reaction. He advocated "the possibility of starting with what we have and working from within to build something better." He gave a down-to-earth example of the efficacy of this approach by pointing out that companies like Ford, now paying starting salaries in five figures to ambitious, talented young men with advanced degrees, have been forced to be more sensitive to the growing spirit of rebellion. Young people won't tolerate being treated like cogs in a machine. "We can't afford to treat them that way because they can always leave, and because we need them more than they need us."

In a speech at Yale he stressed the need for—and the sheer practicality of—equal opportunity in business. People who have money, education and opportunity make better customers, employees and neighbors than people who are poor, ignorant and oppressed. Good employees are hard to find, and imposing irrelevant criteria like race or color limits a company's profit potential. Business has lagged not because of profit motive, but in spite of it, and in opposition to its own best interest. Self-interest, he said, is a more reliable motive than altruism.

What impressed me most about his approach was not only his exhortation to those who who would change the world to change it within the establishment, but his warning to those willing to enter the establishment that they must be prepared to work the change. "We need people who are convinced that the way things are is a shame and a disgrace," he told the Yale students. "It's natural for youth to be impatient for faster progress. That progress doesn't come about because the existing leaders change their minds and their way of doing things, but because one generation grows old and another takes over.

"The correct measure of possible progress of the future is not the actions of my generation," he said, "but the ambitions of yours. The size of the generation gap today suggests that when your generation takes over, the progress could really be major. How much progress big organizations can make toward building a better world is not fixed in the nature of organizations. It depends on you and what you do about it."

Both Henry Fords, men for their times, have recognized their times and the necessity for changing them. They have both met the challenge.

Bibliography

Of the scores of books perused by the author for this study of two men named Henry Ford, the following, though not necessarily completely accurate or consistent, were of particular interest:

Bennett, Harry, as told to Paul Marcus. *We Never Called Him Henry.* New York: Gold Medal Books, 1951.

Greenleaf, William. *From These Beginnings.* Detroit: Wayne State University Press, 1964.

Hickerson, J. Mel. *Ernie Breech.* New York: Meredith Press, 1969.

Marquis, Henry S. *Henry Ford: An Interpretation.* Boston: Little, Brown & Co., 1923.

Nevins, Allan. *Ford: The Times, the Man, the Company.* New York: Charles Scribner's Sons, 1954.

————, and Frank Ernest Hill. *Ford: Expansion and Challenge.* New York; Charles Scribner's Sons, 1957.

————, *Ford: Decline and Rebirth.* New York: Charles Scribner's Sons, 1963.

Olson, Sidney. *Young Henry Ford.* Detroit: Wayne State University Press, 1964.

Richards, William C. *The Last Billionaire.* New York: Charles Scribner's Sons, 1948.

Sorensen, Charles E., with Samuel T. Williamson. *My Forty Years with Ford.* New York: The Macmillan Co., 1956.

Sward, Keith. *The Legend of Henry Ford.* New York: Rinehart, 1948.

Index

398

87899